Rida Inam

Narratives of Disparity

Rida Inam

Narratives of Disparity

Islam and the West in History and Literature

LIT

Die vorliegende Dissertation wurde vom Fachbereich für Sprache, Literatur, Kultur der Universität Gießen angenommen.

This book is printed on acid-free paper.

Bibliografische Information der Deutschen Nationalbibliothek
Die Deutsche Nationalbibliothek verzeichnet diese Publikation in der Deutschen Nationalbibliografie; detaillierte bibliografische Daten sind im Internet über http://dnb.d-nb.de abrufbar.

ISBN 978-3-643-91004-2 (br.)
ISBN 978-3-643-96004-7 (PDF)
Zugl.: Gießen, Univ., Diss., 2017

Klosbachstr. 107
CH-8032 Zürich
Tel. +41 (0) 44-251 75 05 E-Mail:
zuerich@lit-verlag.ch http://www.lit-verlag.ch

Auslieferung:

Deutschland: LIT Verlag, Fresnostr. 2, D-48159 Münster
Tel. +49 (0) 2 51-620 32 22, E-Mail: vertrieb@lit-verlag.de

E-Books sind erhältlich unter www.litwebshop.de

First, I wish to acknowledge my grandparents and all the other remarkable personalities among my elders on both sides of the family, whose examples have been a source of inspiration for me. In my life, I soon realized that confidence, resilience, and ambition are family traits. Having so many amazing personalities to look up to – especially so many strong and brilliant women – has a been a great advantage.

I also dedicate this to my parents, Bushra and Inam, who taught me the importance of seeking a balance in life, especially when it comes to applying my natural talents. Their instructions have stayed with me, sometimes spurring me on and other times taming my overeagerness:

Strive to excel in what you are doing but do not disregard the efforts of your competitors.

Express yourself without fear but do not judge or disrespect anyone.

Exchange ideas with people but do not force your views on others.

Stand up for your beliefs but also admit when you are wrong.

Be proud of yourself but never make others feel second-rate.

Try to fit in but do not become an imitation of other people.

Be tenacious but also know when a cause is lost.

Be confident but not commanding.

Be a feminist but not a misandrist.

Be brave but not imprudent.

I do not pretend to have always lived up to these ideals. I did learn, however, that one should not go to extremes in anything. One choice need not exclude another. I can be both Muslim and Western, because being Muslim does not comprise a blind following of a communal defiance of the West, and being Western is not a submissive compliance to arbitrary standards of assimilation.

Furthermore, I wish to thank my parents for building my character and for teaching me to think outside the box. I also thank them for their endless love and support throughout my life, as well as for the sacrifices they made to build a future for their children. Their lives inspired me to make daring decisions for the sake of progress and to work hard in pursuit of it.

I also thank my two elder brothers whose incessant competitiveness in our childhood ("who can run the fastest/jump the highest/throw the farthest/…") urged me to look for ways to beat them until I started reading their school books, hoping I could outsmart them. The scheme failed, of course, because children do not accept knowledge as an asset worth their admiration or friendship. Still, the competition with my brothers gave me a self-confidence and a sense of equality that a youngest born child may not have developed to the same degree without it.

I also want to express my deep gratitude to my sisters (technically 'sisters-in-law') not only for wonderfully expanding our family circle but also for being so warm and welcoming whenever I visited them to take a break from working on this mammoth and seemingly endless project of mine. Thank you for your love, friendship, and support!

I must also thank my friends who have played a crucial role on my proverbial 'road to Ph.D.' by sharing the same path – literally and figuratively: some of you I met on campus and others on the commute. The former became wonderful intellectual sparring partners with whom I often talked my way out of mental labyrinths. The latter made for a wonderful morning ritual of buying cheap coffee together for the train ride and then talking, laughing and sharing on the way. All of you made me look forward to going to work in the morning, and you provided comfort, distraction, entertainment, companionship, affection, and emotional support throughout the way.

I also wish to thank my students, especially those who became my friends over time. Your questions and feedback helped me clarify my ideas, and getting to know you personally allowed me to learn from your experiences and struggles.

I am also extremely grateful to my supervisors Prof. Dr. Ingo Berensmeyer for all the time and effort he invested in providing clear and precise feedback every time I asked for his help; and Prof. Dr. Yasar Sarikaya, who believed in my abilities from the very beginning of our association and made me part of an amazing team of research and teaching staff. I also thank all my former and current colleagues for three years of fun and productivity at the Department for Islamic Theology and its Didactics.

Another heartfelt thanks to Bashir Mirza and Laeeqa Ahmad, who invested a lot of time in a close reading of my dissertation and offering extensive and very helpful feedback.

A very special thanks to my aunt, Tahira Raza, who can find a solution to any and every problem within minutes, and does not rest until the problem has been solved. Your exceptional competence, altruism, and devotion are truly inspiring. Thank you for everything!

TABLE OF CONTENTS

INTRODUCTION

In Arabia around 570 A.D., one man known only within a close social circle for his honesty and kindness, who until then had been of no influence or importance, became the fountainhead of a stream of changes that altered the course of history. The tangible legacy of this historic development is the Quran: a book that has outlived the man responsible for its existence by fourteen hundred years. His incorporeal legacy is the religion of Islam, which has since spread over many countries and for three centuries rose to prevail over a significantly large part of the medieval world. In the course of history, there have been many encounters between Islam and the West with frequent exchange of cultural elements. However, an ideological rapprochement was seemingly never attempted during these fourteen hundred years. The Islamic world and the non-Islamic West developed and evolved alongside each other, but while the people of these broad-based cultural and religious backgrounds started to mingle, their values and principles today seem to be more contrasting than ever.

It seems likely that wherever different religions and worldviews coexist over long time periods a certain commingling of their respective elements occurs naturally. Geographic boundaries have never served to separate ideas because ideas have always migrated along with people which is why all kinds of religions and beliefs can be found everywhere on earth. But when it comes to the values of Islam and the West it seems as if a significant convergence between them has failed to materialize in an extensive passage of time. It appears that though Muslims and Non-Muslims have mingled demographically, they seemingly failed to assimilate together. Superficial facets of each other's culture have been adopted, but the fundamental bases of their respective values are still believed to be segregated. Today it is largely unknown that the West and Islam have a long history of encounters that shaped their present images of the self and each other. What can history tell us about the forces that underlie their many encounters over time?

It would sound more plausible to study the encounters of Islam with Christianity, of the West with the East, or of the orient with the occident. However, the development of these disparate societies and cultures over many centuries has resulted in a confrontation of the religious values of the East with the secular values of the West.

Muslims and Western people today perceive themselves and each other as distinct and different poles. In fact, instead of growing closer together, the intellectual conflict between Islam and the West has increased in its intensity along with a continuing growth of hostilities between relevant states and confederations formally or informally belonging to one of the two blocs. I will hasten to add that many scholars say that Islam and the West are not two separate entities, definitely and definably so. Though in principle I very much agree with this, I explain my usage of these concepts, which are part of a generalized way of thinking, in chapter two (pp. 13-14 and 18).

The history of encounters of Islam and the West consists of many layers, which is to say that they can be studied from geographical, transcultural, political, sociological, ethnic, theological or other scientific perspectives. The divide between these two groups of people certainly has political as well as historical bases because there is no denying that substantial differences exist in their values and beliefs. The differences in the values and beliefs of Islam and the West will be discussed in this thesis to some extent but I maintain that these differences do not account for the level of division that still prevails after all this time. The main hypothesis of this dissertation is that a conflict between Islam and the West continues to exist in the public discourses in part because of a continued perpetuation of narratives reinforcing the idea that there is an irreconcilable conflict between them. This dissertation seeks to dissect these narratives that maintain the disparity between Islam and the West. I have termed them *narratives of disparity* (NoDs). Their function is to segregate the two entities by constructing their identities as being distinct from one another, by adjusting – or if necessary distorting – the history, values, and/or characteristics of each. NoDs come in many combinations of content and composition but upon closer examination, it becomes obvious that they display recurring patterns.

I chose the word *disparity* for specifically categorizing these narratives because they do not necessarily include a deliberate judgement. Words like *antagonism, conflict* or *hostility* are less neutral and overlook the fact that these narratives are not always constructed, repeated or distributed with a destructive purpose.

Additionally, words like *animosity* infer active aggression initiated by one side, especially if it is the result of destructive deliberation. Consequently, one might be tempted to deduct that one side must be more to blame for this division than the other. It is important to note that these NoDs must be equally present on both sides to create and perpetuate a conflict.

During my research, I have come across four kinds of narratives that have shaped this discourse around the juxtaposition of Islam and the West: these narratives will be subsumed by the umbrella term *narratives of disparity* (NoDs). The underlying argument is that a conflict in worldviews arises because conflicting images of each other are fashioned and propagated in the form of NoDs, which are linked to identity and initiated by ethnocentric impulses. NoDs will be conceptualized in the second subsection of the introduction, as they are based on the interplay of historiography, narrative theory, and literary theory. The first of these two will serve to conceptualize the theory of NoDs. Literary theory will be central to the entire study because a selection of novels will be the object of research.

I have chosen four British novels of a relevant genre. The key role of literary theory within this explanatory concept is to provide the research paradigms necessary for the interpretation of fictionality as well as experientiality and multi-perspectivity in novels to demonstrate how NoDs manifest themselves. Literature does not only depict elements of a current public discourse but can combine historical narratives with contemporary fictional ones.

Creating images of 'otherness' is naturally not specific to only one time or culture. It is rooted in the natural ethnocentric impulse of all human beings. Ethnocentrism is the impulse of wanting to protect and preserve one's own culture from foreign influence or from (real or imagined) threats of extinction. Since this defence mechanism is triggered by reflex, the measures taken in order to protect one's culture are not necessarily executed consciously. And the images of 'the other' which are depicted in the NoDs are not the result of mere fantasy as if randomly plucked out of the air. Such images of what is alien to us – while usually not a detailed depiction of reality – do contain a trace of reality in that they reflect the actual way in which 'the other' is perceived. The view of the beholder is biased by his subjective internalised values creating a tainted image of 'the other' which in turn can reveal information about the beholder himself. Looking at such images of Islam and the East in Western culture – historic and contemporary – it becomes obvious that there has been a visible tendency to distinguish and dissociate the East from the West.

In German paintings of the 18th century, the Islamic orient was often depicted as a luxurious harem, richly filled with food and naked women – in short: everything to please carnal desires. At a time when Europe prided itself on being civilized and chaste, the Islamic world was depicted as a place where lust and greed prevailed.[1] After the age of enlightenment, the self-image of the West was characterized by rationalism and the western image of Islam shifted towards savagery and barbarism. Today, the West defines itself as liberal in matters of sexuality and again the image of Islam represents the opposite: sexual repression. So, it seems that the image of Islam in the West is usually conceptualised to depict an anti-Western worldview.

The Arab-sexuality-trope is still utilized as evidenced in one recent example from the German public discourse which was eventually picked up by international media across Western nations: Björn Höcke, a spokesman of the German right-wing party *Alternative für Deutschland* (AfD), said during a speech in 2015 that refugees are a constant threat to "blonde women". A few weeks later, at the New Year's Eve party in Cologne, hundreds of women became victims of sexual offences by gangs said to be of Arab or North African appearance, obviously Muslim immigrants. This incident became the epitome of this collective fear of the overly sexualized Arab man who is allegedly so repressed that he cannot contain his libido around white women.[2] The incident was also referred to by Donald Trump in several speeches about dangers that immigrants pose. During the first few days after the New Year's Eve of 2015, the discussion seemed to work under the assumption that this was an entirely new experience for the German collective mind, and must be a direct consequence of the recent arrival of more than usual refugees from Muslim countries. Famous German feminist, Alice Schwarzer, was quick to publish a book to that end only four months after the incident. At the same time, however, many voices in the public reminded everyone that sexual harassment is a fixed part of many annual parties, festivals and events of all kinds, including the beloved *Oktoberfest*. This example depicts only one discourse using narratives of disparity. In the course of this study, we will take a look at the intellectual history of Islam where the same tendency to recreate NoDs against the West will also become apparent.

After an analysis of NoDs in historiography, I will extract examples of them from the works of contemporary fiction I have selected. Studying the literature of all the countries that are considered or consider themselves Western is naturally not possible because taking all symbolic systems and cultural contexts into consideration would go beyond the scope of this study as well as my abil-

---

[1] Nochlin, '*The Politics of Vision: Essays on Nineteenth-Century Art and Society*', pp. 33–5

[2] Noack, R. (2016), "*Leaked Document Says 2,000 Men Allegedly Assaulted 1,200 German Women on New Year's Eve*"

ities. Therefore, I compiled a selection of novels which were published in Britain in the years after the events of September 11th, 2001 and found four novels which proved suitable for this analysis.

Even though an analysis of NoDs in historical or political discourse would be interesting, this initial research has been restricted to the genre of fiction because it includes the conceptualisation of the NoD-paradigm. Poetry has been excluded simply because it has less relevance for large masses as it is generally considered "an elitist product reserved for a minority".[3] This study will focus largely on the works of fiction belonging to the so-called middle-brow and the focus will be on the most active genre in British literature at this time: the novel. Britain seemed most suited for this study for two reasons: firstly, the novel as a medium is on a rise there, and secondly, it is a culturally and ethnically diverse market.

Vera Nünning detects a growing popularity of the novel in Britain, even though it had been suspected to have declined because other media were getting more and more established. She attempts to explain this with several factors such as the quality of the novels, their variety and readability and, above all, the fact that the most prominent British authors manage to blend complexity of form and literary sophistication with fascinating stories.[4] Nünning sees the major cause of this (British) phenomenon of the increasing popularity of an old genre not in the artistic qualities of the contemporary British novel alone, but in their most favourable interplay with commercialization. So, while excellent novels are still being created, better marketing strategies are persuading the masses to read and appreciate them: a boom of book clubs, as well as creative ideas of exchanging books with strangers (for instance on public transportation) and then getting together to discuss the contents; there are even entire TV-Shows dedicated to discussing novels. Reading has been made a prestigious activity providing opportunities for socializing. This element of British culture is reflected in the contemporary novel. The state-of-the-nation novel *A Week in December*, by Sebastian Faulks for instance, reflects how reading novels and discussing them is a part of middle-class life in Britain: one character in the novel – a man of Indian heritage who became rich through a flourishing business – hires an English teacher so he can teach him all about novels that have won awards or have been recommended by critics, just so he would have something to talk about with the queen when he meets her.

---

[3] Bickley, *Contemporary Fiction,* p. 12

[4] Nünning and Lusin, eds., *Der zeitgenössische Englische Roman,* p. 1

The other remarkable quality that distinguishes the British literary field from others is its international accessibility. There are many popular authors from different cultural, ethnic, and social backgrounds who publish their writings in Britain, many of whom do not live there permanently. This market provides an uncommonly wide range of perspectives as many authors have lived in several different countries during their lives. Nevertheless, this study will refrain from a cataloguing of authors by their origin, like the genre called "British Muslim Fiction" does. Giving the origins or backgrounds of authors too much importance could lead to assumptions about their intentions or inclinations and thereby bias the readings of these works.

The novels selected for this analysis were all published in Britain but specifically discuss Islam in the West, rather than Islam in Britain. *The Reluctant Fundamentalist*, for instance, is set in the USA and in Pakistan and offers a great reflection on the significance of 9/11. It does not mention Britain or Britishness but discusses the clash between West and Islam in general. This research is on Islam in the West, not on Islam in Britain or Germany. Western identity has replaced European national identities and even Christian identity – especially in discourses that juxtapose it with Islam – which will be discussed historically in chapter three.

The debate about Islam in the West has become more diversified, with over 50 million Muslims living in Europe[5] who take an active part in the social processes of negotiation: every individual struggling for his or her own place in society. Nevertheless, the battle lines in this confrontational discourse are far from being clearly marked: many British-born scholars write in favour of Islam and countless migrants (either Muslim-born or born in Islamic countries) write against it. Due to traumatic experiences that they might have had with families or even regimes who claim to be acting according to Islamic tenets and laws they understandably become hostile towards Islam. In the past decade, we have witnessed a surge of authors gaining fame with Anti-Islamic views. And almost at the same time, there has been a surge of radical Salafi preachers, glorifying Islam, arbitrarily issuing death warrants – so-called *fatwas*[6] – on people who dared to criticize the Quran or the Prophet Muhammed.

---

[5] Statistisches Bundesamt, Europäischer Datenservice, 2015

[6] The Arabic word '*Fatwa*' means 'legal opinion' which a scholar of Islamic law can pass based on methods of Islamic legal theory. A *fatwa* does not necessarily include a death sentence and certainly not defined by it. Nevertheless, since Salman Rushdie's case (known as *the Rushdie Affair*) in the late 80s, this term has been used in the Western discourse as a synonym for 'Islamic death warrant'.

And then there are many people publishing various opinions between these two extremes.

Naturally, when it comes to religion there are as many different opinions as there are minds to harbour them. And while the public discourse is largely steered by subjective opinions and efforts to gain the prerogative of interpretation, the objective of a scientific discussion of Islam is not persuasion of the opposite side but a struggle to understand the complexity of reality. It is important to bear in mind that even in a scientific endeavour there is a risk of being biased and of being suspected of it.

As a Western Muslim conducting a research on Islam in the West, I want to be clear on how to distinguish the interests of scholarship from personal (religious) views. Academics argue about whether disinterested scholarship exists or not. I am more inclined towards the position of denying its existence, but I will not go into the ontological arguments for or against it. Instead, I will precede the research with some notes on the method I will use in order to keep potential causes for bias on the grounds of my intellectual and religious background in check.

I was raised by Muslims. Among other things, I believe in a spiritual realm and regard all religious scriptures as a manifestation of the Divine, including the teachings of Islam, and therefore consider myself a Muslim. However, I do not intend to discuss 'Islam' as the teachings and values in which I personally believe as these can differ greatly from what many other Muslims believe. From all the things that I was taught about this faith while growing up and from the things I learned about it through several phases of critical reflection and questioning, I have fashioned an individual interpretation of faith which is still in the development phase. The result is not a religion by the name of 'Islam' or even 'my Islam' but a personal religiosity which is not to function as a source of knowledge or topic of invention in this study. Depending on the context, the word 'Islam' as used in the course of this research will mean several things – the teachings of the religion, the followers of this religion at a certain time, the core idea of this religion, the sum of all these, or other abstract ideas or entities, and each time it will be made clear which one is being spoken of – but at no point will it denote my religiosity or my personal interpretation or practice of it. Islamic tenets will be discussed, but only by theological approaches[7] which do not assume to be absolute conclusions – unlike the clerical

---

[7] Under the supervision of Prof. Dr. Yasar Sarikaya, as well as Elif Gömleksiz (PhD-candidate in Islamic Theology)

approach of studying religious or theological sources with the intention of proving certain interpretations as superior over others.

In my view, the general discourse around Islam in the West requires more objectivity and honesty in admitting faults on the Muslim side and less condemnation on the secular side. In the past years, Islamic organizations have seemed reluctant to honestly address problems outside their own circles. The past two decades were the fifteen minutes of fame for a few ex-Muslims who presented individual cases of social atrocities, such as honour killings, and present them – usually in the form of autobiographies – as proof of how inherently evil Islam is. Such biographies had quite an impact on people who had no previous knowledge about Islam or Muslims. If a person who never met any Muslims personally and knows nothing about their religion reads the autobiography of ex-Muslims like Sabatina James or Ayaan Hirsi Ali, these women will naturally become the reader's primary source of reference for the subject of Islam. Their success is certainly not an accident. In combination with other influences, such as the rise of the modern phenomenon of Islamist terrorism, and a Europe-wide upswing of right-wing parties with their anti-Muslim populism, it all resulted in an atmosphere of general distrust of the non-Muslim side towards Muslims; and alternatively, defensiveness among Muslims. Over time, many Muslim communities became sensitive to criticism, which might be because they feared that the slightest misdemeanour committed by one of their members can expose an entire community to undue censure or ostracism. Even though these books had little scientific validity, since their line of reasoning was based entirely on subjective experience and isolated incidents, they undeniably had considerable success in spreading prejudices featuring forced marriages, honour killings and/or female genital mutilation (FGM). Wherever these things happen they must be discussed with honesty and precision. The cases must be investigated thoroughly, but only assigning blame on all of Islam has very little chance of solving the central African problem of FGM.

Also, there are many less dramatic problems in the everyday lives of Muslims in Europe, which occur more often and really need to be discussed as well; like the problems that young Muslims face in school regarding dress codes. Some Muslim women want to wear a headscarf and are prohibited to do so in school, while others do not want to wear it but then face criticism at home or in their community. One survey showed that the majority of the women who wear a headscarf in Germany do so without compulsion and gave reasons which indicated internal motivation (self-motivation). Only about 12 percent gave reasons like "to meet the expectations of parents/ partner/ community"[8] which can be interpreted as sources of compulsion or at least of social pressure. However, it is possible that such a survey may give biased results because interviewees who feel compelled to wear a headscarf might also feel compelled to lie about it in surveys. Indeed, there may be a slightly higher number of young women who feel pressurized into covering themselves than detected in the survey. However, the fact that more than two thirds of all Muslim women in Germany do not wear a headscarf can indeed mean that the degree of compulsion is very low, because even if we assume that all women who do wear a headscarf have been forced to wear it, then they are still the minority because the clear majority of Muslim women in Germany does not wear one at all.

Nevertheless, there still are 12 percent of the minority who do wear scarves that do feel pressurized into covering themselves, and they have a problem that needs to be addressed. In the few cases when such things are brought up, the session gets side-tracked, because some critics are keener to expose Islam as being oppressive rather than deal with the problem. At the same time, the Muslims participating in such discussions usually cannot focus on the problem itself because they instantly – sometimes even when there are no critics – become intent on defending Islam. This interplay of defensiveness and condemnation has become routine. The point is that an atmosphere of objectivity and fairness must be established so that discussions about problems in Islamic communities can be honest and helpful without getting distracted by fixed opinions on both sides.

This study is not an endeavour at setting some record straight on Islam. The problem with attempts at removing the infinite number of 'false notions on Islam' is the difficulty to defend the assessment of anything as a 'false notion' according to varying criteria of values. There is no institution in the world holding unquestioned authority over matters of Islam that can assume to rule over such a task, which incidentally does not mean that no one has been trying. But such explanations have often only made matters worse as they only add more information that is also based on controversial interpretations.

The world will probably never agree one interpretation of Islam which is sufficiently evidenced by the huge inner-Islamic divide into countless sects, and even within those sects, there is a great deal of disagreement on many theological questions. This does not have to be a bad thing because its earliest

---

[8] Haug et al. (2009), *Muslim Life in Germany: A Study Conducted on Behalf of the German Conference on Islam, Research Report*, pp. 204–6

adherents and scholars embraced disagreement and diversity of opinion. However, the point of the matter is that Islam cannot be defined absolutely, even though most definitions of it act as absolutes. There are many narratives about what is or is not Islamic. Still, in order to make a coherent case, I must begin by explaining the definitions of both terms 'Islam' and 'the West' which will be applicable throughout the course of this particular study.

First, it is important to point out that there is a difference between the religion of Islam and the practice of Muslims. 'Islam' is not defined by what Muslims do. One is a faith and the other is the religiosity of Muslims. These are often used as synonyms. In this study, Islam will be discussed a great deal but not under the definition of a religion, or a belief system, simply because this is not a theological study. Since I am no theologian, I do not possess the required expertise to analyse, interpret or apply the primary sources and the scripture of Islam.

Similarly, 'The West' will neither be understood as a direction on the compass or a portion of the planet's dry land nor as a cluster of the most influential nations of the western hemisphere. Defining 'Islam' as a belief system and 'the West' as a set of values is insufficient. Followers of Islam are people of many different cultures, countries, ethnicities and historical backgrounds, all of which have over time influenced the interpretation, understanding, and practice of this religion to suit their own cultures. Different sects and cultural forms of Islam have arisen. The conflicts are not always based on merely a theological dissent, which will be elaborated upon in the section regarding the intellectual history of Islam. When we say 'Islam' we are talking about an entity that 1.6 Billion people in the world identify with, without a representation by one agency which could execute some authority to define what is or is not Islamic. For now, it is important to establish that the belief or creed of all Muslims in the world – or even of all Muslims belonging to one sect – is not the same. This is also the case with the word 'West', which is usually applied to denote a set of values or a belief system, much like the word 'Islam' does. And in combination with the definite article, which has a specifying effect, the term 'The West' adopts the same quality which suggests a kind of oneness in its affiliates. 'The West' sounds like it stands for everything that white people, in general, believe in and live by. This is absurd because people of different countries, cultures, ethnicities, faiths, ideologies, and classes coexist here and identify themselves as people of the West. Their views and ideologies continue to vary greatly. Additionally, there is the fact that both terms are naturally liable to change, development and/or adjustments. So, when we say 'Islam' we should differentiate between Islam as it was born in the 6th century AD, from

Islam as it is lived by Muslims in today's Europe, or Islam as perceived by today's non-Muslims of Europe. The same principle applies for the term 'the West', which as a marker of identity is quite new.

Now, one way to avoid such fallacies is to use plural forms of these words, i.e. Islamic worldviews or Western worldviews. But even so, defining them axiomatically as value systems or belief systems in the plural can result in the common error of believing that even though everyone projects a different value system into these terms there must be one absolute out there that embodies the one and only system that deserves the name 'Islam' or 'The West', and that we must attempt to approximate to that. This may or may not be possible to accomplish but that is not the objective of this study.

The goal of this study is to analyse interactions between 'Islam' and 'the West'. For this, we require a dynamic definition that is mindful of how indefinite these terms are. Whilst remembering that there are no transcendental *signifieds* for Islam or the West, the oneness that these terms exude must also be considered for the following reason: even though it does not do justice to the complex reality, it certainly does reflect what is desired by adherents or opponents whenever they define the terms.

It is a pertinent fact that individuals claim the prerogative of interpretation for themselves whenever they offer a definition of what is or is not Islamic or Western. That is why, for the course of this study, the terms 'Islam' and 'the West' will be understood as names of ideal conceptions: everyone usually defines them in accordance with every maxim within their personal and self-contained value system. As an example, we can look at well-known phrases such as "terrorism has nothing to do with Islam". Muslims who say this must have peaceful ideals because not only do they believe that Islam must be peaceful, but they also believe that everyone who says otherwise must be wrong. This is also a narrative because it is selective: it is a representation of what one portion of Islam is to people, but it is presented as though it were a complete picture. In the same fashion, Westerners might say things like "This is America/Germany/Europe. We have freedom/gender equality/human rights here." Such words are usually uttered with a great deal of assertiveness even though they cannot rightfully claim that these nations live up these ideals without fail.

To sum up, an impression of unambiguity is created whenever we hear someone offering a definition of Islam or the West who wishes these terms were definite. This self-assuredness in religious matters is known as *exclusivism*; and in non-religious terms, it might be explained by the impulse known as *ethnocentrism*. It is important to note, that exclusivism and ethnocentrism do not have to be mutually exclusive, as the religious prerogative of interpretation can also be based on ethnocentric impulses: for instance, a Pakistani or Indonesian cleric may display ethnocentric impulses when disparaging the other's religious interpretations.

Exclusivism and *ethnocentrism* are diametrically opposed to the idea of *religious pluralism* or simply *pluralism,* respectively. In the beginning of his article titled *Religious Diversity and its Challenges to Religious Belief* Nathan L. King notes that while in some academic discourses the terms *religious pluralism* and *religious diversity* are used as synonyms, they are assigned clearly distinctive definitions in his article: while *religious diversity* refers to a coexistence of a large number of differing religious views and practices, *religious pluralism* is the capacity to regard all religions or views as equally capable of offering the truth in answer to the ultimate question and/or of imparting salvation to mankind.[9] Since in this study we will be juxtaposing religious views against secular world-views, King's definitions of religious diversity and religious pluralism will be extended to mean diversity and pluralism in non-religious world-views, as well.

In the Muslim world, there is a vast sectarian conflict ranging from theologically discursive dissent to violent hostilities perpetrated with political influence. However, the term exclusivism is usually referred to in the context of **inter**religious diversity. It is part of a tripartite classification – Exclusivism, Inclusivism, and Pluralism – which, according to Netland, was initially developed with regard to Christianity's view on other religions, but can also be found in similar discussions of other religious discourses.[10] In the interreligious sense, exclusivism is when "one religion, typically one's own, or *home religion,* is uniquely privileged over other, *alien religions,* in its truth claims or its salvific efficacy (or both)."[11] The opposite of Exclusivism is religious pluralism. The basic idea of pluralism is giving every religion equal merit, and conversely, exclusivism glorifies the home religion as superior to every other, denigrating dissent of any kind.

> In contemporary philosophy of religion, it is customary to use the tripartite distinction between exclusivism, inclusivism, and pluralism. And providing we recognize a range of variations within each, this is accurate. We should, however,

---

[9] King, '*Religious Diversity and its Challenges to Religious Belief*', p. 2
[10] Netland, '*Inclusivism and Exclusivism*', p. 228
[11] King, '*Religious Diversity and its Challenges to Religious Belief*', p. 2

note that the entire discussion can be conducted in terms of truth claims or salvation claims or both. [12]

Thus, there are several forms of exclusivism, pluralism, and inclusivism. The last concept is a combination of the first two in that it implies that while there is one correct response to the religious ultimate it can be possible to attain it in different ways. It is best explained by giving an example: one form of Christian inclusivism is what D'Costa calls 'structural inclusivism'.

> Structural inclusivists hold that Christ is the normative revelation of God, although salvation is possible outside of the explicit Christian church. Salvation is, or may be, available through other religions per se, but this salvation is always from Christ. This type of inclusivism contains the pluralist legitimation of other religions as salvific structures while also holding to the exclusivist claims of the causal saving grace of Christ alone.[13]

In other words, while inclusivists are unshaken in the conviction that their home religion is superior to all others, they are willing to give credit to other religions if these contain parts of the absolute truth from their home religion.[14]

Now, while there are doubtlessly many inclusivist (and even pluralist) religious traditions that do not restrict truth and soteriological effectiveness exclusively to their own religion, there are still many – perhaps more – traditions that do so. Dissent itself is good and can lead to an increase in knowledge, but ranking one's own view higher than others without a fair competition, leads to disregard of others as mentioned in the following quotation:

> The history of religion is one in which religious adherents have, by and large, believed that the central tenets of the tradition to which they adhere are true, objectively and exclusively so. The central beliefs of religious others are taken to be wrong (and sometimes culpably so), and disagreements have at times involved intolerance and even violence toward those who affirm a different religion. Some of the conflicting truth claims among the religions are rather minor, but many are at a foundational level.[15]

We can see the possible consequences of this hierarchy in historical manifestations of discrimination, persecution or even bloodshed.

In conclusion, the exclusivist attitude might be the one responsible for most conflicts within and around Islam. The conflicts escalate not because of different or even opposing beliefs of the religions of the different groups. We

---

[12] Hick, '*Religious Pluralism*', p. 216

[13] D'Costa, *Christianity and World Religions*, p. 7

[14] King, '*Religious Diversity and its Challenges to Religious Belief*', p. 2

[15] Meister, *Philosophy of Religion*, p. 7

may note that difference of opinion was considered a natural part of early Islam. Even though conflicts did arise during the Prophet's lifetime and shortly after his death, these were mainly because of political or economic interests and not theological dissent. Therefore, conflicts do not arise because of a difference in beliefs or a clash of interests. Escalation of conflicts is usually due to a combination of several triggering factors and we may assume that it is not automatically imminent in exclusivist societies.

In the case of a dissent in beliefs among the different parties which cannot be ignored, there are different ways of handling the situation. Some might seek a dialogue and exchange ideas, some might seek to persuade, others might argue without any plan of action. Eventually, though, one party might run out of intellectual capacities or resources to handle disagreement. And this is the point where some parties resort to desperate and undemocratic, verbally aggressive or even violent methods to silence what they consider unacceptable views. Of course, power and influence are key factors when it comes to handling disagreement. Those in power have the means to respond violently to disagreement especially if they feel there is a threat to their position.

Even though the West is not categorically a religion, the people are still susceptible to the impulse of believing their worldview to be the best, thus ruling out the possibility that it might have flaws. The concept of ethnocentrism, which can be defined in many ways, is one way to explain this tendency. Ethnocentrism essentially denotes the impulse of a people to measure and evaluate everything new by the familiar standards with which they grew up. The result of such an evaluation is biased and the person making it is usually unaware of this bias due to his or her upbringing.[16] To put it in more specified terms, ethnocentrism is:

> a schismatic in-group/out-group differentiation, in which internal cohesion, relative peace, solidarity, loyalty and devotion to the in-group, and the glorification of the 'sociocentric-sacred' (one's own cosmology, ideology, social myth, or Weltanschauung; one's own 'god-given' [sic] social order) are correlated with a state of hostility or permanent quasi-war (status hostilis) towards out-groups, which are often perceived as inferior, subhuman, and/or the incorporation of evil. Ethnocentrism results in a dualistic, Manichaean morality which evaluates violence within the in-group as negative, and violence against the out-group as positive, even desirable or heroic.[17]

---

[16] van der Dennen, Johan M. G., '*Ethnocentrism and In-Group/Out-Group Differentiation*', p. xvi

[17] Ibid., p. 1

'In-group' affiliations can be based on very different markers. An example for a primitive form – which according to van der Dennen's introduction seems to be historically the oldest form of ethnocentrism – are blood-related bonds which might result in blood feuds or blood revenge. Today we encounter more sophisticated forms of ethnocentrism like nationalism or patriotism. Here the markers of bondage are crafted rationalities[18] based on exaggerated images of the 'self' and of the 'other': the 'self' is stylized into the standard for what is 'good', and the 'other' is fitted into a negative stereotype. In other words, ethnocentrism creates a bipolar worldview, where different rules apply for each side. According to Sumner (quoted by van der Dennen), such a worldview involves the existence of two different moral codes, one for the 'in-group' and another for the 'out-group': while it is strongly objectionable to violate the rights of the members of my own group – through theft or even murder – it may be commendable to cause harm to members of the 'out-group'. This double standard may have been functional in the past. It would weaken the 'in-group' if its members were to disregard each other's rights. However, being capable and willing to harm members of the 'out-group' may be considered as serving to protect and even strengthen the 'in-group'.[19]

Quoting Sumner in his brief history of the term, van der Dennen explains that ethnocentrism does not immediately result in hostility and that it could be rooted in the ancient necessity of seeing every foreign group as a threat that might attempt to seize their territory or natural resources. Thus, foreigners had to be viewed with mistrust and scepticism. This would mean, however, that it would take a stimulus more urgent than just the dissimilarity in habitus or appearance to get the 'in-group' to actually attack an 'out-group'[20] – if, for instance, the potential threat becomes a real one when they make an attempt to cut in on assets or to cause harm.

In other words, ethnocentrism is an impulse which has been explored by anthropologists, socio-biologists, psychologists and many others in the past century to explain all sorts of human behaviour especially in the context of cultural clashes or conflicts. There is no need to delve deeply into the different perspectives of those explanations, for there is a wide spectrum of different opinions regarding the capacity of the ethnocentrism theory to account for conflicts.

---

[18] Ibid., pp. 1, 8
[19] Ibid., p. 5
[20] Ibid., p. 4

The case of this study will be built on the following extractions from the literature on ethnocentrism:

- Ethnocentrism essentially is an impulse, which causes people to apply double standards. In the introduction, van der Dennen quotes Pinderhughes who argues that the commitment to one's own in-group often results in the loss of objectivity.[21]
- Even though this is an impulse which impairs our judgement towards others, it is not the only concept to account for hostile behaviour, which requires a separate stimulus to trigger antagonism.
- Reynolds points out that even though ethnocentrism can be explained biologically it does not mean that being racist is a natural impulse which cannot be overcome.[22]

In conclusion, ethnocentrism can explain the impulse of regarding differing cultures as alien or dangerous whilst preferring one's own system simply because it is familiar. Up until this point, it is a natural impulse, albeit one which can be overcome according to Reynolds. The sophisticated and rationalized forms which have arisen from it have different names such as patriotism, nationalism, exclusivism, etc. Paraphrasing Rosenblatt, van der Dennen explains:

> Nationalism, more often than ethnocentrism, involves loyalty to a politically distinct entity, membership in an elaborately organized and relatively populous social grouping, *adherence to a formalized ideology*, and performance of relatively stereotyped allegiance-expressing behaviour.[23] [Emphasis added]

Therefore, while ethnocentrism is an impulse that we may not be aware of, nationalism is a deliberate, sophisticated, and formalized form of ethnocentric force. Nationalism in this sense has an intellectual basis or 'formalized ideology', as van der Dennen calls it.

Nationalism, with all its constituents listed by van der Dennen, has a complex intellectual basis. It often draws the contents of its ideology from history and mythology (heroic figures, epics, etc.). This study will look at the epistemology of these myths and histories and the 'narratives' that they produce. Historical narratives are construed from a certain epistemic pattern and within

---

[21] Ibid., p. 2

[22] Reynolds, et al., eds., *The Sociobiology of Ethnocentrism,* pp. xv–xvii

[23] van der Dennen, Johan M. G., '*Ethnocentrism and In-Group/Out-Group Differentiation*', p. 8

one specific cultural and temporal sign system. A narrative is received or composed based on a human impulse which Taleb calls *narrative fallacy*: "our need to fit a story or pattern to a series of connected or disconnected facts. The statistical application is data mining." He also explains that narrative discipline is distinct from experimental discipline in that it "consists in fitting a convincing and well-sounding story to the past."[24] Selected historical facts are arranged in a sequence, implying correlations or causal links, which cannot be historically proven, adding premises and assumptions along the way, and the result is a story or narrative, which is half history and half fiction. It is history because it is based on historical facts or data, and it is fiction because it is infiltrated with causal links and assumptions from someone's imagination.

The key point in this study will be that the constructor of these narratives is not only the narrator or author but also their recipient or *narratee*. Narratives can be construed by the narrator or *narratee* in accordance with his or her way of thinking, i.e. to make sense of facts – or to alter them if necessary – that one would otherwise much rather deny or ignore to maintain one's worldview. Narratives can also be designed for a specific purpose, for instance, to manipulate or steer opinions in propaganda or demagoguery.

In the context of our discussion about the juxtaposition of Islam and the West, the term Eurocentrism will be used to refer to the non-soteriological equivalent of exclusivism. Eurocentrism refers to the biased perspective assessing everything by today's so-called Western or European standards. A Eurocentric view is at the root of the narrative, which stylizes the idea of 'the West' into an ideal concept that every individual must internalize and, more importantly, which no other worldview can surpass. The resulting outlook is that people can only be truly free, rational, humanistic or modern if they live according to the Western lifestyle.

In this sense, the West and Islam are ideals which are propagated by several different narratives. The battle lines are drawn by external stimuli (conflict of political interests, competition, etc.) which is where the narratives using positive distinction for each to transmit its own superiority come into use. Images of the 'self' and 'other' are composed in opposition to each other. It is largely believed, for instance, that modernism and progress is something that originated and is primarily situated in the West. And there is a tendency to identify Islam or the West respectively with certain values or traits, either good or bad in distinction to the self-image. It is a commonly believed notion that Islam

---

[24] Taleb, *The Black Swan*, p. 309

and the West are inherently opposed to one another. Incidentally, this is further evidence to support the contention that both these are ideals because it does not occur to the followers of an idealized concept that every system is imperfect since it is designed and applied by human beings. Instead of realizing this, they assign descriptive attributes to each other as if these only occur on one side even though most of them are universal. Some of the views or values attributed to either the West or Islam can easily be found elsewhere. Homophobia, to name one, is often assigned to the Islamic worldview, while actually it is also found in significant levels in non-Islamic places like Russia, South America, South Africa, etc. And even countries belonging to the Western confederation have certainly not managed to eradicate homophobic sentiments from their midst and are far from having accomplished full equality in LGBTQ rights. The German government was also strongly opposed to same-sex marriage until very recently. Nevertheless, homophobia has been successfully attached to the image of Islam.

As mentioned earlier, the hostility cannot simply be explained by one impulse but by certain actions that suggested a real threat. The West might have been threatened by the Islamist narrative, on the one hand, which offers Muslims a way to free 'their' lands and resources from the colonial grip of Western countries, by forming one caliphate to fight against this "big bad West". On the other hand, they might feel threatened even by 'moderate Islam' (= a religion with no interest in political power or superiority claims), as it is still growing as a religion, and Muslims who live in Europe and America have not adopted the Western mind-set without question. In the modern age – although not for the first time in history – Muslims feel their religious views to be under attack from the West and thus, in order to defend them, responded with a different narrative built on the idea that Islam is the superior worldview which cannot be flawed. While this basic idea itself may have existed since the beginning of Islam, the narratives like Arab Socialism, Wahhabism, etc. were composed as a direct response to the developments in the West and were new concepts.

This is obviously a very simplistic account and in order to understand this better, we will have to take a closer look at the development of the characteristic attributes of Islam and the West throughout their history in chapter three. The said chapter comprises a reconstruction of the narratives which the terms 'Islam' and 'the West' denote respectively, as these have undergone a very long process of development. Starting with a critical reflection of the definitions they each can have, or have had in the past, this quest for a definition will be approached gradually. We will look at the evolution of the two principle narratives through history and weave them into the fabric of this thesis, before offering literary analyses of selected works of fiction. Even though this section begins with the term 'Islam', both these terms will be dealt with simultaneously. The idea is to trace the diachronic development which led to the definitions of Islam and the West and the narratives that prevail today.

In conclusion, this research is built on the premise that Islam and the West are ideal conceptions and markers of identity. However, these concepts are erratic, subjective and sometimes purport unsubstantiated ideas. They are based upon sets of values, which tend to be exclusive, non-negotiable and binding. These values generate a biased view, which results in narratives that are historically selective, yet coherent and highly credible because they appear to be substantiated and firm.

Nevertheless, the question whether the values of Islam really clash with the values of the West comes to mind. This cannot be answered with a yes or no because it would depend on how Islam and the West are interpreted. One would have to begin by finding one absolute definition of what Islamic and Western values are. There is no one version of Islam and there is no consent about what defines Western values. The latter is derived from several different sources: the catalogue of human rights, the constitutions of western states, Christian values, values of the Renaissance or of the age of enlightenment etc. There is no consensus regarding their definitions, and yet the idea that Western and Islamic values are incompatible is rarely questioned by anyone. This is because the general public is not encouraged to question this idea or the circulated definitions of the terms 'Islam' and 'the West'. Intellectual efforts at maintaining this clash between Muslim and Non-Muslim values have been made on different levels, i.e. political or religious, past or present, the haves and have-nots, etc. The reasons for this are manifold: on the Western side, there were imperialist and colonialist intentions, economic interests, etc. On the Muslim side, it was the loss of political, military and territorial advantage when Europe suddenly (the suddenness was not real in timescales, but a perceived one from the colonized countries' point of view) became more advanced in every discipline of the civilized world in the nineteenth century. What started as a struggle to keep up with the progress of the West ended as a battle of regaining independence from colonial seizures. The ongoing wars involving Muslim majority countries continue to fuel aspirations of seeding distrust and hatred against the respective other. These basic causes, which all arose from a specific historical background, will be discussed in more detail in chapter three.

Therefore, depending on the narrative of what is or is not Islamic/Western these two broad-based entities can be defined as inherently opposed to one another and consequently as incompatible. On the other hand, there are also narratives that disprove this incompatibility. Hence it is important to look at how narratives are composed and distributed.

The focus of this study will be different kinds of narratives, which maintain the alienation between Islam and the West. The use of the term *narrative* for this study also requires interpretation and elucidation. *Narrative* is an object of study in many different fields, and thus has many different applications; and since it will have different applications throughout the course of this interdisciplinary research, I must first map out a theoretical model for this enterprise.

UNDERSTANDING NARRATIVES OF DISPARITY (NODS)

TOWARDS A THEORETICAL MODEL OF NODS

Narrative theory and its object of study have several applications. In the previous section, we had a brief explanation of what a narrative can denote in a general context. But in literary theory, for instance, the term narrative has a precise definition, which will also be relevant, especially during the analysis of the selection of novels in this thesis. Therefore, a clear typology of the term and its different uses is necessary.

This study seeks to explain the development of several different kinds of narratives (regarding their contents, function, and topics of invention) that have caused an oppositional view between Islam and the West. We must begin by mapping out which theories will be applied. First, we need a definition of what narratives are. Fludernik sums up a useful standard definition as follows:

> According to Chatman, there are three main text types: argumentative, descriptive and narrative. Descriptions have no temporal ordering or plot elements; arguments build on logical connections and links; only narratives have temporal structure and a discourse level. Individual sentences or passages may belong to the other text types (there can be descriptive passages in argumentative texts, for example). However, narrative texts proper are based on the combination of story and discourse, a dyad which description and argument do not have, just as they have no 'story'.[25]

"Narratives are based on cause-and-effect relationships that are applied to sequences of events."[26] It is about "how the events of a story are represented regarding selection and (re-)arrangement of narrated details (sequence), as well as space and time."[27] Since the narrator and the *narratee* interpret events, sketching causal links, making assumptions, omitting details, etc., a narrative is created, carrying meaning that goes beyond that which was actually narrated.

---

[25] Fludernik, *An Introduction to Narratology*, pp. 105–6
[26] Ibid., p. 2
[27] Cobley, *Narrative*, p. 12

> Commonly cited examples of narrative in everyday life are films, music videos, advertisements, television and newspaper journalism, myths, paintings, songs, comic strips, anecdotes, jokes, stories of our holidays, and accounts or our day. In more academic contexts, there has been a recognition that narrative is central to the representation of identity, in personal memory and self-representation or in collective identity of groups such as regions, nations, race, and gender. There has been widespread interest in narrative in history, in the operations of legal systems, in psychoanalysis, in scientific analysis, in economics, and in philosophy.[28]

The omnipresence of narratives in everyday life suggests that human beings have a natural tendency towards them. Fludernik argues that the human brain is naturally programmed to record the complexity of correlations in narrative forms such as metaphors, stories, analogies, etc.

> In reconstructing our own lives as stories, we like to emphasize how particular occurrences have brought about and influenced subsequent events. Life is described as a goal-directed chain of events which, despite numerous obstacles and thanks to certain opportunities, has led to the present state of affairs [...]. It is therefore not surprising that psycho-analysis should have incorporated the telling of a patient's life story into the therapeutic process [...].
>
> The significance of narrative in human culture can be seen from the fact that written cultures seek their origins in myths which they then record for posterity. In an explanatory process, rather like that of individual autobiographical narratives, historians then begin to inscribe the achievements of their forefathers and the progress of their nation down to the present in the cultural memory in the form of histories or stories. [...] The nation-state has his own story. [...] Narrative provides us with a fundamental epistemological structure that helps us to make sense of the confusing diversity and multiplicity of events and to produce explanatory patterns for them.[29]

Mark Currie stipulates that "it does not seem at all exaggerated to view humans as narrative animals, as *homo fabulans* – the tellers and interpreters of narrative".[30] In conclusion, human beings have a need to select information, piece it together in a complex form of correlation, sequence, and progression in order to make sense of or give meaning to our past, present, and future. This is why narratives can also be produced and circulated without conscious deliberation.

Narratology "is the study of narrative as a genre. Its objective is to describe the constants, variables, and combinations typical of narrative and to clarify

---

[28] Currie, *Postmodern Narrative Theory,* p. 2
[29] Fludernik, *An Introduction to Narratology,* pp. 1–2
[30] Currie, *Postmodern Narrative Theory,* p. 2

how these characteristics of narrative texts connect within the framework of theoretical models (typologies)."[31] As an area of research, narratology (or Narrative Theory) draws explanatory models from many other areas. It "resembles semiotics in so far as it analyses the constitution of [...] meaning in texts (films, conversational narratives, etc.)."[32] Semiotics – the science of signs and meaning derived from linguistics – would suggest that meaning depends on fixed sign systems of one time and culture. This constitution of meaning is relevant for the literary analysis using models from literary theory.

One such "modern intellectual movement that analyses cultural phenomena according to principles derived from linguistics, emphasizing the systematic interrelationships among the elements of any human activity, and thus the abstract codes and conventions governing the social production of meanings" [33] is structuralism.

> Building on the linguistic concept of the phoneme – a unit of meaningful sound defined purely by its differences from other phonemes rather than by any inherent features – structuralism argues that the elements composing any cultural phenomenon (from cooking to drama) are similarly 'relational': that is, they have meaning only by virtue of their contrasts with other elements of the system, especially in binary oppositions of paired opposites. […]
>
> […] In the study of literary works, structuralism is distinguished by its rejection of those traditional notions according to which literature 'expresses' an author's meaning or 'reflects' reality. Instead, the 'text' is seen as an objective structure activating various codes and conventions which are independent of author, reader, and external reality.[34]

Fludernik explains that since "linguistics has served as a paradigm for narratology, it comes as no surprise that narratologists' models are primarily structuralist and dominated by binary oppositions (story vs. discourse, narrator vs. narratee [...])."[35] In the same fashion, the composition of modernist narratives is also largely structuralist and therefore also based on binary oppositions. One criticism of structuralism is that the binary view of structuralism leads to a fallacy which Jacques Derrida has called Logocentrism:

> Logocentrism is a term that describes the tendency of Western thinkers to privilege one term in a binary opposition over the other term, thus creating a hierarchy

[31] Fludernik, *An Introduction to Narratology*, p. 8
[32] Ibid., p. 9
[33] Baldick, *The Oxford Dictionary of Literary Terms*, (accessed 27 May 2016)
[34] Ibid.
[35] Fludernik, *An Introduction to Narratology*, p. 8

> that organizes thought (e.g. speech over writing, male over female, reason over superstition). [...] In addition, the two terms of a binary opposition define themselves against each other (which [Derrida] calls supplementarity), and any hierarchy is therefore merely arbitrary.[36]

Critics of structuralism see its key weakness, however, in its synchronic and descriptive view.[37] Foucault, for instance, believed that structuralism is restricted because it works within the boundaries of one (cultural or temporal) sign system. The Eurocentric view on history, which was explained earlier is biased by the application of the present European values, with little or insufficient regard to the time interval.

Therefore, history seems to be in many ways merely a collection of narratives; especially so if we look at Jörn Rüsen's definition of history in the series *Making Sense of History*:

> [H]istory is time which has gained sense and meaning. History is meaningful and sense-bearing time. It combines past, present and future in a way that human beings can live in the tense intersection of remembered past and expected future. History is a process of reflecting the time order of human life, grounded on experience and moved by outlooks on the future.
>
> Across the huge variety in which this cultural feature of time we call history has been realized, all its variations share a common mental practice and form: narration. By narration time gains sense. Narratives transform the past into history; they combine experience and expectation – the two main time dimensions of human life. [...] Narratives create the field where history lives its cultural life in the minds of the people, telling them who they are and what the temporal change of themselves and their world is about.[38]

Francois Furet describes this style as history's traditional obedience to "the logic of narrative. What comes first explains what follows." He continues to explain that such a commitment to putting events in a sequence producing logic demands a deliberate selection, arrangement, and presentation of historical facts:

> Since history thus defined has a meaning that predates, so to speak, the set of phenomena that it encompasses, one need only arrange historical facts on the timescale for them to become meaningful within a process known in advance. The very selection of those facts is predicated upon the same implicit logic: the period takes precedence over the object being analyzed; events are chosen according to their place in a narrative defined by a beginning and an end. Little

---

[36] Ritzer, *Encyclopaedia of Social Theory*, p. 591
[37] Ibid., pp. 590–1
[38] Rüsen, *History, Narration, Interpretation, Orientation*, p. 2

> does it matter, therefore, if the events are unique, not comparable, or even lacking in homogeneity with one another, since their significance derives from an external source. But as that significance tends to turn events into markers of change, signaling the dips and breaks along the imaginary route of time, they are chosen for their capacity to embody change and the phases of change. The model of this type of history is political history, both because nation-states are held to be the major agents of change, and because politics, in a wide sense, constitutes the prime repertoire of change: it is the main mode in which modern societies experience and interpret their transformations.[39]

Historiography has also applied various other narrative explanatory models, as well as some non-narrative ones, "such as those which assume that history follows certain natural laws, or those which conceptualize current events as recurrences of crucial moments in a nation's history: 9/11 as a 'repetition' (also in the Freudian or Derridean sense) of Pearl Harbor."[40] However, the classic form of historical narrative, especially when referenced outside the academic historiographic discourse follows the logic of narrative as described by Furet above. Apart from the selection, arrangement, and presentation of historical events in a certain way, the public discourse has another tendency relevant for this research: the inference of temporal succession.

Markers of change suggest a discontinuity of certain tendencies or events in history, which is based on a modernist view of history as progress. Modernism can be defined as "any movement or climate of ideas [...] that supports change, the retirement of the old or traditional, and the forward march of the avant-garde. More specifically, adherence to the ideas and ideals of the Enlightenment. This is the sense that gives rise to the contrary movement of post-modernism."[41] Post-modernists take great issue with the idea of history as merely a temporal succession of isolated and self-contained periods which each have a point of origin and a point of abandonment. This problem of 'periodising' history also reflects in the terms post-colonialism and post-modernism. "In each case, the prefix suggests succession, temporal break, a new period (if not a new start)" [42] though each of these paradigms stand for the abandonment of any notion of historical discontinuity. As a result,

> post-modernism has been seen as simply the latest variant of modernism, and neo-colonialism has been suggested as a more appropriate term than post-colonialism. Although the suggestion is no doubt unpalatable to many, especially the

[39] Furet, *Beyond the Annales*, p. 397
[40] Fludernik, *An Introduction to Narratology*, p. 2
[41] Blackburn, *The Oxford Dictionary of Philosophy*, (accessed 27 May 2016).
[42] Williams and Chrisman, eds., *Colonial Discourse and Post-Colonial Theory*, p. 12

supporters and celebrants of post-modernism, this pattern of an apparent newness masking an underlying continuity might be well-founded.[43]

While fiction writers can legitimately fashion their narratives without restraint, historians do the same with the crucial distinction that their narratives must be supported by sources and evidence. Fludernik concludes that every history traces back to a certain (limited) perspective.[44]

> [Hayden White] maintains that the so-called historical 'facts' and 'events' are only constructed by historiographical discourse and then have meaning attributed to them in a plot which is created by the historian. [...] Every history takes what historians agree upon after the sources have been studied, and interprets this on the basis of speculation or by having recourse to fresh sources or new methods. In contrast to the novel, historical narrative can be proved false if new sources are found. So, the fictionality of history, according to Hayden White, [...] derives from the fact that all plots are constructed, including historical plots in history texts.[45] [Emphasis added.]

To sum up, historical narrative is produced somewhere between the sequence of historical facts on the one hand and the fictionality of the narrativity of history on the other hand. In comparison, literary fiction fashions narratives, which can also be based on similar facts as historical narratives. Since the term narrative can have different applications in different scientific disciplines, it is important to map out some of the theories surrounding it that will become relevant in this study.

Narratology as a sub-discipline of literary studies distinguishes the term narrative from story and plot of a work of fiction. The "'story' consists of all the events which are to be depicted [...] 'plot' is the chain of causation which dictates that these events are somehow linked and that they are therefore to be depicted in relation to each other." The term 'narrative' denotes "the showing or the telling of these events and the mode selected for that to take place."[46] To avoid confusion, I will henceforth refer to 'narrative' in this literary sense either as 'fictional narrative', 'narration' or as 'narrative mode', depending on which one is apt. This 'narrative' in its general use of relating the sequence of the plot is to be differentiated from the usage of this word as propagated beliefs and opinions as in narratives of disparity. This is explained more specifically in the section 'NoDs and Other Applications of the Term'. The term 'fictional

---

[43] Ibid.
[44] Fludernik, *An Introduction to Narratology,* p. 3
[45] Ibid., p. 59
[46] Cobley, *Narrative,* pp. 6–7

narrative' would denote what Fludernik – after compiling characteristics from several literary theorists – describes as

> a representation of a possible world in a linguistic and/or visual medium, at whose center there are one or several protagonists of an anthropomorphic nature who are existentially anchored in a temporal and spatial sense and who (mostly) perform goal-directed actions (action and plot structure). [...] Not all [fictional] narratives have a foregrounded narrator figure, however. The narrator or narrative discourse shape the narrated world creatively and individualistically at the level of the text, and this happens particularly through the (re)arrangement of the temporal order in which events are presented and through the choice of perspective (point of view, focalization). Texts that are read as narratives (or 'experienced' in the case of drama or film) thereby instantiate their narrativity [...].[47]

Since literary narrative hinges on characters, Fludernik explains later that fictional narrative is not necessarily constituted of a sequence of events because experientiality, rather than actions or events, usually constructs them. There is a vast variety of literary strategies to achieve that, even without a narrator figure. "[The] communication of anthropocentric experience [Experientiality] means drawing on fixed patterns of behaviour as well as conveying thoughts and feelings, and depicting perceptions and reflections." The modern psychological novel is an example of such literary narratives.[48] Fludernik believes that narrativity does not depend on the plot because the actions and events of a plot are part of human experience and not vice versa.[49] Experientiality is another characteristic element which distinguishes literary narrative from historical narrative. Fludernik continues to argue that if narrative is understood as that which is construed through experientiality, then history is arguably not narrative:

> Experientiality is filtered through consciousness, thus implying that narrative is a subjective representation through the medium of consciousness. By contrast, academic historiography, which represents facts and arguments but not experientiality, is not entirely narrative. Historiography focuses on the reporting of events, which do not necessarily express narrativity in the sense given above.[50]

While Fludernik argues that even though history can be tainted with fictionality, it ought not to be subjective enough to qualify as narrative. This definition can be complemented by the fact that modernist and structuralist historiography has served in creating so-called grand narratives, which are also

---

[47] Fludernik, *An Introduction to Narratology,* p. 6
[48] Ibid., p. 59
[49] Ibid., p. 109
[50] Ibid.

known as 'metanarratives'. Only the phrase 'grand narratives' will be used in this study to avoid confusion with the self-reflexive writing technique called metanarration, in which the narrator reflects on the process of narration. However, this does not mean that there are no grand narratives in literary theory; the 'busting of the literary canon' is one example as Currie explains:

> One of the major impacts of the new historicisms in literary studies was the busting of the canon: the demythologization of literary value, the breaking of male Anglo-Saxon hegemony in literary studies, the destruction of the boundary between high and popular culture. These were campaigns waged by leftist intellectuals against the traditional values of high culture. The enemy in intellectual terms was totalisation: the idea that the history of literature in its entirety could be represnted [sic] by such a tiny fragment of literature. The literary canon was a grand narrative in the sense that it represented the history of literature as a whole as a linear story constructed by sweeping exclusions. [...] Many of the political problems with the canon were associated with its national character. Within a nation, the canon was understood as a kind of trickle-down economics, where the value and values of great works, as arbitrated by great people with the discrimination to know the good from the bad, functioned as top-down instruction. A kind of narcissism presided over the canon, translating the values of a critical elite into the value of great literature, alleging the universalism of those values.[51]

Other examples of grand narratives are ideas like Enlightenment or Marxism. They are the result of modernist thinking, which is based on the premise that history is progress which dictates that old ideas must be abandoned for the new.

The intellectual movement Modernism subsumes all ideas that celebrate change and progress, meaning "the retirement of the old or traditional, and the forward march of the avant-garde." In this way, modernist views "[adhere] to the ideas and ideals of the Enlightenment."[52] The grand narratives of Modernism are questioned and deconstructed by two counter-movements: Postmodernism and Poststructuralism. The former is primarily known for its aversion of the universality of grand narratives: According to Lyotard,

> the characteristic feature of postmodernity [...] is that the power of the metanarrative [grand narrative] as a legitimating, empowering force is on the wane. Postmodern subjects simply don't [sic] believe in [grand narratives] anymore. They instinctively acknowledge instead the rhetorical function of narrative, and appreciate that alternative narratives could be fashioned from the same groups of events. [...]

---

[51] Currie, *Postmodern Narrative Theory,* p. 108

[52] Blackburn, *The Oxford Dictionary of Philosophy*, (accessed 27 May 2016).

> [...] One of the 'realist' conceits which postmodern writers reject is the impression that narrative somehow unfolds naturally without being shaped by an author, that the task of the narrator is simply to present the reader with a coherent narrative which s/he has come upon. Instead narrative is always the result of selection and interpretation. This is something demonstrated repeatedly by the self-reflexive techniques of the 'metafictional' writers [...].[53]

Nicol describes grand narratives as "a form of ideology which functions violently to suppress and control the individual subject by imposing a false sense of 'totality' and 'universality' on a set of disparate things, actions, and events."[54] Thus, grand narratives enforce an undisputed concurrence of the structural premises that they are based on – be that discontinuity, progress, traditionalism, binary structures or hierarchies. A grand narrative

> is *like a literary narrative* in that it is essentially a means of ordering discrete elements in a particular form and thus presenting a rhetorical case about the way things work or are connected, which legitimates political positions and courses of action.[55] [Emphasis added]

The questioning of grand narratives required postmodernists to come up with an alternative to avoid making post-modernism another grand narrative. Thus, Lyotard believed that grand narratives must be substituted by what he called little narratives (*petit récits*), "which do not attempt to present an overarching 'Truth' but offer a qualified, limited 'truth', one relative to a particular situation." Lyotard assumed that "narratives are never innocent nor natural but always partial, selective, and rhetorical."[56]

This intellectual position is complemented by post-structuralism which is opposed to

> the structuralist view that the unconscious, or the forms of society, will themselves obey structural laws, waiting to be discovered. [Instead], it echoes Nietzsche's hostility to the reduction of human phenomena to lawlike generalizations, associating such views with the philosophical underpinnings of determinist systems such as Marxism, and instead celebrating the formless, or the subjective and spontaneous. Leaning heavily on the psychoanalytic dissolution of the self, it provides one manifestation of the sceptical stance of postmodernism, in particular by refusing any concepts of objectivity, reality, and truth.[57]

Additionally, poststructuralists seek explanations in diachronic histories rather than in relations, structures or sign systems. However, poststructuralism

---

[53] Nicol, *The Cambridge Introduction to Postmodern Fiction,* p. 12
[54] Ibid., p. 11
[55] Ibid.
[56] Ibid., p. 12
[57] Blackburn, *The Oxford Dictionary of Philosophy*, (accessed 27 May 2016).

and postmodernism run the risk of repeating all the fallacies that they repudiate, one of which is related to their names: "In each case, the prefix suggests succession, temporal break, a new period (if not a new start); in each case, however, the idea of historical discontinuity has been challenged". Therefore, modernist views still prevail and continue to forge grand narratives. Therefore, new movements such as post-modernism, post-structuralism, and post-colonialism must be new variants of their respective namesakes, or simply a collection of responses to the same. In the case of post-colonialism, alternative terms, such as neo-colonialism, have been introduced to avoid this fallacy.[58]

While this idea of taking a more self-reflexive and less exceptionalist vantage point has been introduced to the discourse by now, the so-called NoDs, which construct a conflict between Islam and West do not employ the said vantage point but build on the above-mentioned fallacies of post-modernism (and other grand narratives). Juxtaposing two views with regard to postmodernism, Williams quoted Robert Young on the one hand, who says in *White Mythologies* that "Postmodernism can best be defined as European culture's awareness that it is no longer the unquestioned and dominant centre of the world", and the editors of *Past the Last Post*, on the other hand, see postmodernism "as a determined attempt to retain the position and influence of global centrality".[59] The latter describes the function rather than the definition of postmodernism and confirms that it has already become another grand narrative. In conclusion, the post-structuralist idea of questioning grand narratives as well as Lyotard's efforts to avoid replacing old grand narratives with new ones have failed primarily for one reason: questioning or abandoning old grand narratives would have meant the loss of the unquestioned global dominance and moral high ground of European/Western culture, which is necessary in order to legitimize many ongoing worldwide geopolitical and economic activities.

Therefore, grand narratives of Western culture today struggle for a position of superiority under the guise of a struggle for progress or perfection. To construct a hierarchy, narratives must construct binary or multipolar structures as well as characteristics for each. Thus, grand narratives construct ideas for identities.

With reference to several key scholars such as Lévi-Strauss, Bhaba, and Said, Cobley argues that narrative in history and fiction (oral or written depending on the time and the culture) does not only serve the preservation and

---

[58] Williams and Chrisman, eds., *Colonial Discourse and Post-Colonial Theory,* p. 12
[59] Ibid., p. 13

deliverance of information or 'memory'.[60] Cobley explains the key functions of applications of narratives in historiography, stipulating that

> the key 'use' of narrative concerns identity. It is fairly well known in the modern world that social circumstances, and the existence of the self within them, are to a large extent socially constructed by texts and narratives they frequently contain (Shotter and Gergen 1989). Yet it seems that narrative has played an important role in identity-formation for a long time. Commentators on oral culture, as we have seen, repeatedly found that oral narrative served a mnemonic purpose. Yet narrative structures, with their repetitions and stock devices which enabled early oral cultures to remember key points about their present and their history, also facilitated something else. Memory embodied in narrative made a significant contribution to the formation and maintenance of the self-image of peoples, especially when writing may not have been available physically to store records of past events and details of people's most cherished ideals.[61]

Most narratives appeal to people by invoking ideals. Cobley explains the role of narrative in nationalism by explaining that affiliation to one nation requires common markers of identity, which not only include territorial common ground but also common ideals and common history. In my view, this is applicable in the case of Islam and the West as both of these are ideals, which have substituted nationalism as a marker of collective identity. Cobley then goes on to explain that narratives do not always work to unite people but also to promote differences. And this is where he gets to the crucial point of this study:

> [Narrative] has been instrumental in the promotion of difference, helping to preserve some memories and not others, and helping to bind some people into a given community and not others. In fact, narrative has sometimes assisted in upholding an absolutist conception of cultural difference, especially in its contribution to the concept of tradition. In Europe since the Renaissance rediscovery of Greek civilization, for example, the narratives of Ancient Greece have been incorporated into a 'Western tradition' which has frequently been held to be the 'first' and the 'best'. However, assertions of the purity of such a tradition have been so fragile that they have had to be protected by intellectual fortifications in order to prevent infiltration.
>
> Through works such as Martin Bernal's *Black Athena* (1987), it is now well known that European historians, in the nineteenth century especially, systematically 'edited out' the non-white elements of the Western past. The emphasis on Ancient Greece as the cradle of Western culture enabled European historians to expunge the Egyptian, Semitic and African roots of the West's history; what

---

[60] Cobley, *Narrative*, p. 37
[61] Ibid., pp. 37–8

> remained as a result of this process could be put to contemporary use. 'The Greek classics' according to Edward Said, 'served the Italian, French and English humanists without the troublesome interposition of actual Greeks. Texts by dead people were read, appreciated, and appropriated by people who imagined an ideal 'commonwealth' (1994: 235). The 'narrative' of Europe, incorporating some traditions, myths and memories, therefore had a specific goal.[62]

Therefore, it is important to remember that narratives do more than just offer explanations or causal correlations, or give time meaning. They unify members of the 'in-group' and alienate members of the 'out-group'. In fact, they can even function in order to create 'in-groups' and 'out-groups' where there might have been none, to begin with. This is what the NoDs do, as they work to construct a Western identity and a counter-image of Islamic identity as its antithesis. I have divided these NoDs into categories to make them identifiable in discourses and in works of literature where they appear. The NoDs may be recognized as being *petit récits* or little narratives. After all, each has an intellectual, historical and perhaps even factual basis, but they still constitute only part of the truth.

NoDs and Other Applications of the Term

During my research, I realized that I cannot use the term narratives, even in a specified form like Narratives of Disparity, based on a choice of characteristics most suitable for this analysis. Cobley warns:

> All of these findings seem to suggest that narrative has some basic features, including characters and situations, which might tempt one to identify universalizing tendencies in the narrative process. What such a view would fail to apprehend is the many different uses, for different peoples, at different times, that the world's narratives have had.[63]

This study builds on the poststructuralist and post-modern criticism of simplistic, binary, and synchronic paradigms. That is why there was the need to map out a formal model keeping in mind the theories about narrative from several disciplines because they will all become relevant for the analysis of the narratives in literature, and this will also have the capacity of ascertaining

---

[62] Ibid., pp. 38–9

[63] Ibid., p. 37

grand narratives which historiography might have created at some point. Such a narrative is sometimes recognized in itself and sometimes gets projected into the text by the reader, or arguably sometimes it is present in-between these processes.[64]

To help make the distinction between the different, relevant applications of narrative theory, I will briefly sum up all the different applications here:

a. Narrative as a form of written or oral text combines story (temporal order) and discourse and is distinguished from descriptive and argumentative text forms.
b. Historical narrative is construed by historians in order to make sense of time and primarily follows the following formats: *what comes first explains what follows*. History is from beginning to end tied together by facts; compiled, presented and read from one limited perspective, because the interpretation of events takes place under one sign system (semiotics). Therefore, historical narratives, like all plots, are constructed, which is why a certain level of fictionality is inherent, especially if one narrative is presented in a non-reflexive way.
c. Literary Narrative or fictional narrative is a form which is distinguished from plot and story. It occupies a narrative space between the beginning and the end. The narrative is necessarily anchored by characters (human or anthropomorphized, historical or fictional) and the narrative is presented through the consciousness of the characters. Therefore, the literary narrative is based on experientiality of the plot by its characters. It is fictional with the option of making claims in relation to reality.
d. Narration: the process of narrating, or the narrative techniques and modes that are applied.
e. Metanarration, a self-reflexive narrative technique, where the narrator reflects on the process of narration, thereby sensitizing the reader and himself to his subjectivity and biases.
f. Metanarrative or Grand narrative is a narrative on the macro level of a culture, which means it is not narrated in one text or one medium, but it is the narrative that determines the tone of all texts and narratives pertaining to the entire scope of a particular aspect of that culture or sometimes more expansively encompassing the

[64] Fludernik, *An Introduction to Narratology*, p. 109

whole culture. They consist of ideologies that emanate a universality which makes it harder to question or to contest them. Modernism and Enlightenment are examples of such grand narratives, as the premises of these (i.e. history is progress) determined the way that history was told and understood. Postmodernism is the movement which questions grand narratives and instead produces little narratives.

g. Little narratives, seek to create knowledge whilst constantly keeping in mind that this cannot be more than just one part of the truth. Therefore, Postmodernism is a little narrative if it is self-reflexive and does not claim universality.

The classification as *narratives of disparity* (NoDs) denotes a particular kind, found both in history and in literature. In this study, the analysis of novels will be preceded by a synchronic exploration of historical narratives of Western and Islamic identities respectively. In the literary analysis, four kinds of these narratives regarding the clash between Islam and the West will be extracted from novels and illuminated against the backdrop of historical narratives.

The novel as a genre allows intellectual exercises of experiencing different lives and changes in perspective as well as vantage points. The literary narrative in novels is character-centric, thus the depicted plot is primarily experienced and perceived from an individual perspective. This is the micro-level on which the selected novels for this research will be analysed: the constituents of the story world – characters, setting, time, plot, narration, etc. – depict a post-9/11 encounter between Islam and the West where the existence and divisive effect of NoDs becomes apparent. The mimetic qualities of the fictional story world can help demonstrate how the NoDs between Islam and the West manifest themselves in everyday life and cause a rift in the encounter that goes both ways. However, I would like to clarify that most novels and literary narratives do not create or perpetuate NoDs. On the contrary, most novels attempt to inspire a questioning of the prevailing structures and ideas of conflict between Islam and the West.

We will also discuss what literary narratives and NoDs have in common and what distinguishes them. They both have a lot of the same constituents: fictionality, historicity, character-centeredness, tropes, etc. But it is their dissimilarities which expose the weaknesses of NoDs: the perspective of NoDs is almost always restricted to one side, while novels usually offer multi-perspectivity in different ways, NoDs are fractional, biased, and one-sided. Also, literary narratives – even though they are coded in the same selection of tropes and devices, repeatedly – seek to offer different stories, different circumstances, different beginnings, different outcomes, different views, etc. Modern fiction covers a range of new genres and tropes by reinventing old ones or by using old tropes and devices in a new manner or making new combinations. This constant change of perspective, devices, and content inspires a constant questioning of previous narratives. In a way, novels produce little narratives (*petit récits*) as Lyotard called them. In contrast, NoDs which are uniform in content and repetitive in composition offer little or no inspiration for questioning previous narratives, and thus these act like grand narratives.

The cognitive surplus of using novels to analyse NoDs is that literary narratives offer the ideal standards against which the composition, content, and basis can be measured. Thus, this will disclose the weaknesses of these grand narratives which is the best way to deconstruct NoDs.

NoDs can immediately seem credible because people have a natural disposition of construing, sharing and reading narratives and it requires not only a certain level of previous knowledge on the matter but also some intellectual effort to recognize, pinpoint, and disclose the weaknesses in them in order to deconstruct the narrative as a whole. This is probably why NoDs are easily accepted by those already inclined in that direction, whereas they are rarely sound enough to persuade those who think differently. It is important to note that any narrative that was constructed against Islam was probably a response to an Islamist narrative against the West and vice versa. Narratives are rarely deconstructed by those who disagree with them. Instead, they are usually met with a counter-narrative which is equally incomplete and one-sided, thus only able to persuade like-minded people. This does not necessarily mean that there must always be the intention of hardening battle lines between these two groups. Maajid Nawaz reflected in his biography that it is "deeply ironic that Islamist and anti-Islam extremist groups have a symbiotic relationship with each other, feeding off each other's paranoia and propaganda: far-right extremism, Islamism, more far-right extremism, more Islamism and so on."[65] NoDs have a good chance of survival because narrative and counter-narrative feed on each other, thus effectuating their continued existence.

NoDs consist of a coherent and plausible presentation of selected ideas from a subjective point of view. They are subjective because they highlight some nuances whilst omitting or obscuring others, thus giving an imbalanced account favouring or reassuring one side of at least two. NoDs are based on a

[65] Nawaz and Bromley, *Radical,* pp. 137–8

selection of arguments, evidence and deductive reasoning, which are put in a specific order designing a well-founded and coherent argument, carefully veiling the weak points or glitches by means of rhetoric or pseudo-scientific trickery. Arguments are backed up by historical data, demographical figures and often even polls. However, the approaches of statistical analysis are also subjected to a vast methodology. Therefore, every time we hear statistics we should check the source and make sure the study was conducted in a scientifically valid and impartial manner. Since people usually refrain from making such inquiries, it is easy to throw around numbers or percentages in order to make a convincing point. In the public discourse, it is largely believed that numbers cannot lie. In October 2014 a heated TV-debate about Islam on the weekly show *Real Time with Bill Maher* with guests Sam Harris (Neo-Atheist author) and Ben Affleck (an actor) became an internet hit because Affleck reprimanded the other two for Anti-Muslim racism. The host quoted a poll that showed over 70% of the Pakistani population believed that apostasy should be penalized by death.[66] Maher then drew a causal link between this result and negative effects of the Quran because Pakistan is officially a so-called 'Islamic Republic'. However, considering the fact that the illiteracy rate in Pakistan is somewhere above 50% – varying between 40% and 70% among different age groups and the sexes[67] – it would become rather difficult to trace this grave development back to the Quran which most Muslims do not read but only recite in Arabic. But even the translation of the Quran cannot simply be read without a proper knowledge about its hermeneutics. In any case, one should inquire as to how this data was collected. Because in a country like Pakistan, with such a complex demographic (a huge variety of ethnicities, languages, cultures, religious creeds, as well as a vast spectrum of different social, economic and educational conditions), it is difficult to select a proper representative sample or a sample that covers all tiers of a sector of the population. Even though this result is certainly worrying, it cannot be conclusively linked to the teachings of the Quran. Therefore, 'facts' or numbers can be controversial. Different sources deliver different numbers depending on the circumstances of the data collection. Statistical analysis suggests that there are too many factors involved in real life to produce numbers with a one-hundred-percent validity. Therefore, neither the statement 'Islam is a threat to the West' nor the contention that 'Islam is a religion of peace' is wrong as long as both of these

---

66 The Pew Forum on Religion and Public Life, '*The World's Muslims: Religion, Politics and Society*', p. 55

67 UNICEF (2013), *Pakistan Statistics UNICEF*, (accessed 10 November 2017).

statements are based upon valid and plausible arguments. Such positions are held up by narratives, carefully scripted especially for sustaining and defending one position, which is necessarily only part of the entire truth (if there is such a thing). The purpose might also be persuasion, although it is hardly ever the result because these narratives usually appear very persuasive only to those who already think accordingly.

Narratives of Disparity can be based on different arguments, ideas or topics of invention. They do not necessarily have to be sophisticated or even tasteful. Hate-speech, for instance, can be based on a narrative. Often people can make racist resentment sound plausible by giving reasons and arguments for the way they feel. I have detected a few constant features on which narratives about the clash between Islam and the West are based, and as mentioned earlier I have divided them into the following four subcategories:

Narratives of Distinctive Identity

Intellectual attempts at defining Islam or the West by the very elements that seem to distinguish them from each other can be subsumed under the term Narratives of Distinctive Identity. The result is a bipolar worldview with a clear divide between Islam and the West. If the West is defined, for instance, as characteristically modernist, progressive and rational, then the logical inference is that Islam is and always has been traditionalist, reactionary and dogmatic. The idea of an irresolvable incompatibility of Islam and the West is often built on these efforts to define the two by their differences (real or fabricated).

Narratives of Inadequacy

These narratives seek to inextricably unite selected negative qualities with the identity of the 'out-group'. One example is the effort of asserting a general inadequacy of Islam compared to the West by referring to deficiencies in so-called Islamic countries or using individual cases of Muslims committing crimes or displaying unsavoury behaviour. Narratives of inadequacy – for instance, the one stating that Islam is misogynistic (silently adding: *in a way that the West could never be*) – imply that this failing is so inherent in Islam that it cannot be corrected unless the Muslim identity is shed off.

Narratives of Mutual Distrust

These narratives are fashioned from a selection of different historical and geopolitical events, which seemingly prove that Islam or Muslims have both the means and the intention to harm or infiltrate the Western people, infect the mind-set or sabotage society. For example, *'Islam is a threat to the West!'* Conversely, the narratives circulated in Muslim countries build on a selective history of oppression, colonization, and exploitation; they often also focus on the alleged harm that Western values might do to the values of Islam and to the integrity of Muslims who live there. Distrust is defined here as a combination of an absence of trust with the presence of fear or paranoia.

These narratives are applied at a higher level of escalation in this perceived conflict between these two sides, as they mean to justify any means to protect not only the people but also the values from pervasion or extinction.

Narratives of Superiority

These assert an unquestioned and indisputable superiority of the 'in-group's' ideals over every other ideology, civilization or religion of the past, present or future. These narratives are firmly established under the protection of a transcendental entity: in case of Islam, this is either God or the Prophet Muhammad, while in the case of the West these can be replaced by secular ideals that are made sacrosanct, e.g. enlightenment, freedom, rationalism, modernism, etc. Any attack, criticism or simply a refusal to bow to these idolized entities can evince outrage and be criminalized by labeling them as 'treason' or 'blasphemy'.

Much like the other three kinds, narratives of superiority utilize selected events from history in order to inspire the young generation's zeal for the noble cause of the West or the sacred mission of Muslims all over the world. Romanticized stories of bravery, sacrifice, and heroism are recurring patterns in these narratives. However, in contrast to the other three kinds, this last category sometimes builds on tautological or circular arguments instead of real evidence or clearly delineated arguments.

Some Examples are American Exceptionalism, Islam Supremacy, Pan-Arabism, *Leitkultur,* White Supremacy, Muslim Exceptionalism etc.

This last kind is difficult to overcome because it appeals to narcissistic impulses rather than ethnocentric ones. While the latter is a natural impulse the former has pathological capacities. Neither has a rational foundation or justification.

The four of these can be a sequence, or there can be narratives applying elements from more than one of these. Thus, Islamism, Pan-Arabism and the Global War on Terror as well-known examples would probably be a combination of 3 and 4, while some of them might also draw elements from the other two.

It is important to note that even though the explained examples for NoDs have been reconstructed from the West's point of view, the Muslim side has equally incomplete and biased NoDs against the West, some of which are direct responses (i.e. counter-narratives) to the anti-Muslim views in the West. They are different in content because they are based on different historical narratives and different motives and different grand-narratives, which is why the above examples could not be formulated in a neutral format ('the respective other' instead of 'Islam' or 'Muslims'). While in the Western discourse Islam is perceived as a threat to the people and the values of the West, many Muslims perceive the West as a brutal oppressor and exploiter, or as a threat to world peace and social justice. This is why one Muslim Narrative of Superiority is known as Arab Socialism: a counter-narrative to Western values and a direct strike against capitalism. The point is, that this tension is maintained by both sides equally, even if we are now discussing only one side. The upcoming part will explain the differences in the content of the NoDs of the two sides. But first I must add one note.

These four kinds of NoDs have been identified because of their recurring appearances in historical, political and literary discourse. There can be more than these or these could also be classified in an entirely different manner. The point is, that these four are not mutually exclusive and describe the most predominantly used topics of invention to compose narratives that serve to segregate Islam and the West.

Historical Perspectives on Islam and The West

Historical Narratives in Literature

> You have not been to Rhodes? You must go. It seemed to me unlike the other islands we had visited. Its cities were fortified, protected by ancient castles; they guarded against the Turks, much like the army and navy and air force of modern Greece, part of a wall against the East that still stands. How strange it was for me to think I grew up on the other side! [68]

This project is a study of NoDs in post-9/11 literature. What this means from a literary theorists' perspective will be discussed in chapter four. First, we need to discuss what this periodization means from a historical perspective. Earlier, we established that a modernist understanding of history is a 'stagist' view: history in stages which are completed, overcome, superseded, etc. Generally, it means that modernist historical narrative is premised on the idea that old traditions are substituted by new and progressive concepts and thence discontinued and the idea that historic developments took place within definite time periods of varying lengths.

The number of narratives and the number of novels to be analysed in this study had to be restricted not only for reasons of practicality but also so the basic hypothesis can have a validity at all; the basic hypothesis is that Islam and the West are not inherently disparate, but that narratives construct them in a way that they seem like oil and water. Before testing this hypothesis, we must make clear that it is not universally valid but merely an explanatory model, which can only be tested in a predefined context. The said context will be restricted temporally to the post 9/11 era, but that does not mean that this study is predicated on the idea of discontinuity. On the contrary, I believe that the years after the 2001 terrorist attacks against the USA in New York and Washington DC brought out in the open the continued existence of traditional sentiments regarding racial diversity, equality, and imperialism, which many believed had long been overcome.

To understand the present situation between the primary values of Islam and the West, it is important to look at their respective developments. After

---

[68] Hamid, *The Reluctant Fundamentalist,* p. 26

having explained what is meant by the terms 'Islam' and 'the West', we will now look at the gradual development which led to a bipolar perception of these two broad-based entities.

The previously quoted description of the traditional historical explanation in the form of a narrative by Furet, combined with the criticisms concerning a structuralist and binary view, as well as a modernist fallacy of discontinuity in history, led me to a different approach to this chapter. Norman Davies set up the following standards for a comprehensive historian today:

> Any narrative which chronicles the march of history over long periods is bound to be differently designed from the panorama which co-ordinates all the features relevant to a particular stage or moment. The former, chronological approach has to emphasize innovative events and movements which, though untypical at the time of their first appearance, will gain prominence at a later date. The latter, synchronic approach has to combine both the innovative and the traditional and their interactions. The first risks anachronism, the second immobility.
>
> Early modern Europe has served as one of the laboratories for these problems. Once dominated by historians exploring the roots of humanism, protestantism [sic], capitalism, science, and the nation-state, it then attracted the attention of specialists who showed, quite correctly, how elements of the medieval and pagan worlds had survived and thrived. The comprehensive historian must somehow strike a balance between the two.[69]

I have decided to build on this and attempt a historical view on the ideals of Islam and the West in a synchronic but also diachronic mode. The reason for this is no desire to claim to be a comprehensive historian as Davies' described, but because this seems the best way to avoid the fallacies of historical narratives thus far. As argued in previous sections, the construction of images of the 'other' is correlated to the construction of images of the 'self'. Since many contemporary public speakers on both extremes of the conflict between Islam and the West draw their inspiration from some historical narrative about the 'self' or the 'other', it can easily happen that this inquiry into their history becomes merely another counter-narrative based on the same subjectivities.

In order to avoid creating a counter-narrative against the national ethnocentric histories, painting pictures in which 'the other' is to blame for conflicts between them, we will take a look at selected markers of change in the history of each. Change is particularly important because it is so difficult to come by. Even the smallest modification in the way we think, live, assess, act, believe, etc. can take decades to come into effect. In some cases, we will even see that

---

[69] Davies, *Europe,* pp. 6–7

change can be deceptive: many concepts that we were certain had already been implemented, never reached below the surface.

The paradigm shifts in history which will be discussed here were chosen because they are recurring references used in some narratives of disparity in the selected works of literature. We will look at paradigm shifts on one side of this conflict and how it affected the other and vice versa. As we will see, the development of each side eventually began to be affected by the respective 'other', which is why it is not easily possible to dissect a history of Islam from the history of the West. We will look at developments which eventually led to the emergence of today's 'most precious' values, so important that people are ever willing to go to war for them.

We will begin with the history of the West because one of its most precious sources of pride, namely democracy, predates Islam by almost a millennium.

DEFINING 'THE WEST' FROM A DIACHRONIC VANTAGE POINT

> European history knows no such burst of vital energy until the era of the Renaissance. For Greece, apparently, did not develop slowly and methodically. It blazed.[70]

'The West' as a denomination for a set of ideals or a culture and identity is quite new. It was a substitution of the ideal of Europe as one, which in turn substituted the ideal of Nationalism, etc. There is no need to go into the detailed history of ancient Greece and the Roman Empire. I will only summarize the roots of civilization as we know it which date back to them, around a millennium before Christ. The most commonly cited points of reference for the ideas of Western civilization are Ancient Greece or Hellenism, Enlightenment and the Judeo-Christian tradition.

Ancient Greece blazed with developments that allowed humankind to influence the laws of nature to its advantage:

> Greek philosophy, or 'love of wisdom', grew up in opposition to conventional religious attitudes. Socrates (469 - 399 BC), son of a stonemason, was sentenced in Athens to drink hemlock for 'introducing strange gods' and 'corrupting youth'. Yet the Socratic method of asking penetrating questions in order to test the assumptions which underlie knowledge provided the basis of all subsequent

[70] Ibid., p. 98

> rational thought. [...] According to his disciple Plato, Socrates said: 'All I know is that I know nothing.' It was the perfect start for epistemology.
>
> Plato (c. 429-347 BC) and Plato's own disciple Aristotle (384-322 BC) together laid the foundations of most branches of speculative and natural philosophy. With [Plato's Academy and Aristotle's Lyceum] in mind, it has been said: 'the legacy of the Greeks to Western Philosophy was Western Philosophy'. [...] His [Plato's] encyclopaedic works range from metaphysics and ethics to politics, literary criticism, logic, physics, biology and astronomy.[71]

Greek philosophy came up against the religious myths around the Olympian Pantheon of its time. The Renaissance in the 15th and 16th centuries in Europe was marked by a revival of these Greek philosophies, which had been kept at bay by several schools of Christianity as they posed a threat to existing power structures. Even the ideas of Enlightenment were later resisted by some Christian churches. Many centuries passed after Ancient Greece was defeated by the Roman Empire when Cleopatra conceded defeat, and the knowledge of Hellenism was forgotten until its rediscovery by scholars during the Muslim reign in Europe from the 8th century to about the end of the 15th century.

In the meantime, the two great monotheistic religions developed in Europe. After Muslims conquered parts of Spain, they managed to erect societies where Christian and Jewish people would not suffer disadvantages from Muslim rulers. They tightened their grip only when their powers began to crumble. Their efforts were in vain because after a long period of steady decline of all Muslim empires, they were torn apart by sectarian conflicts and corrupted political systems. These and other developments were preceded by the crusades and the Reconquista in the eleventh century:

> The end of Umayyad rule in Spain in 1031 led in due course to what is known as the Reconquista. An important step in this was the fall of Toledo to the Christians in 1085, because many Muslim and Jewish scholars continued to live there and could be contacted by Christian scholars from France and elsewhere. In the century after the fall of Toledo, many translations of Arabic books began to be made into Latin. The Qur'an was one such and was followed by refutations. Western Europe certainly gained a fuller knowledge of Islam than it had previously had, despite its earlier contacts; but at the same time, it formed a negative image of Islam which has influenced European thought until the present century.[72]

---

[71] Ibid., pp. 110–1

[72] Watt, *Islam: A Short History,* p. 120

According to Armstrong, the sectarian and political conflicts among Muslims during the crusades had made it hard for them to "band together against an external foe"[73]. She thus continues:

> This became tragically apparent in July 1099, when the Christian Crusaders from western Europe attacked Jerusalem, the third holiest city in the Islamic world after Mecca and Medina, massacred its inhabitants, and established states in Palestine, the Lebanon and Anatolia.[74]

At the time, however, the Crusades were not perceived as a religious cause by the Arabs, and as Armstrong also explains:

> The Crusades were disgraceful and formative events in Western history; they were devastating for the Muslims of the Near East, but for the vast majority of Muslims in Iraq, Iran, Central Asia, Malaysia, Afghanistan and India, they were remote border incidents. It was only in the twentieth century when the West had become powerful and threatening, that Muslim historians would become preoccupied by the medieval Crusades [...].[75]

The Crusades are doubtlessly a part of a Muslim narrative against the West, but they are also referred to by Christians, the most famous example being George W. Bush Jr. who spoke of a crusade before invading Iraq.[76]

The Spanish Inquisition set in with the purpose of cleansing their history and culture from the impacts and the people that the Muslim reign had left behind. To this day, remnants of the Arab legacy can be found in European culture and language, but their origin is seldom acknowledged and thus largely unheard of. The Byzantine Empire fell apart but then the Ottoman Empire was founded in 1299 as a Muslim counterforce, keeping the battlefront between Islam and Europe alive. The Ottomans remained capable enough to stand up against the West and other enemies. They even expanded their territory and made progress in science.

> Under his [Suleiman al Qanuni's (1520-66)] rule, the empire reached the limits of its expansion, and Istanbul enjoyed a cultural renaissance, which was chiefly characterized by superb architecture [...]. The court also patronized painting, history and medicine to a high level, built an observatory in 1579, and was intrigued by the new European discoveries in navigation and geography. There was an eager exchange of information with the West during these expansive years when,

---

[73] Armstrong, *Islam*, p. 79
[74] Ibid.
[75] Ibid., p. 81
[76] McSmith, A. (2001), *Short Attacks Bush for 'Crusade' Quote*, (accessed 11 November 2017).

despite Europe's achievements, the Ottoman state was the most powerful in the world.[77]

The discoveries in navigation and geography led to the discovery of the New World in 1492 and many other discoveries and inventions followed. The Middle Ages were over, and the West was certainly gaining a lot of confidence. Shortly before America was discovered, the printing press had been invented which led to a distribution of knowledge on a larger scale. Scientific discoveries like Copernicus' model of the universe (1543) followed, and also a critical look on religion with Martin Luther's efforts of translating the Bible into German to get more people to read it for themselves. He could not have spread this message far and wide without the printing press. This birth of Protestantism was, though perhaps inevitably, met with a lot of resistance from the orthodox forces, leading to many religious conflicts in Europe for a century, culminating in The Thirty Years' War during the first half of the 17th century.

We are already halfway through the period known as Renaissance, which denotes the rebirth of Ancient Wisdom. The rediscovery of Plato's rational thought made way for the scientific revolution in the 17th century, which was based on experiments as the basis of knowledge, and "gave them greater control over the environment than anybody had achieved before".[78] The end of the 18th century brought several new ideas of huge political impact: Adam Smith's *The Wealth of Nations* (1776) laid the foundation for modern economy. Immanuel Kant introduced *An Answer to the Question: What is Enlightenment* (1784), encouraging individuals to think for themselves and break free from heteronomy. Secular views had emerged by this time. "Progress, including open-ended material progress was one of the ideals of the Enlightenment. Mankind was judged perfectible, among other things, through the application of the new science of economics." Thus, economics sprung from the logic of exploitation through 'the rape of nature'.[79] The next decades witnessed two revolutions, the American and the French, where the people stood up against the ruling forces. It seems like the new perspective no longer condoned accepting positions, fates, and hardships. These had previously been believed to be assigned by God; suffering, endurance, and patience were considered virtues. Freedom was a new ideal and fighting to the death for it became the new virtue.

---

[77] Armstrong, *Islam,* p. 112
[78] Ibid., p. 122
[79] Davies, *Europe,* pp. 99–100

Then, when in 1798 Napoleon Bonaparte occupied Egypt and left again after only three years, "he brought with him a corps of scholars, a library of modern European literature, a scientific laboratory and a printing press with Arabic type". Napoleon's forces also came with "a superbly efficient modern army".[80] In his study of the encounters of Islam and the West, Bernard Lewis argues that this time was a crucial moment in the Arabs experience of the advancements of the West. They found themselves facing all the European achievements of the past three centuries. It demonstrated the enormity of the advance of the West, which the Arabs had not been aware of before. Eventually, the realization from this led Muslim leaders to the conviction of trying to catch up with them.[81]

In the second half of the 19th century, Darwin's *Origin of Species* (1859) offered a well-founded counter-narrative to the theology of creation. Again, the supposition of discontinuity would be deceptive as several strands of Creationist beliefs still have many adherents who do not believe in evolution. Additionally, the enormous change in the making of civilization also showed in European Literature of the late 19th century, when science fiction became a popular genre (e.g. Jules Verne), asking questions about what science can do, rather than what God can do.

> The new society of Europe and its American colonies had a different economic basis. Instead of relying upon a surplus of agricultural produce, it was founded on technology and an investment of capital that enabled the West to reproduce its resources indefinitely, so that Western society was no longer subject to the same constraints as an agrarian culture. This major revolution in reality constituted a second Axial Age [...]. It had not been planned or thought out in advance, but had been the result of a complex process which had led to the creation of democratic, secular social structures. [...] By the time this technicalization of society had resulted in the industrial revolution of the nineteenth century, Westerners felt such assurance that they no longer looked back to the past for inspiration, as in the agrarian cultures and religions, but looked forward to the future.[82]

The people in Europe had been used to calling upon God for rain and a rich harvest, but gradually started to depend on their work and knowledge instead. This gave the Europeans a great deal of confidence. The modernization of the society found a new virtue: efficiency. The new system of science and industry had been erected but it could not be run without people for menial labour and buyers for the produced surplus of goods. A society of this kind could not be

---

[80] Armstrong, *Islam*, p. 126
[81] Lewis, *What Went Wrong?*, pp. 31–2
[82] Armstrong, *Islam*, pp. 121–2

run by a small elite. More people had to be educated which led them to want to have a say in the decisions of the government. Armstrong explains the link between human resources and democracy as follows:

> If a nation wanted to use all its human resources to enhance its productivity, it had to bring groups who had hitherto been segregated and marginalized, such as the Jews, into mainstream culture. Religious differences and spiritual ideals must not be allowed to impede the progress of society [...]. Thus, the ideals of democracy, pluralism, toleration, human rights and secularism were not simply beautiful ideals dreamed up by political scientists, but were, at least in part, dictated by the needs of the modern state.[83]

This led to a direct and grave impact on the Islamic world in the form of colonization. "The progressive nature of modern society and an industrialized economy meant that it had to expand continuously. New markets were needed, and, once the home countries had been saturated, they had to be sought abroad."[84] This was all a very complex and long-winded process. The colonized countries provided raw material and bought cheap manufactured products in exchange which essentially broke down the local industry. Also, the colonies had to be transformed and modernized to meet the needs of the metropolitan state, but these attempts only reached the elite circles. Therefore, modernization never reached the entire society which led to a further marginalization of the lower circles. Suffice it to say that the larger parts of the colonies' population had to suffer under their rule and consequently never took a liking to them.[85] After this, Muslims became…

> …exposed to the contempt of the colonialists, who were so thoroughly imbued with the modern ethos that they were often appalled by what they could only see as the backwardness, inefficiency, fatalism and corruption of Muslim society. They assumed that European culture had always been progressive, and lacked the historical perspective to see that they were simply seeing a pre-modern agrarian society, and that a few centuries earlier Europe had been just as 'backward'.[86]

The idea of Europe "is a relatively modern idea. It gradually replaced the earlier concept of 'Christendom' in a complex intellectual process lasting from the fourteenth to the eighteenth centuries." After the Enlightenment set in, the divided community became rather embarrassed to be bound by their common Christian identity and needed a different anchor. "After that, the awareness of

---

[83] Ibid., pp. 122–3
[84] Ibid., p. 123
[85] Ibid., pp. 123–4
[86] Ibid., p. 125

a European, as opposed to a Christian community, gained the upper hand" until "Rousseau announced in 1772: 'There are no longer Frenchmen, Germans, and Spaniards, or even English, but only Europeans.'" [87] This does not mean, however, that Christianity became irrelevant as a source of identity altogether. As Davies explains:

> Geographical Europe has always had to compete with notions of Europe as a cultural community; and in the absence of common political structures, European civilization could only be defined by cultural criteria. Special emphasis is usually placed on the seminal role of Christianity, a role which did not cease when the label of Christendom was dropped.[88]

For many people, Christianity remained a crucial aspect of bringing together the different cultures of the peoples of Europe. Davies quotes T.S. Eliot as an example who said:

> It is in Christianity that our arts have developed; it is in Christianity that the laws of Europe – until recently – have been rooted. It is against a background of Christianity that all our thought has significance. An individual European may not believe that the Christian Faith is true; and yet what he says, and makes, and does, will all ... depend on [the Christian heritage] for its meaning. Only a Christian culture could have produced a Voltaire or a Nietzsche. I do not believe that the culture of Europe could survive the complete disappearance of the Christian Faith.[89]

With all the many different and sometimes opposing cultural, intellectual and spiritual markers with which it was attempted to pin down what constituted Europe, it becomes evident that it was an Ideal more than a reality: "[Europe] has often been taken as a synonym for the harmony which was lacking. 'Europe' has been the unattainable ideal, the goal for which all good Europeans are supposed to strive." [90] Interestingly, not everyone in Europe bought into the narratives behind this ideal. One example being Britain: While the European identity became the source of feelings of supremacy for most countries in order to justify their political pursuits, the British may not have needed this because they had their Empire and after that the memory of that empire to draw their feelings of supremacy from. As Davies puts it, "they were definitely Europeans, but with prime extra-European interests."[91]

---

[87] Davies, *Europe,* pp. 7–8
[88] Ibid., p. 9
[89] Ibid.
[90] Ibid., p. 10
[91] Ibid., p. 13

A passage in the autobiography of a British Muslim who was radicalized and joined an Islamist group in his teens of 2012 named Maajid Nawaz (co-authored by Tom Bromley), demonstrates the fictionality of historical narrative as well as the experientiality of literary narrative. Nawaz recalls a memory of a history class in school which affected him greatly:

> Part of the history syllabus was British Imperial history, and so we studied British India. [...] We studied events like the Indian 'Mutiny', where even the name of the event is significant. In the Indian subcontinent, the event is referred to as a 'The First War of Independence', rather than a mutiny implying false rebellion. During one lesson, as we were discussing India and the Raj, the teacher asked the class, 'How many of you here are proud of our Empire and its achievements?' Everyone put a hand up, except for me. 'Is there anyone who isn't?' All looked around as I put mine up. This moment stuck fast in my mind. I sat there in class and pondered for a while that 'No matter how well I get along with these people, no matter how much I hide my beliefs, they will always see me as belonging to a race they *civilized*.'[92]

Nawaz not only describes how the history of the British Empire is narrated in the UK as opposed to that in India or Pakistan, but he describes the way he experienced it as a British citizen of Indian descent. The Imperial past of the UK has also been stylized into a narrative, so that it can inspire pride instead of resentment. This may be a necessity because Imperialism continues to this day and it must be defended rather than disparaged. The question which Nawaz raises in this chapter of his biography is not so much, how honest or scientific this approach is, but how it affects the ethnically varied society of today's Britain.

After the concept of Europe came in to fulfill the new needs of the population for an identity to unite some European nations in their causes, the concept of 'the West' emerged with the arrival of the United States of America (USA) in the politics of Europe in the 20th century. Interestingly, the term 'Western civilization' or 'the West' is marked by its very selectiveness, because if we look at how much of Europe is Western in the sense of the term 'Western civilization', it is only a minor part of Europe:

> For the best part of 200 years, European history has frequently been confused with the heritage of 'Western civilization'. Indeed, the impression has been created that everything 'Western' is civilized, and that everything civilized is Western. By extension, or simply by default, anything vaguely Eastern or 'Oriental' stands to be considered backward or inferior, and hence worthy of neglect. [...]

[92] Nawaz and Bromley, *Radical,* p. 146

> Historians most given to thinking of themselves as from 'the West' – notably from England, France, Germany, and North America – rarely see any necessity to describe Europe's past in its entirety. They see no more reason to consider the countries of Eastern Europe than to dwell on the more westerly parts of Western Europe. [...] Whatever Western civilization is, therefore, it does not involve an honest attempt to summarize European history. Whatever 'the West' is, it is not just a synonym for Western Europe. [...] This is a very strange phenomenon. It seems to assume that historians of Europe can conduct themselves like the cheese-makers of Gruyère, whose product contains as many holes as cheese.[93]

So even though the West and Europe are not synonymous they do draw their markers of identity from some of the same intellectual sources. Since ancient Greece was also an era that witnessed progress of an immense magnitude, it was also a time that inspired narratives of disparity:

> The notion that Greece was all liberty, and Persia all tyranny, was an extremely subjective one. But it provided the foundation of a tradition which has persistently linked 'civilization' with 'Europa' and 'the West'.[94]

> The idea of 'the West' is as old as the Greeks, who saw Free Hellas as the antithesis of the Persian-ruled despotism of the East. In modern times, it has been adopted by a long succession of political interests who wished to reinforce their identity and to dissociate themselves from their neighbors. As a result, 'Western civilization' has been given layer upon layer of meanings and connotations that have accrued over the centuries. There are a dozen or so main variants.[95]

Davies then names a dozen variants of Western markers of identity with their key influences on its identity today:

1. The Roman Empire: The countries that once belonged to the Roman Empire, which included France and Spain, are seen as part of 'The West', while other European countries which the empire never reached, like Poland or Sweden, are usually not associated with the West.
2. Christian civilization which became the antithesis to the East after the rise of Islam.
3. The Catholic World: "In this version, the West was equivalent to Catholicism, where the frequent divorce of ecclesiastical and secular authority facilitated the rise of successive non-conformist movements, notably the Renaissance, the Reformation, the Scientific Revolution, and the Enlightenment. [...] None of these key movements made an

---

[93] Davies, *Europe,* p. 20
[94] Ibid., p. 102
[95] Ibid., p. 22

early impact on the Orthodox world." The Catholic influence embedded Latin as a language of the elite into European culture.[96]

4. Protestantism caused a rearrangement of clusters of countries as they became independent from the Catholic Church.[97]
5. "'The French variant of Western civilization' based on the ideas of the Enlightenment and its manifestations in the French Revolution in the late 18th Century. Both secular movements have had a lasting effect on the West. In this time, French became the language of the European elite."[98]
6. "The imperial variant of Western civilization was based on the unbounded self-confidence of the leading imperial powers during the long European Peace prior to 1914. It was fired by a belief in the God-given right of the 'imperial races' to rule over others and in their supposedly superior cultural, economic, and constitutional development."[99] Even though it is technically not the first narrative of superiority, it certainly is the one within which we can recognize the current forms of supremacy most clearly. "For the rich imperial club in the West was marked by its advanced industrial economies and sophisticated systems of administration; the East by peasant societies, stateless nations, and raw autocracy."[100]
7. The Marxist variant which was a direct counter-narrative to the imperial variant. It was implemented as an ideology in the Soviet empire[101] and by them also in East Germany after the Second World War. Germany's past experience with communism seems to have caused a lasting anti-left attitude. The past elections have shown that the German population is more likely to go right, instead of left if they are disillusioned with the establishment.
8. The first German variant of Western civilization began with the First World War. "Its advocates harbored no doubts about Germany's civilizing mission in Eastern Europe, whilst their rivalry with France, and their rejection of liberalism and 'the ideas of 1789', led to a distinction

96 Ibid., pp. 22-3
97 Ibid., p. 23
98 Ibid.
99 Ibid.
100 Ibid.
101 Ibid.

between *Abendlich* (Occidental) and *Westlich* (Western) civilization."[102] This notion of distinct identity between Occident and Orient has been taken up again today, by the PEGIDA (*Patriotische Europäer Gegen die Islamisierung des Abendlandes*) movement who warn against an "Islamization of the *Abendland*".

9. The White Anglo-Saxon Protestant variant of Western civilization which began when Germany assumed a position of hegemony in Europe and the USA joined forces with Britain against them. This alliance built on their shared interests and markers of identity, such as the language and the religion. It revived during the Second World War and later with the NATO and "it inspired a characteristic 'Allied Scheme of History' which had held sway for the rest of the century".[103]
10. The second German variant of Western civilization was the Nazi ideology of racial supremacy.[104] It caused the perhaps most infamous genocide in history: the holocaust, murdering around 6 million Jews. The holocaust became a frequent point of reference within Zionist narratives where it can be used to silence criticism, for instance. When Nobel laureate, Günter Grass wrote a poem in 2012 lamenting that as a German he is not allowed to criticize Israel's politics because of the holocaust, Israel declared him persona non-grata the same year. On the other hand, the anti-Semite counter-narrative which denies the holocaust ever happened sadly also continues to exist.
11. The European variant of Western civilization which began in the late 1940s and ended with the collapse of the Iron curtain.[105]
12. The American variant of Western civilization developed from the Anglo-Saxon variant when a new constellation of countries formed under the leadership of the USA with its ideas of democracy and capitalism.[106]

Davies then sums up the premises on which these kinds of markers of identity are built:

> From all these examples, it appears that Western civilization is essentially an amalgam of intellectual constructs which were designed to further the interests of their authors. It is the product of complex exercises in ideology, of countless identity trips, of sophisticated essays in cultural propaganda. It can be defined

---

[102] Ibid.
[103] Ibid., p. 24
[104] Ibid.
[105] Ibid., p. 25
[106] Ibid., p. 24

> by its advocates in almost any way that they think fit. Its elastic geography has been inspired by the distribution of religions, by the demands of liberalism and of imperialism, by the unequal progress of modernization, by the divisive effects of world wars and of the Russian revolution, and by the self-centered visions of French *philosophes*, of Prussian historians, and of British and American statesmen and educators, all of whom have had their reasons to neglect or to despise 'the East'. In its latest phase, it has been immensely strengthened by the physical division of Europe, which lasted from 1947-8 to 1991. On the brink of the twenty-first century, one is entitled to ask in whose interests it may be used in the future.[107]

This last question is very interesting, and I am certain that after 9/11, Norman Davies will have known one possible answer. He noticed four years before 2001 that there is a pattern in these narratives:

> A set of assumptions recurs time and again. The first maintains that West and East, however defined, have little or nothing in common. The second implies that the division of Europe is justified by natural, unbridgeable differences; the third that the West is superior; the fourth that the West alone deserves the name of Europe. [...] Every variant of western civilization is taken to have an important core and a less important periphery. Great powers can always command attention. Failing powers, lesser states, stateless nations, minor cultures, weak economies do not have to be considered even if they occupy a large part of the overall scene.[108]

THE RISE AND FALL OF ISLAM'S NARRATIVE OF SUPERIORITY

In Ancient Greece, the great philosophers of Hellenism came up with ideas that play a fundamental role in the values of the Western world today: democracy, rationalism, medicine, agriculture, architecture, science, etc. to name a few. The interesting thing about their history is that while they are such precious Western assets, people forget a crucial part that Muslims played in their survival.

One crucial transition of life in Europe was the adoption of agriculture which even led to soil erosion in Greece in the early sixth century BC. Ecology "created the first form of artificial habitat – the cultivated countryside" leading to "a permanent food surplus and hence the potential for demographic

[107] Ibid., p. 25
[108] Ibid.

growth". The surplus of produce required a medium of exchange other than goods and services. Money in the form of coins was known to have been used by the ancient Greek as well as by the Romans.[109] The ability of humankind to cultivate nature to its advantage like this became a part of the Judeo-Christian tradition, which "stressed Man's supremacy over the rest of Creation".[110] Interestingly, Europeans like Montesquieu believed in the 18th century that Europe's climate was of such magnificence that it seemed as if nature had predestined the continent for supremacy.[111] Subsequently, the economic developments in Europe required many nations there to find new markets and new lands, leading to the colonization of agrarian countries.

Karen Armstrong believes that cultures and societies reformed the old paganism because it was "no longer adequate in the larger and more complex societies that evolved once people had created a mercantile economy capable of supporting this cultural effort." Armstrong explains that the economies of the agricultural pre-modern societies depended on a surplus of produce, making the labour of the peasants so vital, that the latter could not be encouraged to take part in their high culture. This division between workers and elite was why the faiths that arose in times of social and economic growth were concerned with social justice and compassion. She continues to explain that since Arabia is mostly a desert, the people there did not have an agrarian surplus which required a complex system of economic justice. Thus, the innovations of what Armstrong calls the first Axial Age passed the Arabians by unnoticed.[112] The surplus of produce and thus a prospering commerce could evolve in Arabia when the two great empires – the Persian or Sassanid Empire in Iraq and the Byzantine Empire in Syria and Egypt – became so caught up in wars and conflicts against each other that their trade had to be rerouted through Arabia. And then the tribe of the Quraysh began to develop a market economy, making Mecca the economic centre of Arabian trade.[113]

> Mecca had become a thriving mercantile city, but in the aggressive stampede for wealth some of the old tribal values had been lost. Instead of looking after the weaker members of the tribe, as the nomadic code prescribed, the Quraysh were now intent on making money at the expense of some of the tribe's poorer family groupings, or clans.[114]

---

[109] Ibid., p. 101
[110] Ibid., p. 99
[111] Ibid., p. 45
[112] Armstrong, *Islam,* pp. 6–7
[113] Watt, *Islam,* pp. 10–1
[114] Armstrong, *Islam,* p. 3

With the growing injustice, Arabia developed the need and the inclination towards a sophisticated faith of social justice of its own. Armstrong elucidates:

> This social concern had always been an essential part of the visions of the great world religions, which had developed during what historians have called the Axial Age (*c.* 700 BCE to 200 BCE), when civilization, as we know it, developed, together with the confessional faiths which have continued to nourish humanity: Taoism and Confucianism in China; Hinduism and Buddhism in the Indian subcontinent; monotheism in the Middle East; and rationalism in Europe.[115]

Apparently, the Arabs knew of some of these monotheistic religions which came from one god. Even though the Arabs were polytheistic in the pre-Islamic period, they did believe in a high God as well and assumed the prophets and scriptures which were given to Jews and Christians must come from this "High God of their pantheon" whom they knew as Al-ilāh (later Allah). So, the Arabs believed in the truthfulness and divine origin of the Jewish and Christian faith. The Jews and Christians who encountered Arabs fairly often were aware of this advantage and "taunted the Arabs for being left out of the divine plan."[116] When the Arabs developed a society with an actual market economy they suddenly had the need for an Axial Age faith. The pre-Islamic Arabian structures in which "one tribe fought another, in a murderous cycle of vendetta and counter-vendetta" were not capable of raising issues like social justice as the monotheistic religions were. And it "seemed to many of the more thoughtful people in Arabia that the Arabs were a lost race, exiled for ever [sic] from the civilized world and ignored by God himself."[117] So, when the Quran was revealed to Muhammad, he was convinced that he was not bringing the Arabs a message that was entirely new, but one which had been delivered to Jews and Christians by their own prophets. He made aware that "if the Quraysh did not mend their ways, their society would collapse (as had other unjust societies in the past) because they were violating the fundamental laws of existence."[118] To that end, he taught people that it was wrong "to build a private fortune, but good to share wealth and create a society where the weak [...] were treated with respect."[119] Armstrong concludes:

---

[115] Ibid., p. 6
[116] Ibid., p. 3
[117] Ibid.
[118] Ibid., p. 4
[119] Ibid.

> Social justice was, therefore, the crucial virtue of Islam. Muslims were commanded as their first duty to build a community (*ummah*) characterized by practical compassion, in which there was a fair distribution of wealth. This was far more important than any doctrinal teaching about God. In fact, the Quran has a negative view of theological speculation, which it calls *zannah*, self-indulgent whimsy about ineffable matters that nobody can ascertain one way or the other.[120]

This is why Islam has a strong political and juridical presence. The key difference between Islam and Christianity is the ultimate aspiration behind it:

> The life and achievements of Muhammad would affect the spiritual, political and ethical vision of Muslims for ever [sic]. They expressed the Islamic experience of 'salvation', which does not consist of the redemption of an 'original sin' committed by Adam and the admittance to eternal life, but the achievement of a society which puts into practice God's desires for the human race. This not only redeemed Muslims from the sort of political and social hell that existed in pre-Islamic Arabia but also provided them with a context within which they could more easily make that wholehearted surrender to God which alone can fulfil them.[121]

William M. Watt sums up:

> It is roughly correct to say that in Islam the place of theology is taken by law and jurisprudence. Those who deal with the intellectual aspects of the religion are jurists and not theologians, and at the centre of higher education is jurisprudence and not theology. In other words, Islam is more concerned with orthopraxy than orthodoxy. This comes about because the early development of Islam and Christianity took place in very different circumstances. The first Christians lived in the Roman Empire, where there was an effective system of law of excellent quality, and for three hundred years the Christians had no political responsibilities. The first Muslims, on the other hand, lived in Mecca, Medina and other parts of Arabia, where nomadic customary law was breaking down because there were now communities based mainly on either commerce or agriculture. From the time of the Hijra the leading Muslims were responsible for the affairs of a political community, and consequently we find in the Qur'an rules for dealing with the practical problems which arose. As the centuries passed these grew into a complete system of law, both public and private, as well as prescriptions for the practice of religion.[122]

The Quran claims to be only a reminder of an old message that has been sent to humankind for centuries and "did not put forward any philosophical arguments for monotheism; its approach was practical, and, as such, it appealed to the pragmatic Arabs." The Quran says that 124,000 prophets (which

---

[120] Ibid., pp. 5–6
[121] Ibid., p. 20
[122] Watt, *Islam*, p. 87

Armstrong believes is a symbolic number indicating infinity) have been sent to humankind all over the world and that the message is always the same: God letting people know, how they should live on earth. Some other prophets are mentioned by name, but only those who were known to Arabs.[123] This is why Muhammad never asked Jews or Christians to convert to Islam; he believed that their revelations were equally valid.[124] They were known as the *ahl al-kitab*, which means People of the Book. The authenticity of their scriptures was not questioned. Conversion was not encouraged until the middle of the eighth century.[125] They still believed that God had to seek out the people of Arabia himself in order to elevate them to a higher form of existence. Yet simply imitating the other religions was no option because the pre-modern societies did not know the concept of progress in the form of cutting ties with old traditions and then marching onwards. Traditions and culture were part of collective identity, therefore, in those times, no one would have thought it a good idea to just abandon them for new ways.

> It is only our more modern culture that can afford to prize originality and jettison tradition wholesale. In pre-modern society continuity was crucial. Muhammad did not envisage a violent rupture with the past or with other faith communities. He wanted to root the new scripture in the spiritual landscape of Arabia.
>
> Hence Muslims continued to perform the customary rituals at the Kabah, the cube-shaped shrine in the heart of Mecca, the most important centre of worship in Arabia. It was extremely ancient even in Muhammad's time [...].[126]

To sum up, Muhammad saw the revelation as a warning to the Arab people who had corrupted their own tribal values so much that they no longer functioned as a social order. Their system would collapse if they did not change it and the way to do that was to follow a creed offering guidance from God. Because they looked on the Jews and Christians as more advanced and prosperous social orders, they were convinced that their advantage was by courtesy of God's guidance. This belief in the success of a people depending on whether they have divine power on their side has stayed with Muslims throughout their history. This is why in the early years of Islam it was considered pointless to dwell on efforts to find a consensus about the nature of God, or any other normative views on transcendental questions.

---

[123] Armstrong, *Islam,* p. 7
[124] Ibid., p. 9
[125] Ibid., p. 26
[126] Ibid., p. 9

> [F]ar more crucial was the effort (*jihad*) to live in the way that God had intended for human beings. The political and social welfare of the *ummah* would have sacramental value for Muslims. If the *ummah* prospered, it was a sign that Muslims were living according to God's will, and the experience of living in a truly *islamic* [sic] community, which made this existential surrender to the divine, would give Muslims intimations of sacred transcendence. Consequently, they would be affected as profoundly by any misfortune or humiliation suffered by the *ummah*, as Christians by the spectacle of somebody blasphemously trampling on the Bible or ripping the Eucharistic host apart.[127]

While the Quran itself insists that the Prophet was simply a person merely sent by God to warn people and had no peculiar right to claim any role of political power or function, Muhammad gradually became more involved in political matters as he was frequently called upon by the people, because they believed he was the voice of God.[128] So, even though his involvement in politics was a consequence and not the purpose of his calling, the role of a spiritual political leader gradually became a tradition.

> The Qur'an says hardly anything about the control of the affairs of the Islamic state. In the Constitution of Medina, Muhammad was one clan chief among nine, though he was also accepted as the prophet and it was stipulated that disputes were to be referred to him for settlement. The Qur'an (8:1,41) states that a fifth of the booty taken in raids was to be paid to him. With his successes against the Meccans, his power gradually increased, and in his last years there was little opposition to his decisions. Much of this autocratic power was inherited by the caliphs with the consensus of the community. By Arab custom, the chief usually consulted with the leading men of his tribe, and there seems to have been a little of this in the caliphate. Apart from this, however, Muslim rulers through the centuries have tended to practice a form of autocracy, *although because there are no precise Qur'anic rulings*, some modern Islamic states have managed to establish a form of democracy.[129] [Emphasis added]

The development from a spiritual leader to a political autocrat was complete by the time of the Abbasid Caliphate (750 – 935). This Caliphate took the forms of an absolute monarchy which was new to Islam. "Where the Prophet had always been addressed informally by his given name, like any other mortal, the caliph was styled the 'Shadow of God on earth'." Courtiers prostrated before Harun al-Rashid and kissed the ground he walked on. Not even the Prophet was treated this way, nor would he have condoned it. But even though

---

[127] Ibid., p. 6
[128] Ibid., p. 11
[129] Watt, *Islam*, p. 100

it was technically un-Islamic, the new caliphate's economic and political success seemed enough to justify its form and existence.[130] So throughout their history, Muslims considered every regime as Islamic as long as it prospered. Consequently, when a system failed they considered it a sign from God telling them they had strayed from his path. This explains why Muslim regimes are so successfully using religion as the primary source to justify their political causes. When the Muslim world realized that the West had left them behind, they habitually turned towards religion for solutions.

> From the time of the Prophet Muhammad, Muslims had seen current events as theophanies; they had encountered a God who was present in history and had issued a constant challenge to build a better world. Muslims had sought a divine meaning in political events, and even their setbacks and tragedies had led to major developments in theology and spirituality. When Muslims had achieved a type of polity that was more in accordance with the spirit of the Quran after the decline of the Abbasid caliphate, they had agonized less about the political health of the *ummah* and felt free to develop a more interior piety. But the intrusion of the West into their lives raised major religious questions. The humiliation of the *ummah* was not merely a political catastrophe but touched a Muslim's very soul. This new weakness was a sign that something had gone gravely awry in Islamic history. The Quran had promised that a society which surrendered to God's revealed will could not fail. Muslim history had proved this. Time and again, when disaster had struck, the most devout Muslims had turned to religion, made it speak to their new circumstances, and the *ummah* had not only revived but had usually gone on to greater achievements. How could Islamdom be falling more and more under the domination of the secular, Godless West? From this point, a growing number of Muslims would wrestle with these questions, and their attempts to put Muslim history back on the straight path would sometimes appear desperate and even despairing. The suicide bomber – an almost unparalleled phenomenon in Islamic history – shows that some Muslims are convinced that they are pitted against hopeless odds.[131]

This tendency of Muslims to look toward religion for answers regarding political problems – instead of answers to theological or spiritual ones – is one reason why Islamist narratives are so powerful.

One of the reasons for al-Rashid's successful reign was not only the security of existence he provided for the people, and the ruthlessness with which he quashed uprisings, but also his investments in knowledge. He funded arts and scholarship, leading to a cultural renaissance.[132]

---

[130] Armstrong, *Islam,* pp. 46–7
[131] Ibid., p. 130
[132] Ibid., p. 47

> Literary criticism, philosophy, poetry, medicine, mathematics and astronomy flourished not only in Baghdad but in Kufah, Basrah, Jundayvebar and Harran. *Dhimmis* [Armstrong translates this in the Glossary as 'protected subjects'. Dhimmis were non-Muslims – but members of the *ahl al-kitab* – who lived under the protection of Muslim rulers, usually because they paid a special tax for this protection] participated in the floresence [sic] by translating the philosophical and medical texts of classical Hellenism from Greek and Syriac into Arabic. Building on the learning of the past, which had thus become available to them, Muslim scholars made more scientific discoveries during this time than in the whole of previously recorded history. Industry and commerce also flourished, and the elite lived in refinement and luxury.[133]

This diligent scholarship resulted in different intellectual approaches to theology as well. Many intellectual movements formed and fought against each other in ways to approach Islamic jurisprudence and exegesis. Rationality was discovered but also resisted against. A very long winded intellectual history, interspersed with politics unfolded.

One key factor which, in my view, led to a stagnation of Islamic (legal) thought was the abandonment of *ijtihad*: The followers of Abu Hanifah [namesake of the Hanafi school of law] believed it to be "essential for jurists to use their powers of 'independent reasoning' (*ijtihad*), arguing that they must have the freedom to make new laws, even if they could not be based on a *hadith* or a Quranic utterance."[134]

> [The term *ijtihad*] comes from the same root as *Jihad* and its basic meaning is 'effort', but it came to have the technical meaning of a qualified jurist's exercise of his independent judgement on a legal matter. This was something which had been done by the founders of the legal schools. In the early tenth century, however, it came to be held that the gates of *ijtihad* had been closed, and this implied that there were to be no further attempts to found a distinctive school. In the nineteenth and twentieth centuries, when many new problems arose, there were discussions about whether the gates of *ijtihad* could be reopened. The conservatives opposed the idea, but the liberals, backed by the pressure of events, insisted on a reopening of the gates, and this, in fact, came about.[135]

Over time, all the different intellectual movements settled on the establishment of four legal schools, which are all accepted by Sunni Muslims. Sharia law is considered a process – rather than a fixed and normative code – in which legal decisions are made based on a study of an individual case and deductive reasoning based on a thorough research of primary sources and previous legal

---

[133] Ibid.
[134] Ibid., p. 49
[135] Watt, *Islam,* pp. 90–1

decisions. Consequently, there can be no canonized volume of Sharia Law that might be recognized by all Muslims.

When Muslim reigns became less concerned with social justice and more concerned with autocratic power, legal Islamic scholarship which may have revealed how un-Islamic their reign was, had to be limited. One example of this method was the rule of the Mongols:

> [The Mongols were] powerful enough to put new constraints on the *ulama*. The Sharia was no longer permitted to be a potentially subversive code. By the fifteenth century it was agreed that the *ulama* could no longer use their own independent judgement (*ijtihad*) in creative legislation; it was said that 'the gates of *ijtihad*' were closed. Muslims were obliged to conform to the rulings of past authorities. The *shariah* had in principle become a system of established rules, which could not jeopardize the more dynamic dynastic law of the ruling house.[136]

William M. Watt and Karen Armstrong disagree about the time of the closing of these gates, which probably differed in all parts of the Muslim world. Referring to the restriction on founding new legal schools, Watt dates it to the tenth century, while Armstrong, referring to the Sharia becoming rigid and normative, dates it to the 14th century. The closing of the gates of *ijtihad* was obviously also not something that came into effect in every aspect of Muslim life and politics overnight but rather gradually.

Another reason for it was the increase of sectarian conflicts, which Watt maps out as follows:

> Although theology was subordinate to jurisprudence according to the usual Muslim outlook, in time there came to be a large body of scholars who gave much thought to the exposition of the intellectual aspect of Islamic belief – that is, to theology. The development of theology in Islam, however, was rather different from that in Christianity, because from the beginning Islam was a political as well as religious community. The consequence of this was that the earliest theological arguments normally had political implications. As has already been noted, the question of whether the Qur'an was created or uncreated was basically a political dispute.
>
> [...]
>
> The first appearance of sectarianism is usually taken to be in 656 when an army in Iraq was led by the caliph 'Ali. This army had just defeated the forces of the Meccan group opposed to 'Ali's assumption of the caliphate and was preparing to march against his rival, Mu'awiya. A considerable body of men seceded or went out (kharaju) from the army because they disapproved of some decisions 'Ali had taken. These are regarded as the first of the sect of the Kharijites or Khawarij (the singular is Khariji), which proliferated during the Umayyad period

[136] Armstrong, *Islam,* p. 85

> and had many subdivisions. 'Ali met some of the grievances of the first group and they returned to his army; but shortly afterwards a second group with similar grievances 'went out', refused to be reconciled and were eventually massacred.[137]

The Shi'ite belief often argues that the Quran is not the direct word of God and thus open for re-interpretation by one divine caliph. "The various Shi'ite groups also had their laws, but formal law was less important for them because their Imam had the power to overrule previous decisions. Thus, there is in Shi'ism, no great body of laws and legal thinking comparable to what is found in Sunnism."[138] This belief was instrumentalised by the Abbasid Caliph al-Ma'mun (813-33) in order to establish an autocracy, which was meant to help him get the growing conflict in the empire under control. He began an inquisition known as the *minha*, where judges had to pledge in public that they believed that the Quran was created. According to Watt, this was not a theological approach but had exclusively political motives, because the Shi'ites of that time believed that a caliph is a divinely inspired person whose decisions are binding on all Muslims. If the Quran was created by Muhammad, another divinely inspired person, then the present Caliph was free to change it and all Muslims were obligated to obey. The *ulama*, or scholar jurists following the Sunni schools of jurisprudence held the view that the Quran is not created but the unchangeable word of God and therefore resisted al-Ma'mun, believing that they alone could interpret the unchangeable Quran. They rose to power when the *minha* was abandoned in 850, possibly because it failed to fulfill the hopes for a reconciliation of rival interests. "Its abandonment was tantamount to making the Sunnite form of Islam the official religion of the caliphate, and giving the '*ulama*' an assured place in it."[139]

In the seven centuries before the gates of *ijtihad* were gradually closed scholars and learned men were explored and transformed the world of science. The late 8th century marked the beginning of Islam's Golden Age of science. Baghdad became a center of learning known as the House of Wisdom (*Darul Hikmah*). A great number of scientists, teachers, and doctors rose to fame in this period. The tenth century witnessed the works of Ibn Sina (known as Avicenna in the West), the twelfth those of Ibn Rushd (Averroes in the West) and the fourteenth of Ibn Khaldun. It is no coincidence that these scholars have a special name in the West because their scientific achievements in medicine,

---

[137] Watt, *Islam,* pp. 101–2
[138] Ibid., p. 87
[139] Ibid., pp. 41–2

astronomy, mathematics, physics, philosophy, historiography, sociology, etc. were later built upon by scientist in the West. The translations and commentaries of the ancient wisdom of Hellenism which Muslims had produced were crucial in bringing the ancient wisdom back to Europe, which the Renaissance is known for. They all have a share in the advancement of the West in the centuries that followed:

> The effective introduction of Arabic numerals into Europe to replace the Roman numerals came about through the publication in 1202 of a book by a merchant from Pisa who had studied under a Muslim teacher in Algeria. The most important impact on Western Europe was probably that of Islamic medicine. There were already medical schools but they were distinctly backward. Contact with Islamic medicine greatly raised their standards and extended their competence. Numerous Arabic works were translated into Latin, but the predominant one was The Canon of Avicenna, which until about 1600 had more influence on the European medical schools than the works of Galen and Hippocrates. It was only gradually, too, that European hospitals were established and brought up to the standards set by Muslim hospitals.
>
> In Western Europe before 1100 [AD] little was known about Aristotelian logic, but not much else about Greek philosophy. After that date, however, Christian theologians became interested and studied the numerous translations from Arabic which were now being made. Among these were the philosophical works of Avicenna, including the exposition of his views by al-Ghazali, and nearly all those of Averroes. By the thirteenth century, there was a vigorous intellectual movement which was soon to develop further what had been learned from the Muslims in science and philosophy, though not for a time in medicine.[140]

Many great works of philosophy were built on Averroes' Aristotelian commentaries and were highly influential throughout the thirteenth century in Europe. Even though they raised doubts and faced resistance by some and admiration and inspiration for new intellectual horizons by others, the accomplishment of Islamic scholars was largely acknowledged.

> By the fourteenth century, however, the Western European outlook was beginning to change. The poet Dante (1265-1321), in his great work *The Divine Comedy*, at one point speaks of the philosophers and mentions Avicenna and Averroes, but at the same time he has the names of a dozen Greek philosophers, and calls Aristotle 'the master of those who know'. By this time there were already one or two translations made directly from Greek, and the trickle became a flood after the conquest of Constantinople by the Ottomans in 1453, when many Greek manuscripts were brought to the West. There then developed what can only be called a revulsion of feeling from things Arabic and Islamic. Latin Christendom

---

[140] Ibid., pp. 120–1

> completely lost awareness of all that it had been given by Islamic thinkers, seeing instead everything as having come directly from the Greeks. This virtual denial of the Islamic contribution is now urgently in need of correction.[141]

The invention of the printing press and the renaissance coincided with an intellectual decline of the Muslim world. While the Western world was gradually looking towards science for inspiration, the Muslim world remained somewhat fixated on trying to solve problems by mending their religiosity. The thirst for knowledge which the Muslim scholars of the Middle Ages had demonstrated decreased gradually.

The Ottoman Empire was also built on the autocratic models of the Byzantine and Mongol empires. The Ottoman Empire was founded in 1299, and thus very shortly before the West started using gunpowder in battles. Until the 16th century, the Ottomans thrived and expanded their territory. They even reached the gates of Vienna in 1529. They started off with an efficient rule, a tolerant order with a well-organized bureaucracy. But eventually, they too made the mistake of instrumentalising religion for the purposes of unification.

> Like the two other empires, the Ottomans also gave their state a special Islamic orientation. Under Suleiman, the *Shariah* received a more exalted status than in any previous Muslim state. It became the official law of the land for all Muslims, and the Ottomans were the first to give regular form to the *Shariah* courts. Legal experts – the *qadis*, who dispensed the law, and the teachers in the *madrasahs* – became an official government corps, creating a moral and religious link between the sultan and his subjects. This was especially valuable in the Arab provinces, where the partnership between the state and the *ulama* helped people to accept Turkish rule. Not only did the *ulama* have the backing of the sacred law and so gave legitimacy to the regime, but it was often the case that the *ulama*, who were native to a particular province, acted as essential intermediaries between the indigenous population and the Turkish governor.[142]

The Ottoman people were all happy and proud to belong to a state under Islamic rule because of the old promise of success for societies who live under Islamic law. The successes of the Ottoman Empire were enough to convince the people of its sanctity, which is probably why no one seemed to notice that such a state did not resemble the first Islamic society under the Municipal code of Medina, which Muhammad had established. Instead, it continued the tradition of using the Islamic ideal in order to justify autocratic regimes, which Harun al-Rashid was the first to perfect. Pointing out the irony, Armstrong

---

[141] Ibid., pp. 121–2

[142] Armstrong, *Islam*, p. 112

concludes: "Thus the *Shariah* was made to endorse the system of absolute monarchy (now more powerful than ever before) which it had been originally designed to oppose."[143]

The *ulama* did notice, however, that their own power was restricted to making only legal decisions which did not oppose the interests of the Sultan. When some of them began to look to modernist approaches and to display intellectual resistance, the Empire responded by restricting the educational system, and dropping the studies of philosophy, to begin with. A steady decline set in: an agrarian society proved unable to provide for such a vast empire. The military grew weaker and as the economy suffered, corruption increased. It was a slow decline but by the eighteenth century, it was undeniably apparent. At this point, Muslims started to ask themselves, what they are doing wrong and what the West is doing better. While Westerners had been traveling and studying the East frequently for centuries, as pilgrims or for trade, Muslims usually did not travel to the West much. Islam was being studied by the West but not vice versa. They started it in the 18th century.[144] However, this also took a lot of time to make a difference. For a long time, Muslims struggled with the question of piety, fearing that traveling there could be a form of apostasy. So first, Muslims who sought improvement had to begin by making an argument about why it did not constitute apostasy. But the reluctance to travel was only slowly overcome, sometimes impeded by specific fears, such as the possible import of syphilis from the New World.[145] So, even though they knew something had to be changed, it took them a while to put it into practice. After many efforts in translating books, it gradually became possible to observe the competition. Now they had a concrete question in mind, concerning the source of their wealth and strength. Bernard Lewis observes:

> Traditional answers to such a question would have been in religious terms. All problems are so to speak ultimately religious, and all final answers are therefore religious. The final answers given by traditional writers to the older formulation of the question were always 'let us go back to our roots, to the good old ways, to the true faith, to the word of God.' With that, of course, there was always the assumption that if things are going badly, we are being punished by God for having abandoned the true path. That argument loses cogency when it is the infidels who are benefiting from the change.[146]

---

[143] Ibid., p. 113
[144] Lewis, *What Went Wrong?*, pp. 23–7
[145] Ibid., pp. 37–9
[146] Ibid., p. 45

In my view, it is this compulsive habit of linking everything to religion and measuring themselves and others by arbitrary standards of piety is and always has been a big impediment that has been keeping the so-called Muslim world from making significant and lasting progress.

The peripheral regions of the Ottoman Empire were the first to feel the deprivations caused by the decline of the economy. Local reformers decided to take matters into their own hands again and eventually succeeded. The Arabian Peninsula was freed from the Ottoman rule by Muhammad ibn al-Wahhab (1703-92), the namesake of Wahhabism, "a puritan religion based on a strictly literal interpretation of scripture and early Islamic tradition." Al-Wahhab set out to restore his own view of the *ummah* that was established by the Prophet himself. To this end, he refused to accept any sources which date back to a time after the Prophet. He also used aggressive methods to spread his ideas, some of which have been taken up by contemporary fundamentalists.[147] The Ottomans finally also attempted a reform known as the *Tanzimat*. It succeeded in offering the people of Turkey a unifying marker of identity: the land they were all born in. They shifted their focus from religion to nationalism.

Al-Wahhab was a rather isolated case of regressive reform. When the Ottoman Empire demerged into several states, the local attempts of reform differed greatly from country to country. Morocco, for instance, was reformed by a Sufi named Ahmad ibn Idris (1760-1836). In Libya, Muhammad ibn Ali al-Sanusi (d. 1832) founded the Sanusiyya movement, which is still predominant in Libya today. Interestingly, some of these movements developed ideas which were similar to the modernist ideals of the West even though they had no knowledge of the West and derived them from the Sufi tradition of Islam. "They insisted that the people rely on their own insights, instead of relying on the *ulama*. Ibn Idris went so far as to reject the authority of every single Muslim thinker, except the Prophet." He encouraged people to abandon old traditions if they were no longer helpful and "taught the people to model themselves on an ideal human being rather than yearn for a distant God, in a sort of devotional humanism."[148]

This development is one reason why the Islamic world of today is so heterogeneous regarding the practice and interpretation of Islam, varying from country to country. This is why Libyan Muslims practice Islam differently than Turks or an Afghans. Often the differences in interpretation are not assigned

---

[147] Armstrong, *Islam*, p. 114
[148] Ibid., p. 115

to the reformers who influenced the notion of religion in those countries. Instead, it often leads to an entanglement of religion and culture or ethnicity. Either way,

> [t]here was, [evidently], no intrinsic reason why Muslims should reject the ethos of the new Europe. Over the centuries, they cultivated virtues that would also be crucial to the modern West: a passion for social justice, an egalitarian polity, freedom of speech, and, despite the ideal of *tawhid* [the divine unity, which Muslims seek to imitate in their personal and social lives by integrating their institutions and priorities, and by recognizing the overall sovereignty of God], a *de facto* or (in the case of Shiism) a principled separation of religion and politics. But by the end of the eighteenth century the most alert Muslims had been forced to recognize that Europe had overtaken them.[149]

Much like the closing of the gates of *ijtihad*, their reopening could also not take effect without impediment or resistance. It was prompted by the modernist thinkers of Islam in the 19th century. This development began when the Islamic world became more and more aware of the West's advantage. A few futile attempts at matching up were initiated, but they all were unsuccessful because many Muslims still failed to grasp how fundamentally transformed the West had become. It was an entirely different kind of civilization which took three centuries to develop. All the attempts to imitate this development by Muslims remained too superficial to have the desired effect.

In the 19th century, more reformers sought to modernize the interpretations and practice of Islam, usually after having traveled and even studied in Europe. The most important of these were Jamal Uddin al-Afghani, Muhammad Iqbal, Muhammad Abduh and Rashid Rida. Al-Afghani is usually the one given credit for demanding that the gates of *ijtihad* be reopened. Muhammad Iqbal (1876 - 1938), a poet and philosopher from India, …

> […] had been deeply influenced by Western thought and had received his Ph.D. in London. Yet he believed that the West had elevated progress at the expense of continuity; its secular individualism separated the notion of personality from God and made it idolatrous and potentially demonic. As a result, the West would eventually destroy itself, a position that was *easy to understand after the First World War*, which could be seen as the collective suicide of Europe. Muslims, therefore, had a vital mission to witness to the divine dimension of life, not by retiring from the world to engage in contemplation, but by an activism that implemented the social ideals of the *Shariah*.[150] [Emphasis added]

---

[149] Ibid.
[150] Ibid., p. 132

Presumably because of aversion to colonialization and imperialism and later all the wars that raged in the secular West, it became more difficult to promote its ideas to the people of the colonized countries in a good light.

Even though these Islamic modernists would certainly not all agree with each other on everything, they all had the same objective: finding a new approach to Islam which would enable Muslims to compete with the West again. They all believed that the success of the West had to mean that God was trying to tell Muslims they had strayed from the path. The differences between the ideas of these thinkers were usually on questions about whether the Quran and the Prophet encouraged independent thinking and reasoning; other matters of dissent concerned the role of religion in politics, the contextual interpretation of religious sources etc. Their attempts were usually rather complex and required a great deal of study. Most of them involved the application of reason based on research. Such concepts were – if at all – adopted only by people of the educational elite. The masses responded to the only simple reform which appealed to Muslims of every level of society: founded by Hasan al-Banna (1906-49) in Egypt, the Society of Muslim Brothers soon became a mass movement reaching Muslims throughout the Middle East:

> Al-Banna knew the Muslims needed Western science and technology, and that they must reform their political and social institutions. But he was also convinced, like the reformers, that this must go hand in hand with a spiritual reformation. [...] Al-Banna insisted that Islam was a total way of life; religion could not be confined to the private sphere, as the West contended. His society tried to interpret the Quran to meet the spirit of the new age, but also to unify the Islamic nations, raise the standard of living, achieve a higher level of social justice, fight against illiteracy and poverty, and liberate Muslim lands from foreign domination. Under the colonialists, Muslims had been cut off from their roots. As long as they copied other peoples, they would remain cultural mongrels.[151]

Later the society fell into disrepute when a minority of its adherents engaged in terrorism. But their ideas were revived with slight alterations. As the global situation became more and more caught up in religious, ideological and economic conflicts, the narratives that appealed to the Muslim masses the most, were the ones that were rather hostile towards the West.

The 20th century was a time which sowed the perhaps most fertile seeds of antagonism between Islam and the West. The century began with the discovery of oil in Iran, for which the British managed to secure the grant. Five years

---

[151] Ibid., pp. 132–3

later the Constitutional Revolution began to secularize the country and "limit the power of the Monarchs and give the Iranians parliamentary representation".[152] Only fifteen years after the beginning of the 20th century, several European countries found themselves embroiled in the First World War. Shortly thereafter, the Ottoman Empire collapsed. Secularism started to spread across Europe and in 1923 the Republic of Turkey was established by Mustafa Kemal under a strictly secular system. The 1930s were marked by a collapse of the Western economy, known as The Great Depression, and by the rise of the Nazis in Germany. Hitler presented the Jews as scapegoats for economic hardships and slowly set the fatal machinery in motion which began by marginalizing and discriminating Jews; it continued with their demonization and dehumanization and ended with their prosecution and genocide with the ferocity and precision of a witch hunt.

Meanwhile, the Indian Subcontinent, one of the largest of British colonies, was struggling for independence with Mohandas "Mahatma" (*Maha Aatma* meaning 'great soul') Gandhi as the main leader of this movement. He applied strictly non-violent forms of protest, which came to be known as civil disobedience. India gained independence in 1947 but not before Muhammad Ali Jinnah, who was a British educated jurist just like Gandhi, persuaded the British to divide the country so that the Muslims of India could represent their interests in their own democratic state. Even though a plan to establish a secular state with some seats reserved for religious minorities in the parliament was being negotiated, it was abandoned after all, because most people did not seem to believe Hindus and Muslims capable of running a country together. And so British-India was divided into India and Pakistan. This partition saw one of the most intensive and bloodiest massacres in history in the consequent migrations, especially in the province of Punjab which had to be divided. Interreligious conflicts between Hindus and Muslims erupted all over India. Muslims, Sikhs, and Hindus who happened to live on the 'wrong' side of the new border had to leave their homes and roots behind and migrate with their families and possessions. Therefore, even though the Muslims and Hindus of the Indian subcontinent might have really been unable to run a fair democracy together, their partition into India and Pakistan has done nothing to resolve the tensions between them.

The population of both countries needs to be schooled in interreligious tolerance and religious pluralism which would undoubtedly take decades to

---

[152] Ibid., p. 128

plan, implement, refine and thrive. Both Gandhi and Jinnah envisaged a secular democracy following the British example, but since both died within a year of the establishment of the two autonomous countries, their enterprises remained incomplete.

After the Second World War, the power distribution in the West was under a process of reconfiguration. A tug of war began between communist Soviet Russia and the capitalist USA. The United States of America gained air superiority after 1945 and have gotten involved in military conflicts in more than a dozen countries since. In the end of the Second World War, they even released two atom bombs killing hundreds of thousands in Japan; the first and only use of nuclear weapons in history. The following years, after the establishment of the state of Israel in 1948, the Middle East Conflict began and continues to this day.

Modernization in the West was underway: it was a process that was slowly covering all aspects of the society. In the 1960's, the Civil Rights Movement took on the injustice of racial discrimination in the USA. Martin Luther King applied Gandhi's method of civil disobedience in the desegregation movement. In 1979, the Soviets intervened in Afghanistan which led the USA to fund and arm Islamist militias of the region, so they could defend their borders. They later formed the group that owned up to the 9/11 attacks two decades later. In the 1990s the Bosnian war culminated in the massacre of Srebrenica where thousands of Bosnian Muslims were slaughtered. This incident was used by Islamists in order to recruit young Muslims from European countries to fight for the Islamist cause. The 20th century witnessed several displays of failed politics in the East and the West. It also witnessed the rise of a relatively new phenomenon: Islamist Terrorism. The beginning of the 21st century was marked by the 9/11 attacks. The aftermath has been reflected upon in the introduction and will be discussed in the literary analysis of Post-9/11 Literature.

In conclusion, the developments of the 20th century from beginning to end increased the hostility between the two sides, even though the East witnessed several attempts to attune itself to Western ways, so they might compete on an equal footing. The West too made attempts to modernize the (former) colonies. But they all failed for several reasons:

> Where Europeans and Americans had been allowed to modernize at their own pace, and to set their own agendas, the inhabitants of the colonized countries had to modernize far too rapidly and were forced to comply with somebody else's programme. But even Western people had found the transformation of their society painful. They had experienced almost four hundred years of political and often bloody revolutions, reigns of terror, ethnic cleansing, violent wars of religion, the despoliation of the countryside, vast social upheavals, exploitation in

> the factories, spiritual malaise and profound anomie in the new megacities. Today we are seeing similar violence, cruelty, revolution and disorientation in the developing countries, which are making an even more difficult rite of passage to modernity. It is also true that the modern spirit that developed in the West is fundamentally different. In Europe and America, it had two main characteristics: innovation and autonomy (the modernizing process was punctuated in Europe and America by declarations of independence on the political, intellectual, religious and social fronts). But in the developing world, modernity has been accompanied not by autonomy but by a loss of independence and national autonomy. Instead of innovation, the developing countries can only modernize by imitating the West, which is so far advanced that they have no hope of catching up. Since the modernizing process has not been the same, it is unlikely that the end product will conform to what the West regards as the desirable norm.[153]

The modernization in the West was based on ideas that scorned authoritarian stances and thus led to a wave of reforms elevating the suppressed classes in the West. They were initiated and led by the people, not by the ruling classes (bottom-up): The French Revolution, the American Revolution, Abolitionism, the Suffragette movement, and desegregation being only a few examples. In the Muslim world, however, modernization was presented as a predefined target stipulated by the ruling class (top-down). Additionally, the condition of the West was not seen by Muslims as something worth struggling for. The West was perceived as being war-torn during the first half of the 20th century, and as war-mongering throughout the second. This latter perception has been a powerful element in anti-Western narratives.

The Nazi propagandists had perfected the application of narratives of disparity for their cause, using and applying theories from the science of psychology which was quite new at the time. Freud's *Civilization and its Discontents* and his nephew Edward Bernays' works on propaganda were studied by Goebbels. Bernays had formulated his theories on propaganda for commerce. He is known as the father of public relations, he may even be regarded as the father of advertisements and endorsements. The concept of propaganda has not been used in this study in the context of the intellectual groundwork that may be involved in promoting the disparity between Islam and the West for two reasons:

a. Ever since the Nazi regime, the term propaganda has a number of connotations that do not fit into the basic theory of this study: for instance, the term propaganda is usually associated with a vicious intent.

---

[153] Ibid., p. 124

b. Propaganda is fashioned deliberately and is usually a top-down method of a government or large public organization.

Narratives of disparity as understood here can work top-down as well as bottom-up or even in the space in-between; they may be contrived deliberately and also subconsciously.

A wider look at history demystifies the illusion of discontinuity. Symptoms of injustice and oppression, racial segregation, ethnic cleansing, witch-hunts, scaffolding and medieval torture all continue to exist. The philosophy which builds the foundation of our civilization has changed; the values that people identify themselves with have changed and thus the narratives which justified previous means of oppression had to be adjusted. Oppression was not discontinued when the values of freedom and equality were prioritized. Instead, it changed its name and was made compatible with the new values. Top-down oppression never stopped. Monarchs can impose it on their subjects; the bourgeoisie on the poor; elected leaders like Hitler and Mussolini have subjected their citizens to it in a democracy; political parties often resort to various means of fiscal and legislative suppression and too many economies only make the rich richer and the poor poorer; religious leaders can exploit their positions by invoking God's favour; many communities persecute minorities and powerful nations and bodies dictate terms to weaker ones. It is known that lobbies fund think-tanks, which are often factories producing grand narratives to substantiate their cause. Lobbies usually also buy University faculties who help formulate and justify their narratives. Even liberal politicians sometimes aid these processes by either denying the existence of oppression (*Colour Blindness Paradigm*) or by giving it a different name and making it sound necessary and plausible. 'Torture' is not only still used but it has been perfected with the application of medical and psychological know-how. It is called 'enhanced interrogation' which – unlike the medieval kind – is a necessary measure to keep the population safe from terrorism. Racial segregation continues to exist in the form of 'racial discrimination', and in the generally continued perception of certain people as 'different' – a perception that necessitates the continued use of words like 'ghettoization', 'interracial marriages', 'mixed race', etc. The most widely used method to protect ethnic cleansing or genocide is by denying it ever happened or renegotiating the definition of genocide. Genocide as a criminal offence was recognized in the late 1940s which is why most governments refuse to take responsibility for genocides which happened before that time, like the Armenian genocide of 1915 which the Turkish government refuses to acknowledge; or the genocide of the Herero and Nama people in the German colony of Southwest-Africa between 1904 and 1908, that Germany also refuses to recognize as a genocide to evade the costs of restitution. In some arguments, the term genocide is tied to the death toll, so that up to a certain number of confirmed deaths it is not considered enough to justify this label. All these are only a few examples from recent history of some of the most powerful Western countries. The fact that oppression exists in Islamic countries need not be proven because no one in the West ever believed the narratives that served to justify injustices committed by 'the other'.

The above-mentioned examples show that narratives serve to mitigate decisions that violate an existing moral code or code of ethics that a nation or civilization holds sacred. In some cases, the exchange of one single word has been sufficient to reconcile inhuman actions with the very humanist values that serve to bestow pride and power on peoples and nations.

ENCOUNTERS OF ISLAM AND THE WEST – A MAKING OF NARRATIVES

> What did he look like, you ask? Well, sir, he ... But how odd! I cannot now recall the man's particulars, his age, say, or his build; to be honest, I cannot now recall many details of the events I have been relating to you. But surely it is the **gist** that matters; I am, after all, telling you a history, and in history, as I suspect you – an American – will agree, it is the thrust of one's narrative that counts, not the accuracy of one's details. Still, I can assure you that everything I have told you thus far happened, for all intents and purposes, more or less, as I have described.[154]

Narratives of disparity are direct derivatives of historical narratives and a result of their historiography. I would like to sum up the main historiographic foundations for the narratives which fuel the disparity between Islam and the West to this day. Subsequently, their applications will be detected in a selected number of novels which were published in England between 2001 and 2009.

Throughout the history of Islam and of the West, there have been many encounters between the two sides. An exchange of ideas has never been lacking, and yet there is one meta-narrative that states that whenever there is an encounter of Islam and the West there will automatically be conflict because the inherent values of each are so different that they will clash inevitably. My

[154] Hamid, *The Reluctant Fundamentalist*, pp. 134–5

hypothesis, however, is that the basic and constant values of Islam are compatible with Western values and that it is only by designing narratives about their incompatibility that they are successfully kept apart.

In the previous chapters, we have seen that even though there have been several attempts at overcoming the chasm that seems to lie between the two sides they were followed by schemes that wiped out the markers of the previous approach. Similarly, the Spanish Inquisition served to wipe out the marks that the Arab conquerors had left in Europe in medieval times and in the 20th century, the Wahhabi movement wiped out all the efforts of Islamic modernists to bring European influences upon the Muslim world.

> If Hitler commissioned positivist histories which argued for the linear evolution of the Aryans from the dinosaurs, he was repeating a historiographic strategy which had always applied to the description of European culture. The construction of a culturally cohesive national society often has to colonize its extra-national origins as well as its national competitors, treating Jesus, Homer and Joyce as part of the story of English literature, as universal rather than national subjects.
>
> Canon-busting can be understood then as part of a general assault on grand narratives that advance such universalistic pretensions.[155]

In a very similar fashion Muhammad Iqbal insisted in the early 20th century that

> Islam was just as rational and advanced as any Western system. Indeed, it was the most rational and advanced of all the confessional faiths. Its strict monotheism had liberated humanity from mythology, and the Quran had urged Muslims to observe nature closely, reflect upon their observations, and subject their actions to constant scrutiny. Thus, the empirical spirit that had given birth to modernity had, in fact, originated in Islam. This was a partial and inaccurate interpretation of history, but no more biased than the Western tendency at this time to see Christianity as the superior faith and Europe as always having been in the vanguard of progress.[156]

Thus, Islam does not denominate one religion, but it is the title of any number of narratives which people construct in order to maintain their view regarding Islam. These narratives can be very different in nature, and yet they are all referred to as "Islam" by their authors. Two prevalent understandings of Islam today are radical Islam on the one hand and moderate Islam on the other hand. Radical Islam is based on the "ideological narrative", a term coined by Maajid Nawaz, which tells the story of how all Muslims must come together under one caliphate in order to compete with Western imperialism and

---

155 Currie, *Postmodern Narrative Theory,* p. 108
156 Armstrong, *Islam,* p. 132

regain world leadership (Arab socialism or Pan-Arabism). This narrative is based on the notion that the current situation of Muslims in the world was a sign of God being unhappy with the faith of Muslims today. Based on this, the propagators of this narrative argue that to regain a position of superiority in the world, Muslims must improve their faith; and since the modern faith made God unhappy, they have to try and recover the original faith as close to the time of the Prophet as possible in order to accomplish that. The religion as practiced by the average non-political believer is referred to as 'moderate Islam'. This term exists only to counter the ideological narrative which hijacked the name of this religion for its own cause. Thus, 'moderate Islam' is the counter-narrative to Islamism. In addition, there are literally thousands of other narratives that define what is or is not Islam between these two ends, which are constantly battling one another.

While Samuel Huntington seemingly neglects this diversity, his explanation of the conflict between Islam and the West in *The Clash of Civilizations and the Remaking of World Order* offers an accurate depiction of the majority of Islam's representatives' role in the standoff. Huntington considers that both sides engage equally in this struggle for global hegemony and thus guarantee its continuation. He also looks at the history of this encounter which began as a conflict between Christianity and Islam, and notes that the causes are not only their differences but also their similarities:

> The causes of this ongoing pattern of conflict lie not in transitory phenomena such as twelfth-century Christian passion or twentieth-century Muslim fundamentalism. They flow from the nature of the two religions and the civilizations based on them. *Conflict was, on the one hand, a product of difference,* particularly the Muslim concept of Islam as a way of life transcending and uniting religion and politics versus the Western Christian concept of the separate realms of God and Caesar. *The conflict also stemmed, however, from their similarities.* Both are monotheistic religions, which, unlike polytheistic ones, cannot easily assimilate additional deities, and which see the world in dualistic, us-and-them terms. Both are universalistic, claiming to be the one true faith to which all humans can adhere. Both are missionary religions believing that their adherents have an obligation to convert nonbelievers to that one true faith. From its origins, Islam expanded by conquest and when the opportunity existed Christianity did also. The parallel concepts of "jihad" and "crusade" not only resemble each other but distinguish these two faiths from other major world religions.[157] [Emphasis added]

Huntington observes that the conflict between Islam and the West is based equally on the similarities and the differences between the two. His thesis will

---

[157] Huntington, *The Clash of Civilizations and The Remaking of World Order*, pp. 210–1

be supported by a demonstration of NoDs which can be fashioned with either. The discourse around New Year's Eve of 2015 in Cologne offers one example:

A. A narrative of inadequacy was fashioned proclaiming that Arab men assaulted women that night, because, unlike German or European men, Arabs are inherently disrespectful towards women.

B. The counter-narrative in the discourse cited a number of sexual assault during the annual *Oktoberfest* in Bavaria in order to prove that sexual harassment is not causally linked to some ethnic or religious affiliation. It is also a narrative of inadequacy as it portrays the West as bigoted and sanctimonious.

Narrative A was fashioned with the intention of discrediting refugees in order to justify the demand for a stricter asylum policy. Narrative B was fashioned in order to retaliate Narrative A and to discredit its instigators as politically incorrect. Neither narrative serves to dissolve the disparity between the two parties. On the contrary: both narratives reinforce the disparity by promoting a binary worldview of '*we and they*' in their own way. Also, neither narrative can help the victims or solve the problems at hand regarding misogyny or security. After a long public discourse lasting several months, the conflict itself remained largely unresolved but the disparity and mutual distrust were hardened.

The following conclusion of Huntington's diachronic dissection of the conflict and its roots can also be read as a list of the grounds upon which NoDs are established:

> A comparable mix of factors has increased the conflict between Islam and the West in the late twentieth century. First, Muslim population growth has generated large numbers of unemployed and disaffected young people who become recruits to Islamist causes, exert pressure on neighboring societies, and migrate to the West. Second, the Islamic Resurgence has given Muslims renewed confidence in the distinctive character and worth of their civilization and values compared to those of the West. Third, the West's simultaneous efforts to universalize its values and institutions, to maintain its military and economic superiority, and to intervene in conflicts in the Muslim world generate an intense resentment among Muslims. Fourth, the collapse of communism removed a common enemy of the West and Islam and left each the perceived major threat to the other. Fifth, the increasing contact between and intermingling of Muslims and Westerners stimulate in each a new sense of their own identity and how it differs from that of the other. Interaction and intermingling also exacerbate differences by members of the other civilization. Within both Muslim and Christian societies, tolerance for the other declined sharply in the 1980s and 1990s.[158]

[158] Ibid., p. 211

Huntington believes that Muslims continue this conflict because they believe they deserve global hegemony but keep failing to acquire it:

> The underlying problem for the West is not Islamic fundamentalism. It is Islam, a different civilization whose people are convinced of the superiority of their culture and are obsessed with the inferiority of their power. The problem for Islam is not the CIA or the U.S. Department of Defense. It is the West, a different civilization whose people are convinced of the universality of their culture and believe that their superior, if declining, power imposes on them the obligation to extend that culture throughout the world. These are the basic ingredients that fuel conflict between Islam and the West.[159]

And the West continues the conflict because it feels threatened by Islam which "is the only civilization which has put the survival of the West in doubt, and it has done that at least twice."[160] Therefore, Huntington sees one reason for the revival of this conflict: "[The] fundamental questions of power and culture. [...] Who is to rule? Who is to be ruled?" And he sees another reason for the conflict:

> [There are] two different versions of what is right and what is wrong and, as a consequence, who is right and who is wrong. So long as Islam remains Islam (which it will) and the West remains the West (which is more dubious), this fundamental conflict between two great civilizations and ways of life will continue to define their relations in the future even as it has defined them for the past fourteen centuries.[161]

Huntington appears to have detected narratives on both sides that have caused an escalation of the conflict: "Growing Muslim anti-Westernism has been paralleled by expanding Western concern with the 'Islamic threat' posed particularly by Muslim extremism."[162] The interplay of narratives vs. counter-narratives reproduces the clash.

The modernist and liberal narratives of Islam were more successful in the West because they were talking from a position of power over the world. Though they failed to establish peace or justice and equality they did succeed in evincing their aspiration of a superior way of thinking hence a superior way of like and maintaining their position of power. This may explain why sources in the West sold liberal narratives more successfully to their people. On the other hand, liberal narratives that Muslim intellectuals attempted to spread were not appreciated by the majority often evoking an aversive response to

---

[159] Ibid., pp. 217–8
[160] Ibid., p. 210
[161] Ibid., p. 212
[162] Ibid., p. 215

anything remotely akin to the 'other's' values, as if they showed a position of acceptance or subordination to the West. Consequently, the liberal or modernist narratives resulted in a backlash toward orthodoxy, sometimes even toward radicalism, in the so-called Muslim world. This is because orthodox and radical groups refuse to accept the superiority of the West, and present narratives of Islam's superiority instead. A display of 'bravery' in the form of defiance against the West is a powerful element in those narratives. The many inner-Islamic sectarian conflicts complicated things even more. Young people especially leapt to adopt the supremacist narrative which made them feel strong and proud of being Muslims, rather than the liberal one which required enough humility to see the defects of the Muslim world as well as realize it would require strength and intellectual efforts to make amendments.

Muslims of today like to refer to the achievements of the scientists and scholars of Islam's Golden Age to prove that progressivity is not incompatible with Islam. This narrative has been countered by critics of Islam who interpret Muslims' inability to have been able to sustain or regain that glory or subsequently even to match up to the West as proof that their achievements in the Golden Age were merely a historical fluke.

Another such narrative is blaming the decline of the Muslim world on the colonization, even though it did not set in until after the decline had already been underway. And though it may be true that the West capitalized on the economic weakness of Muslim countries during colonization, it is still not entirely accurate to claim that the decline of the Muslim world was exclusively due to the intervention of the West. It is evident that throughout history, many Muslim regents themselves were responsible for taking detrimental decisions.

The West, on the other hand, purports several narratives that perpetuate the idea of its positive distinction from other people, mind-sets, or thought systems. In order to establish its superiority over other civilizations, these narratives utilize a set of values – primarily democracy, freedom, individual rights, and secularism – which are supposedly better than any other set of principles which mankind has ever taken credit for. The impulse of ethnocentrism is obviously a universal phenomenon. However, it has been very effective in the spread of these narratives and by now they are so well rooted in people's minds that it almost always considered axiomatic that European or Western values stand above everything else. The so-called Eurocentric view has been rather quick in judging Muslim leaders and their claims of Islam's superiority over every other belief and of it being worth dying or even killing for. Meanwhile, Western countries are at war with countless countries in the name of freedom, because they are convinced that freedom and all their other values are worth killing for. The issue is that in both cases the values that are written all over the flags waving in battlefields are never observed entirely. They are only useful in order to maintain the narratives justifying the actions. After all, without a worthy cause and without a set of principles supporting it, it would not be called 'war', but simply 'mass murder of innocents' and 'theft of a foreign land and its resources'.

Every measure that followed 9/11 was essentially a failure and led to a further destabilization of the Near East. Post-9/11 is not a demarcation of discontinuity, but it did mark some very radical and sudden changes: it changed the sense of security in the USA and in Europe and it changed their people's sense of justice and equality. The post 9/11 era has also given centre stage to one narrative of superiority called Neo-Atheism. It is based on a notion most prominently argued by Richard Dawkins in *The God Delusion* that states that the ultimate root of all bloodshed and injustice is religion. The less extreme version of this is narrative is claiming the superiority of rationalism over religious fervour.

In conclusion, there is no inherently inimical relationship nor a reason for conflict or necessity for war between the religion of Islam and the ideals of the West except what might be propagated by means of narratives especially construed for the purpose or creating enmity. There are narratives which perpetuate a supposedly irresolvable conflict between the values of Islam and the West. I do not wish to give a counter-narrative to any of these, but the objective of this thesis is to identify and analyse the narratives of disparity and examine their content and structure. "As historians are periodically being told – without their really heeding the warning – there is no such thing as a 'pure' fact. A historical fact is an intellectual decision and decision is what distinguishes history from the wholesale publication of manuscript material."[163] This thought could be extended to any number of academic disciplines: there are no pure facts but only intellectual decisions. Therefore, one could argue against certain narratives by providing counter-narratives, but one cannot simply declare them to be false. So, in lieu of Graham MacPhee's warning against what he calls "the paradigm of Post-9/11 Exceptionalism",[164] this research treats the shocking events of September 11, 2001 not as an isolated climax of imperial politics, but as a point of reference which made resentments visible and gave rise to sets of narratives that asserted the disparity between Islam and the West anew.

---

[163] Furet, *Beyond the Annales*, pp. 403–4
[164] MacPhee, *Postwar British Literature and Postcolonial Studies*, p. 116

Islam and The West in Selected Contemporary British Novels

> Being a novelist I consider myself superior to the saint, the scientist, the philosopher, and the poet [...]. The novel is the one bright book of life. (D.H. Lawrence)

Gerald Schneiders noticed that the history of religious and political controversies regarding Islam in Europe has a parallel in the history of literature. Dante Alighieri depicted Muhammad in *The Divine Comedy* as an eternal resident of hell, subjected to unfathomable tortures. Schneiders sees the next milestone in the tradition of anti-Muslim literature in Humphrey Prideaux's *The True Nature of Imposture, Fully Displayed in the Life of Mahomet* of the late 17th century. As a widely known volume by a renowned historian, Prideaux's text was the primary source for Voltaire's works, in which he said that one's natural common sense must be completely shaken up with the turn of every page of the Quran, which he deemed indigestible. Also, as he mentioned to the Prussian King Frederick II in a letter in 1740, Voltaire was convinced that Muhammad was nothing but a Tartuffe with a sword. These examples are only two of many.[165]

The past has a direct effect on our present, and yet the past is not tangible and cannot be visited or faithfully reconstructed. Historiography is one form in which the past exists and effects the present. Transformations and changes in society and social structures are usually also debated in the public sphere and consequently in all kinds of media. The past two decades in British fiction are a very interesting period to study in this respect because many vast changes and transitions occurred in this relatively short time and society has had to keep pace and adjust. The novels chosen here might arguably qualify as historical novels because they are novels that attempt to explain the present or in some cases a potential future by means of a diachronic analysis of developments.

> History is other, and the present familiar. The historian's job is often to explain the transition between these states. The historical novelist similarly explores the

[165] Schneiders, *Islamfeindlichkeit,* p. 13

> dissonance and displacement between then and now, making the past recognizable but simultaneously authentically unfamiliar.[166]

This quote reflects a diachronic historiography, but we have established earlier that history can also be told in a structuralist synchronic mode. A historical novel, however, can look at only one period and still take on a postmodernist perspective. In any case, as Paul Cobley had explained, it is a human instinct to want to fit historical facts into a narrative. This is why history is a popular inspiration for creative writers.

> A historical novel might consider the articulation of nationhood via the past, highlight the subjectivism of narratives of History, underline the importance of the realist mode of writing to notions of authenticity, question writing itself, and attack historiographical convention. [...] One might suggest an alternative narrative of the rise of the novel focused through historical fiction, for instance, a form concerned with social movement, dissidence, complication and empathy rather than the more individualistic novel form we are familiar with, born of autobiographical, personal, revelatory narratives. Certainly, figures that we might see as key exponents of the novel form, such as Gustave Flaubert, or Leo Tolstoy, considered their historical fictions not to be novels at all, but experiments and crucial interventions in important cultural debates.[167]

The novels analysed here are responses to the developments after 9/11 which was a resounding paradigm shift in the world's history. Therefore, these novels are historical novels, except that the time interval between history and the present, in this case, is rather minimal. Since it is only a selection of novels and not all novels which address Islam in the West today, this dissertation is only a fraction of literature's reflection of these narratives. Based on the premise that narratives of disparity can be found everywhere – in the public discourse, in political agendas, in stories or myths, in historiography and in fiction's depiction of reality – this research will attempt to explain the encounter and relationship between Islam and the West by pinpointing narratives of disparity in contemporary British novels. I have chosen the novel as a genre because of its focus on experientiality and its characteristic element of world-making. Frankly, the conflict between Islamic and western values is also a product of fictional world-making since in principle there is no inherent conflict unless one is construed in narratives. Additionally, the conflict is not tangible but something that is experienced by the collective mind.

In the following chapters, I will analyse a selected number of novels and present my reading of them regarding the *narratives of disparity* they feature.

---

[166] de Groot, *The Historical Novel,* p. 3
[167] Ibid., p. 2

Each of the chosen novels, depicting a conflict between Islam and the West in various ways, can be analysed in relation to all the narratives because these are often interconnected as well. Each novel will be discussed with a focus on the representation and discussion of several elements such as religion, ethnicity, identity, Islam, and the West. Since novels are anthropocentric in their nature, the focus will be on the way the characters perceive these elements, instead of focussing on how the author represents them. The analysis of each novel will begin with a list of major characters, a plot synopsis, and reflections on the modes of discourse. After this, the literary narrative will be inspected with regard to narratives of disparity vis-à-vis Islam in the West.

The analysis of the first novel focuses primarily on the narratives of the so-called War on Terror in the aftermath of the 9/11 attacks. The term 'War on Terror' was coined by the 43rd US-President, George W. Bush Jr., shortly after September 11th, 2001, when a series of attacks on several targets in the United States, resulted in the loss of around three thousand civilian lives. The Islamist terrorist organization Al-Qaeda soon claimed responsibility for these attacks, and suddenly the USA was facing a new enemy. The planning and execution of these attacks, which included the hijacking of three passenger planes of US-Airlines and the destruction of the twin towers of the World Trade Centre – the two largest skyscrapers in the heart of New York City – changed the way the nation looked upon its enemies in the middle east, because they demonstrated a level of sophistication which no one had thought them capable of before and at the same time revealed the USA's weaknesses. Suddenly they had been challenged by a seriously dangerous opponent and the odds had changed.

The Global War on Terror became Bush Jr.'s legacy of global impact. In the aftermath of the 9/11 attacks, two huge battlefronts of the world manifested themselves: Al-Qaeda against the United States of America and this gradually transformed into "Islam against the West" in the minds of the Western population. Even today, fifteen years onwards, many political parties in Europe and the US do not distinguish Islam from Islamism, Islamist Extremism or Islamist Terrorism.

The Middle East had been torn by conflicts long before this attack and several Western Nations had been interfering in (and sometimes controlling) their politics and economics for decades. The so-called 9/11 attacks mark a paradigm shift of historic significance inasmuch that up until then no one had suspected there might be an enemy strong enough to challenge the USA, much less capable of planning and successfully executing a strike killing thousands of civilians. Now that the USA had been challenged in a way that had revealed their weaknesses, they were facing several tasks: In order to reassure a shocked nation of the government's ability to protect its people and to regain their trust, they had to expose the ones responsible for this attack and bring them to justice, thus reclaiming a position of superiority in the world. The most difficult task was to make the people of USA feel safe again. The task of maintaining a certain image of superiority or invincibility was of a certain priority to the US government, especially because this particular enemy – the Al-Qaeda leader Osama bin Laden – had been armed and financed by the USA during the Soviet-Afghan War in the 1980s. The War on Terror was launched to accomplish these tasks.

Wars are predicated on strategies that affect many levels of people's lives: not only does a war include military actions against the enemy but it begins with the need to propagate a set of narratives in order to recruit people to join in its endeavours as well as to justify all its costs. The narratives in this case included among others:

- Asserting that Iraq possessed nuclear weapons and Saddam Hussein's government had to be overthrown because it posed an immediate threat to the USA
- Propagating the necessity of incarceration and torture of terrorism suspects for the sake of national security
- Justifying racial profiling and surveillance

Meanwhile, Hussein, Ghaddafi, bin Laden and other like personalities had also spread narratives of Arab Socialism, Pan-Islamism or Pan-Arabism, which resulted in the construction of several counter-narratives in Western nations. Thus, the narrative of the USA and its allies being at war with *Islam* (instead of *Islamist Terrorism*) was in part because Islamist terrorists do not distinguish between Islam and Islamism but believe themselves as following the sole representatives of 'the one true Islam'.

The 9/11 attacks are a turning point in the plot of the upcoming novel *The Reluctant Fundamentalist*, in a way that they mark a shift in the balance of power. While all the previous theories vis-à-vis Orient vs. Occident, Islam vs. the West, or colonies vs. metropolitan state – like Said's *Orientalism* and Huntington's *Clash of Civilizations* – were conceptualized in a framework wherein one side was in a position of power or dominance over the other, this thesis is based on a different premise, because the 9/11 attacks revealed an opponent who was suddenly on an equal footing simply because he refused to assume a subordinate position. The confrontation between Islam and the West is now happening on an equal footing, not only on the military battlefield but also on an ideological level: Islamism is the answer to American supremacy, in that it is a narrative of superiority in its own right. The use of narratives of disparity is not specific to only one side of the conflict; for every US-American NoD there is a Muslim counter-narrative which further propagates disparity, rather than equivalence.

Most of the novels discussed in the upcoming chapter have been subjected to many thorough and fascinating analyses, most of which focus on their many post-colonial implications. While post-colonialism is certainly a constructive paradigm in order to interpret them, my readings go beyond the intended meaning of the story. Obviously, a work of fiction is packaged in a generic framework which must be known to the writer and the reader, so the message can be decoded. It is obvious and generally recognized that Hamid's novel TRF, for instance, can be productively interpreted from the post-colonial perspective, as Hamid was probably aware of while writing. Since my reading of the novels is based on the theoretical paradigm of *narratives of disparity*, which is obviously unknown to the authors who wrote the novels being analysed here, the implication of the reading is a different one. This analysis is no interpretation by means of a pertinent code. If narratives of disparity have been dictating the discourse around Islam and the West for much longer than the past 16 years of the post-9/11 era, then they will be visible in the story world of a novel depicting encounters between Islam and the West. I will not be reading from the literary texts as much as I will be reading into them.

Each chapter for the analysis of a novel will entail a summary of the plot, a reflection of the chosen narrative devices, a discussion of previous interpretations, as well as extractions of narratives of disparity from the plot. The order and priority of these elements vary between the analyses of the different novels.

The Reluctant Fundamentalist (2007) by Mohsin Hamid

A Reading of Hamid's *The Reluctant Fundamentalist (TRF)*

> I did not grow up in poverty. But I did grow up with a poor boy's sense of longing, in my case not for what my family had never had, but for what we had had and lost. Some of my relatives held onto imagined memories the way homeless people hold onto lottery tickets. Nostalgia was their crack cocaine, if you will, and my childhood was littered with the consequences of their addiction: unserviceable debts, squabbles over inheritances, the odd alcoholic or suicide. In this, Jim and I were indeed similar: he had grown up outside the candy store, and I had grown up on its threshold as its door was being shut.[168]

Mohsin Hamid's second novel, titled *The Reluctant Fundamentalist (TRF)* was first published in 2007 in London and decorated with the Anisfield-Wolf Book Award. It has been subjected to many analyses applying different existing models of interpretation. This chapter is not an interpretation of the text in that sense as it does not attempt to analyse what the author may or may not have intended. This analysis is an extraction of narratives of disparity vis-à-vis Islam and the West from the plot of the novel. *TRF* features an encounter of these two entities, which is depicted before and after the 9/11 attacks in NYC. The attacks cause a trauma, which affects every element and figure of the story world creating a dramatic binary worldview. Sarah Ilott argued that many works of literature in the post-9/11 era constructed stories as an antidote to the trauma by construing grand narratives and that *The Reluctant Fundamentalist* is different from most of these in that it encourages the reader to "leave the wounds open" instead of seeking closure. Ilott argues that this is accomplished by an activation of the reader to make up his/her own mind, and by refusing to provide any closure by the end of the novella.[169] In fact, Ilott's fascinating reading of the novel offers a very sound interpretation of how Hamid might have intended a deconstruction of post 9/11 narratives that were

---

[168] Hamid, *The Reluctant Fundamentalist,* p. 81

[169] Ilott, '*Generic Frameworks and Active Readership in The Reluctant Fundamentalist*', p. 582

supposed to offer closure. My reading is focused on the content level and the discourse level of the novel in order to disclose how narratives of disparity – which comprise a fragmentary worldview – are constructed in it due to a perception impeded by psychoses of the protagonist.

The protagonist and first-person narrator, a 26-year-old named Changez – among other entities in the novel – develops forms of mild personality disorders that cloud his judgement: for one, he develops a form of cultural or ethnic narcissism, as in his view the 9/11 attacks marked a shift in the balance of power, after which his ego no longer allowed him to pursue his *American Dream* of becoming a US-American himself. The novel discusses psychoses as a driving force behind decision making and acting; psychoses that can be caused by the trauma of loss, as Erica did after her boyfriend died, and the USA did after the 9/11 attacks. Changez suffers the same blow due to the loss of his *American Dream* which consisted of more than making a fortune and a successful career: he had dreamed of settling down with a white woman, of being accepted and of becoming part of the US-American elite. A dream, which was crushed in the aftermath of the 9/11 attacks, as well as by Erica's illness. All three turned to the past for consolation and as a source of inspiration and strength: the US-American nation chose its past as a source of identity and became exclusivist in its nostalgia. Erica did not just escape life, but retreated into nostalgia and chose the past over the present and the future. And finally, Changez, who chose his past life in Pakistan over his future in the USA.

The novel begins in Lahore about four years after the 9/11 attacks, as Changez approaches a US-American man – who remains unnamed – because he looks lost. Changez Khan (Urdu version of the name Genghis Khan) is a Pakistani young man of exceptional intelligence, as evidenced by his excelling achievements in education in Pakistan as well as in the USA. He departed for the USA in the late 90s, aged 18, to study economics at Princeton and to settle there. After his graduation, he secured a job at a prestigious business consultancy firm in New York. Only eight months later he deliberately disposes of his job and returns to Pakistan early in 2002, because he gets disillusioned during the aftermath of the 9/11 attacks. Another four years onwards, as a bearded 26-year-old lecturer of a University in Lahore, Changez is telling this story to the US-American stranger, sitting with him in a café called *Old Anarkali* in Lahore. They get together for one tea but end up sitting through more than one serving together. Since the stranger is unwilling to share any information about himself, Changez is left to guess most of the things we learn about him: his considerable height and strength, as well as his haircut, indicate that he is a soldier, which he indirectly and inadvertently confirms at one point (p. 147).

The choice of name for the café they are sitting in will also be subjected to analysis. Anarkali literally means pomegranate blossom and is the name of a famous character from an old Indian myth. She is said to have been a courtesan who fell in love with crown prince Salim of the Mogul Empire. Her story has been featured in poetry, prose, plays, and movies. The character has been a part of Indian mythology, art, and culture for centuries, from ancient literature to contemporary theatre. The symbolism of her fictional narrative will also be interpreted.

As a listener to Changez' lamentable tale, the US-American soldier functions as a synecdoche for the US-American forces that are active in Pakistan. The soldier readily accepts Changez' invitation for tea and later dinner. He is unwilling to share his own story and the occasion that brought him to Pakistan, but he gladly listens to Changez' detailed narrative. During their interlude in the café, the soldier sits with his back to the wall and startles very easily. Minor things like the approach of their waiter and a short blackout make him jump. Every time he is startled he reaches to the inside of his jacket with his right hand as if to retrieve either a wallet or possibly a handgun – the existence of which is indicated on several occasions in the story but never explicitly confirmed. The soldier does not only represent the commanding voices of the US-American War on Terror, but also the US-American sentiments of distrust and their constant fear of bearded South-Asian or Arab men. Even though the soldier was distrustful towards Changez from the start, the number of reasons for him to distrust Changez increases as the story progresses, because in the embedded story Changez' character arc evolves from being an optimistic and USA-friendly romantic to a disillusioned and hostile anti-American activist. By the end of the narration, Changez explains that he can use his current position at a University to recruit students for campaigning against US-American geo-politics.

By contrast, the plot of the embedded story is centred on the question of how Changez came to live in the USA and what led him to move back to Lahore, focusing on two failed enterprises: one is a romantic relationship with Erica whom he met on a trip to Greece after graduation and continues in NYC after their return; the other is his job at Underwood Samson which he secured shortly before his trip to Greece and begins immediately after his return. The plot of the nested narrative stretches over a period of around eight months, starting with his job interview with Jim who later becomes his boss and ending when Changez decides to resign and return to Lahore after only eight months at his first job after graduation. The 9/11 attacks occur halfway through these eight months and become a turning point for all the elements that were at the core of his life at the time: his cultural identity, his relationship with Erica, and his career.

Initially, he had been excited and happy to be in New York City where he did not stand out as a foreigner. Changez started off with great focus and diligence. He worked hard throughout their training regimen and was repeatedly ranked the best trainee. He also enjoyed having an expense account and spending horrendous amounts on fancy food, drink, and clubs. Changez completed a project in Manila with outstanding success, but not without feeling guilty about adopting elitist etiquettes to maintain the position at the top of the chain of command. Up to this point, his identity crisis is only subtly present between the lines. This crisis suddenly surfaces with a vengeance when he sees the 9/11 attacks live on the news the day before his departure from Manila. He tells his listener in the frame narrative that, to his own surprise, seeing the attacks had made him smile. Seeing the soldier's reaction, Changez tries to make his listener understand that he did not smile because of the harm this attack had done to people. He explains that it was the shift in the balance of power which the attack represented that filled him with a sense of amazement.

Upon his return from Manila, Changez sees that the 9/11 attacks had changed the woman he loved and the cosmopolitan air of NYC. Both had become unwelcoming towards Changez who had also begun to change. In late October, as he watches US-American troops attacking Afghanistan, he notices the disproportion of the confrontation and the "sports-event-like coverage" of the same and finds himself empathizing with the "fellow Muslim nation" of Afghanistan (p. 113), causing him "to tremble with fury". His immediate reaction is to try and stifle his emotional outburst of solidarity with Muslims by getting drunk (p.114). This intuitive response is not only ironic, as the people he refers to as his "fellow Muslims" would be likely to denounce drinking, but it is also a sign of Changez' hypocrisy, which will be discussed in more detail in the upcoming sections. His hangover the next morning causes him to be late for work for the first time.

These resentments gradually affect his work as they make him lose focus and interest. A sudden increase of verbal abuse by strangers on the street and rumours about a growing wave of discrimination against Muslim employees makes him worry about losing his job. However, his concerns turn out to be groundless as Changez is ranked the best among the trainees again after completing a project in New Jersey. He receives a bonus, which he uses to pay off all his student loans. At this point, Changez had already been too preoccupied to be happy about his success, because the standoff between India and Pakistan grows more serious. He visits his family in Lahore in late December 2001 and by January 2002 is already reluctant to return: he wants to stay with his family, so he can help protect them in case a war breaks out. Upon his family's insistence, however, he boards a plane to NYC where he notices many young men his age. It makes him ponder the selflessness of Pakistani families to be sending their sons abroad in an impending war because they are considered the ones most likely to benefit from the opportunities there. Upon his return, he is once again rejected by Erica whose mental health is steadily deteriorating. Changez has trouble accepting the breakup and is extremely disinterested in his work. Jim offers Changez one of only two spots in a new project in Chile, which is a great responsibility that he would be handling alone. Changez readily accepts the assignment albeit with less enthusiasm than Jim had expected. He travels to Chile first class with Jim but is unwilling and unable to take pleasure or pride in his status or the extravagant indulgences.

Changez' mental paralysis sets in once and for all while he is in Chile. Unable to work, he spends a lot of time getting updates on the imminent war between India and Pakistan, as well as reading up on the history of Chile.

Chile used to be an important port on the sea route from the Pacific to the Atlantic Ocean until the Panama Canal provided a shortcut. Changez is fascinated by the country which displays a history of grandeur and beauty. And even though that grandeur is no longer there, its remnants give the country a history and character that Changez finds captivating. The news about the stand-off between India and Pakistan unsettles him, especially the fact that the US government does not signal its support for Pakistan, which would have probably caused India to stand down; but despite having military bases in Pakistan, the USA seems perfectly indifferent to the danger threatening its ally and host. Eventually, these musings make Changez realize that he was not grounded enough in his identity to steady Erica who was looking for someone to hold on to. At the same time, Changez gets in touch with his family at home, who are suffering financial hardships while expecting an outbreak of war. He decides to transfer all his savings to his family because it is the only way he can feel useful to them.

The ultimate turning point is a conversation between Changez and the Chilean owner of the company named Juan Bautista: he compares Changez to the *janissaries* of the Ottoman Empire causing him to feel like he had been fighting for the army that was exploiting his fellow countrymen. The Janissaries were an army of soldiers who had been abducted from their Christian families in their infancy and raised as Ottoman soldiers. Thus, they ended up fighting for the same rulers who had taken them away from their families and sometimes fighting to oppress people of their own origin. This realization is the final measure of disillusionment from Changez' American Dream.

Throughout his narration, Changez repeatedly refers to himself as an *ex-janissary*. All the young men he had seen on the plane when he was returning to New York from Lahore complete this simile: Changez had noticed many men his age on the plane to New York and had felt it was ironic that the very demographic sector that would have been expected to stay to protect their home, family, and country in a war was being sent away. They were expected to use their intellect to build a life far away from uncertainties. Ever since Changez heard of the *Janissary* army he felt it was a cowardly escape and treason, as they were all going abroad, leaving their families behind to go on a different mission, like an army of renegades.

The morning after his conversation with Juan Bautista, Changez announces he will not work any further, and against all attempts of his co-workers and Jim to dissuade him he heads back to New York, fully aware that he will be losing his job and visa. Even though it is difficult for him to leave the company, his sensibilities are at no point a serious threat to his resolve.

He goes to visit Erica at the institution to say his goodbyes but learns that she went missing two weeks after his last visit and that her clothes were found neatly folded in a pile on a rock. The most probable explanation is that she committed suicide. Changez is deeply hurt and struggles to accept that she is no more alive. At the same time, the media coverage of their military intervention, the rhetoric of the government, and the US-American self-portrayal and politics continue to anger Changez. The wound of losing Erica and the hostility he faces from the once welcoming face of the USA make him aggressive. Eventually, he decides he is extremely opposed to US-American politics and resolves to go back to Pakistan and do something to resist it. His transformation from "a lover of America" to an adversary of US-American politics is complete.

At this point in the frame narrative, the soldier probes Changez about how he had intended to put his resolve of stopping the USA into practice. Changez impedes the story here by getting up to walk his guest to his hotel.

> What exactly did I do to stop America, you ask? Have you really no idea, sir? You hesitate – never fear, I am not so rude as to forcibly extract an answer. I will tell you what I did, although it was not much, and I fear it may well fail to meet your expectations. But first let us leave this market [...]. (p. 191)

Changez continues to tell the soldier on their way to the hotel how the conflicts in Iraq, Afghanistan, India, and Pakistan continued to unfold in the subsequent years after his return. They were all connected by the US-American War on Terror. Changez explains that as a University lecturer who is popular among his students, he managed to motivate some of them to participate in "demonstrations for greater independence in Pakistan's domestic and international affairs" (p. 203). Changez does not only invest a lot of his time and suffering – he took a beating trying to break up a fight once and even spent a night in prison – for the student movement in Lahore, but he also constantly puts his job at stake with these activities. One of his student recruits had gone missing a short time before and a local News Channel had come to one of their rallies and interviewed people. They aired and replayed a political comment made by Changez, in which he denounces the alliance of Pakistan and USA. It is obvious how committed and determined he is. However, Changez assures the soldier that he is strongly opposed to violence and only recruits bright and non-violent students for this cause and concludes his narration of the embedded story.

Soon after, the plot of the frame narrative also ends when they reach the gate of the hotel. At this point, the paranoia and mutual distrust climax: as they arrive the US-American gets uneasy because he sees that the waiter and some other men are following them. Changez keeps talking to calm him down, but it starts to sound less convincing. The novel ends when the men start closing in on the US-American in front of his hotel and he reaches under his jacket, presumably to take out his gun.

The entire frame narrative is centered on the nature of their encounter, which is permeated by mutual distrust. Because of the casual way in which Changez speaks to the man, it initially appears to be harmless curiosity or even kindness. As the story proceeds, however, it gradually becomes clear that there is another level of narrative underneath the one that is being delivered. After a while, the reader has reason to suspect that Changez as the narrator cannot be relied upon. In my reading, Changez approached the soldier with the intention of engaging him in a battle of sorts, since a soldier's function is to fight against the enemy. Changez' narration is his way of waging war against the USA, as he is fighting his enemy by intellectual means. Changez' narration seems to be telling the soldier that Pakistan or Muslims, in general, refuse to be ruled by the West any longer and that they will not be silenced or defeated easily.

The story within the story is longer than the story itself and the so-called *narrative space* is expanded. The reader has plenty of space to piece together the actual plot which may differ from the narrator's accounts. The novel is a contemporary dramatic monologue,[170] which is a narrative form known from poetry. The dramatic monologue is a form of homodiegetic narration, in this case by Changez Khan who delivers the story and can only know what he can perceive. The monologue takes place in the frame narrative in which Changez Khan is the only one who speaks. Every event and every dialogue that is taking place in this frame narrative is recounted by the first-person narrator. The narrator repeats every question using indirect speech before he answers it and describes every event before or while he reacts to it. Within the nested narrative, however, the I-narrator recounts the dialogue through direct speech.

The classic form of a dramatic monologue works with a technique known as *unreliable narration*. The ultimate effect of unreliable narration is mostly the gradually progressing and inadvertent self-exposure of the narrator.[171] As in the classic form of *unreliable narration*, the unreliability of Changez' narration is based on a subliminal bias, meaning the narrator is unaware of the falsehood of his story. Changez is still rather young and his judgement is biased by a powerful delusion and romantic fantasies. This form of narration is distinct from that of a so-called *Bildungsroman,* which is also usually a form of fictional autobiography and thus an I-narration. The characteristic element of a *Bildungsroman,* however, is the upward character arc of the protagonist from immaturity to maturity. Thus, the retrospection takes place from a higher vantage point, allowing for a self-reflexive and illuminating insight into the accounts. In the case of a dramatic monologue, on the other hand, the character arc – if present at all – is a downward one, like the proverbial *descent* into madness. Consequently, the events are recounted in the same frame of mind as they were experienced, thus limiting the capacity of self-reflection to a minimum. Even though Changez can pinpoint the role that selected moments played acting as a succession of catalysts, each shaping the plot of his story, he does not re-evaluate his past decisions while narrating. For instance, during his narration, he can name the final catalyst leading him to leave the USA: hearing someone compare Changez to *janissaries*. However, he offers no re-evaluation or critical analysis of the choice he made back then. The time lapse between Changez' experiences from the embedded narrative and his narration in the frame narrative is not only rather short (four years) but also did not comprise a process of mental or emotional growth as suggested by several indicators, like Changez' still being in denial about Erica's death.

---

[170] Ilott, '*Generic Frameworks and Active Readership in The Reluctant Fundamentalist*', p. 572

[171] Nünning, *Unreliable Narration,* p. 6

The described mode of representation does not allow for a multidimensional sketching of the major characters. The figures are described as Changez remembers them or remembers hearing of them as one of the characters never met Changez in person. The narrator's view is unreliable because it is biased by his narcissistic and hypocritical disparagement of the US-American people and culture, as well as his inability to accept the fact that a relationship with Erica was deemed impossible by her mental ailment and not by any question of his ethnicity or religion.

During the narration, the reader must slowly assume a viewpoint that differs from the narrator's, because the story reveals a strong bias in the narrator's perspective. In this example, the narration additionally seems *unreliable* in a deliberate sense as by the end the reader feels the narration was meant to deceive and divert the US-American soldier. Changez Khan starts off looking like a protagonist, but by the end it dawns on the reader that he might just as well be an antagonist, plotting to harm the soldier.

The strong bias in unreliable narration is due to the following inhibitions: a selective and fragmentary memory, exclusivist value system and cultural norms which the narrator has internalised and – most importantly – a psychosis or a pathological personality disorder, which is mostly narcissism.[172] The psychosis is the result of a dramatic experience: the plot of a dramatic monologue comprises a dramatic event which marks a turning point in the development of the central character and functions as a trigger for the narrator's descent into madness. The dramatic event serving as a trigger in this novel is the terrorist attacks in New York and Washington on 11th September 2001. Their aftermath changed the way Changez was treated by strangers, causing him to feel like an outcast, even though his colleagues and friends did not seem to treat him any differently.

At a very early point in his narration, he describes his educational and economic background; the former reveals his narcissism and the latter his hypocrisy. While Changez offers no description of his personality, he does sum up his educational and economic background. In fact, he opens the nested narrative with reflections on how hard it was for him to get selected for a spot at Princeton University. His narcissism becomes apparent when he calculates the limited places which the university opens for students from abroad every year. He is convinced of being at a higher level of accomplishment compared to every US-American student who secured a place at Princeton that year because

---

172 Ibid.

international candidates compete with a larger number of competitors for a lot fewer places reserved for their kind. He sums up his first year at Princeton with the following words: "As a result, the non-Americans among us tended on average to do better than the Americans, and in my case, I reached my senior year without having received a single B." (p. 4). Even so, Changez' narcissism can seem subtle, but that is only because the story is told from his perspective and he is entirely unaware of it. It is a defining element of unreliable narration that the main characters are discernibly complacent and condescending without being aware of it.

Regarding his financial background, he explains that his grandfather had been a wealthy barrister and his family members – including the women, as he stresses to his Western listener – are all working professionals. He explains that because of the decline of the Pakistani rupee the life of working professionals became less and less extravagant over time. His family still wanted to retain its image as being wealthy and did everything to cover up its shortfalls. Changez continued this way in the USA as well. This part hints at the second personality disorder apart from being a narcissist: Changez is also a hypocrite. There are several indicators for this, some of which have been mentioned earlier: he works hard throughout his four years at Princeton to earn enough money besides studying so he can pretend to be rich; he drinks alcohol whilst also believing it to be a sin; in the frame narrative their table at the bistro is approached by a begging child and he says it was wise of the US-American guest not to give him any alms but then does so himself; at one point he pretends to be Chris in order to seduce Erica; and most revealingly, he judges his fellow graduates in Greece for their lavish spending and ill-treatment of elderly staff, and later takes great pleasure in using the company's expense account. Also, anyone who has ever visited Pakistan knows that it is a false claim to say that elderly members of staff are treated with respect by their employers there. Pakistan is a society with an enormous class divide, featuring a common form of etiquette to maintain the boundaries between classes. Most families in Pakistan have servants functioning as housekeepers, cooks, nannies, janitors, or sometimes as everything at once. The people hired as servants are poor and illiterate people ranging from all ages: children, young adults, adults, or even elderly people. They hold a lower station in the house and many people in Pakistan are very strict in maintaining the boundaries between the servants and masters by strictly abiding by the following customs: servants are not allowed to use the same furniture and facilities as their masters. They sit and sleep on the ground, and eat their meals (usually leftovers) in a separated sector of the home after the family members have eaten. Even small children of the employer's family treat the servants irrespective of any age gap in the same authoritative manner as their masters. All servants will usually call the small children of their masters by a common form of address like *Sahib/Sahiba, Bibi/Baba* (which all roughly translated mean 'sir/madam'), *or Baji/Bhai* (meaning older sister/brother) or other terms of address depending on regional dialect. The fact of the matter is that poor elderly people are not necessarily treated with the same respect as wealthy elderly people. The Pakistani 'business etiquette' serves to divide the upper class from the lower class and, in that respect, be deemed to invalidate the principle of respect for age. Therefore, judging his US-American companions for taking an authoritative tone with elderly staff is hypocrisy on Changez' part. Hamid does not mention these very common Pakistani customs of keeping and treating servants this way, but the hypocrisy shows in the way that Changez criticizes his companions behind their backs and not as individuals but as US-Americans:

> 'But you *told* us,' they would say to Greeks twice their age, before insisting things be done their way. I, with my finite and depleting reserve of cash and my traditional sense of deference to one's senior, found myself wondering by what quirk of human history my companions – many of whom I would have regarded as upstarts in my own country, so devoid of refinement were they – were in a position to conduct themselves in the world as though they were its ruling class.
>
> But it may be that I am inclined to exaggerate these irritants in retrospect, knowing the course my relationship with your country would later take. (pp. 23-24)

At this point, Changez fails to mention whether he bothered to confront his companions when they did something he disliked. The narration suggests that he kept quiet about it, which hardly shows character. Even so, if Changez disliked their behaviour in any way, he might have disparaged them as individuals rather than claiming that their cultural or national identity compels them to a specific failing. Humankind is prone to vanity and superiority complexes irrespective of their culture, ethnicity or religion. His hypocrisy allows him to construct negative stereotypes about US-Americans which are part of the groundwork of narratives of superiority.

A person's judgement can be severely biased by adverse traits like hypocrisy, prejudice, and narcissism. In addition to these, Changez' intellectual capacities are impeded by his state of denial about Erica's death. While this aspect is something he does seem aware of, he is still unable to shed his delusions. Changez clearly understands some of his past feelings while he is recounting the story, and in retrospect, he can explain the effects that some events had on the choices he made in life. But in the following passage, it becomes apparent that he is still unable to accept that Erica is no more alive because he fantasizes about her showing up at his doorstep with a backpack someday. Recounting his mother's wish that he gets married he describes his emotional state thusly:

> Not, of course, that I actually believe I am having a relationship, in the normal sense of that term, with Erica at this moment, or that she will one day appear, smiling and bent against the weight of her backpack, to surprise me on my doorstep. But I am still young and see no need to marry another, and for now, I am content to wait. (pp. 199-200)

The final disclosure of his state of mind is when his embedded narrative ends with his recollection of his comment being covered on TV and replayed many times: he says he was disappointed upon not hearing anything from Erica afterwards, because he – against all rationality – had been hoping she would decide to resurface after seeing him on TV. His paranoia stems from his equally boisterous suspicion that the US-Government is watching him and will now come after him in retaliation for this statement. Even though his neurotic inability to accept Erica's death is comprehensible from a psychological point of view because her body was never found, it goes a long way to disclose the aberration in his rational and intellectual capacities. Again, this is a classic effect of a dramatic monologue that by the end of the tale the reader realizes that this is actually a 'madman'[173] recounting his story, putting everything he has related into a new and awry perspective. At last, we understand that nothing he has narrated in his story can be considered as certain or an accurate representation of events.

By means of the chosen mode of representation, unreliable narration in a dramatic monologue, the narrative delves on the question of what the world looks like to a man whose undoubtedly high intellectual capacities are ultimately impeded by psychoses, as well as coloured by hypocrisy, narcissism, denial, and ego-centrism. The result of such biases in the eye of the beholder is a world which is divided into good vs. bad, me vs. you, us vs. them; there are no shades of gray. Such a worldview is so different from the complexity of reality that it cannot be maintained without turning a blind eye on certain facts and fashion partially true narratives that highlight some facts whilst omitting others.

---

[173] Placed within inverted commas because the term is archaic and inapt in this particular case because Changez' ailment is a latent form of schizophrenia, rather than something as vague and dramatic as 'madness'.

BINARY VIEWS ON ISLAM AND THE WEST IN HAMID'S *TRF*

The story is immersed in the tensions arising from contrasting elements like financial constraints and wealth; hard work and indulgence; egoism and altruism; family and foreigners, etc. Changez experiences all of them and eventually makes his choice in life. He chooses the first of each by choosing to live in Pakistan instead of the USA. Changez has experienced life by shifting from one extreme to the other so that the world must necessarily seem binary to him. And even though the term 'Islam' is never used in this novel, it speaks of Islam in a very specific manner. Much like the novella Erica has written, Hamid's novel "leaves space for your thoughts to echo" (p. 58). There are obvious references to Islam, for instance, those regarding Changez' attitude towards drinking alcohol:

> You seem puzzled by this – and not for the first time. Perhaps you misconstrue the significance of my beard, which, I should in any case make clear, I had not yet kept when I arrived in New York. In truth, many Pakistanis drink; alcohol's illegality in our country has roughly the same effect as marijuana's in yours. Moreover, not all of our drinkers are western-educated urbanites such as myself; our newspapers regularly carry accounts of villagers dying or going blind after consuming poor-quality moonshine. Indeed, in our poetry and folk songs *intoxication* occupies a recurring role as a facilitator of love and spiritual enlightenment. What? Is it not a sin? Yes, it certainly is – and so, for that matter, is coveting thy neighbor's wife. I see you smile; we understand each other, then. (pp. 61-62)

Islam as a theme is present in the novel, and there is a reason for the absence of its name in it: Hamid discusses Islam as a marker of identity rather than as a religion with a soteriological, spiritual or even cultural function. The distinctive element that separates Changez from his US-American co-workers, fellow students, and friends is not his culture or ethnicity, but his formal and outward affiliation to Islam. His Muslim identity only becomes a problem after 9/11 because the people of the USA begin to associate Islam with terrorism. Changez never faces exclusion over matters of cultural difference or over questions of prohibition or repression. In fact, he imagined himself getting married to Erica without once considering any possibility that his parents might object; he drank alcohol not only in the USA, but we learn that he had an arrangement for illegally purchasing alcohol in Pakistan as well; his mother asks him whether he is gay and even that possibility is not described in the novel as a dramatic potential for disaster. Clearly, there is no cultural clash between Muslim and Western values that drive or even impact the plot of *The*

Reluctant Fundamentalist in any way. In comparison, many British novels, plays, and movies from the pre-9/11 era are centred on a dramatic depiction of cultural or religious conflict regarding interracial marriage, homosexuality and/or exclusion and discrimination based on cultural or ethnic difference – e.g. *White Teeth, My Beautiful Launderette, East is East, Bend It Like Beckham*, etc. These examples stem from pop culture and do not represent a general literary trend, but I will certainly argue that a popular trope in pre-9/11 fiction centered on Muslims in the West was a conflict between conservative Muslim parents and their non-religious, westernized children. This is also the case in one of the novels to be analysed in this dissertation titled *Maps for Lost Lovers* by Nadeem Aslam. The post-9/11 generation of young Muslims in the West was rather the opposite: a large part of the Muslim youth in the West became attracted to a conservative interpretation of Islam with a vengeance because it offered them an appealing narrative of Islam's superiority, after a supposedly failed struggle to assimilate.

Religion as a theme is discussed in *TRF* without the label of any religion. The story is evasive of themes such as virtue, sin, heaven, hell, or redemption and thus manages to steer clear of a theological discussion of religious doctrine or even mention of any religion. Instead, this novel suggests that religious adherents are the same in their weaknesses and also in their commitment to doctrine as non-religious people to their values, which can have similar consequences for people in their lives at individual or social levels. It seems that Hamid chose to address religion in a non-theological way in order to draw a parallel to the doctrine of capitalism, which is prevalent in the USA and in other parts of the West. Thus, Hamid defines Islam (or religion) as a focal point in the life of the people in the East, which they refer to for guidance in all aspects of their lives: it provides values, priorities, and directives.

In this paradigm, Islam or religion does not have a soteriological basis, which means it is not exclusivist in itself. Instead, the exclusion of others stems from the feelings of superiority. Hamid draws a parallel to civil religion which provides the same kind of focal point in the life of US-American people which is tied to patriotism, capitalism and the priorities that these dictate (loyalty, freedom, efficiency, rationality and profit maximization) resulting in a set of directives which differ from religious ones. Imperialist and selfish attitudes have become intertwined with these values thanks to influences like Ayn Rand's philosophy of objectivism based on a re-evaluation of traditional virtues like compassion and kindness. Rand often took part in the public discourse, where she once defended the US-American history of the exploitation of Native Americans. Her novel *Atlas Shrugged* is highly popular in the USA especially since many famous capitalists have endorsed Rand's novels as their inspiration. So, even though Rand's novels were not too popular in her lifetime, their attractiveness increased over time. In January 2010 the website Aynrand.org issued a press release stating that *Atlas Shrugged* had set a new record of five hundred thousand copies sold in the USA the year before.[174]

The drawing of a parallel between capitalism and religion is indicated in several parts of Hamid's novel. Capitalism with all its attractions and its values is personified in Jim, the executive of Underwood Samson & Company who recruits Changez from college. He had worked himself up from rags to riches and likes Changez because he too is struggling and Jim recognizes his talents and a ruthless tendency. Changez had bonded with Jim during his job-interview over their shared experience of working hard to be able to afford a lifestyle to cover up their financial predicament. Noticing that Changez is losing interest in work Jim tries very hard – under certain risks – to coax him back. Jim's rationality and professionalism have made him immune to compassion. Despite his fondness for Changez, he has no trouble firing him for his refusal to work. Jim functions as Changez' mentor and his aim is to teach Changez the rules and values of capitalism. Jim wants to make sure Changez does not stray from the path of meritocracy in which success is measured in money. At one point, Jim gives him a motivational speech about the virtues of capitalism which Changez calls "sermon" (p. 111). While Changez is changing a tire that had been punctured by people out of spite, Jim tells Changez how the economy evolved and became the metaphorical heart of the human body while the workers became the "tailbone" – a body part rendered useless by evolution. (p. 110) While Jim wants to make Changez feel better by reminding him that he is now part of the elite, these words linger in Changez' mind for weeks and eventually make him feel uneasy. The comparison of this speech to a sermon might also refer to its exclusivist elements: Jim's ideology of success measured in wealth is an exclusivist and elitist ideology, which considers egotism and a disregard of others a virtue, and compassion and an effort for equality a sin, because it is essentially a weakness when it comes to the pursuit of capitalist interests. For a while after Jim's "sermon", Changez manages to live by it and ignore the resentments of the little people who may lose their jobs depending on Underwood Samson's calculations and consultation. The religious terminology seems to indicate draw a parallel between doctrinaire religion and materialistic capitalism, suggesting that both are equally divisive and dehumanized.

---

[174] https://ari.aynrand.org/media-center/press-releases/2010/01/21/atlas-shrugged-sets-a-new-record

The fact that Jim failed to lure Changez into staying with promises of large salaries is an interesting turn of events. It stands as the fictional failure of capitalism to integrate minorities because it offered them materialistic gain in exchange for a loss of individuality and identity. The simile with the *janissaries* suggests that there is an armed conflict between Changez' 'side' and the American people and being a part of the capitalist machinery of the West was the same as betraying his side or becoming a renegade. Changez overlooks the fact that capitalism itself treats everyone the same way: Jim had explained in his "sermon" to Changez that some people are the heart of the system, while others are limbs; and some become obsolete like the human tailbone. Clearly, Jim saw potential in Changez to reach a position at the heart of the system irrespective of his background. Capitalism in its most radical form, however, can tend to dehumanize individuals by measuring them only by their monetary value; but in doing that, the system does not discriminate against people based on race or religion. On his part, Changez had interpreted the capitalist machinery as the force that fights to suppress the third world, including his home country in a "Clash of Civilizations" which is far from what Jim had in mind. Changez has forged that narrative himself based on the simile of the *janissaries*. So, in this novel, the Clash of Civilizations as predicted by Huntington is based on narratives of disparity constructed by Changez' troubled mind.

Another non-religious matter in which Hamid uses religious terminology is the subplot regarding Changez' only romantic interest: his love affair with the young aspiring novelist Erica. She is still mourning the loss of her boyfriend Chris who died of cancer one year before Erica meets Changez. Her lingering feelings for Chris are repeatedly referred to as a religion. Erica's depression over the loss of Chris surfaces after the events of 9/11. She is willing but unable to be intimate with Changez. After one failed attempt at physical intimacy which Erica initiated, Changez pretends to be Chris and they manage to sleep together once. Erica then admits herself in a clinic but soon after wanders off and disappears. It is suggested that she committed suicide by jumping into the waters. As far as Changez knows, her body is never found. Erica (part of the word AmErica), the woman of Changez' dreams, is the personification of his American Dream which he chases in vain. Similarly, Chris (ChrisTian or ChrisTopher Columbus) represents Changez' US-American alter ego which he feels he is expected to adopt in order to fit in. Since Chris is described in absentia by Changez who had never met him in person, we do not learn much about him in detail, except that Changez sees him as his rival. Changez feels humbled by Chris but this is never based on his attributes or qualities but simply on the fact that, unlike Changez, Chris had had a relationship with Erica. At one point, Changez' momentarily adopts him as an alter ego: since Erica tells Changez that she has not been able to get aroused since Chris died, Changez asks her to close her eyes and pretend he is Chris, so they can engage in sex, which was satiating but tasteless. This seems to be the point when Changez realizes how achieving anything by becoming someone else is unsatisfying. He mentions that Erica became more reserved after this, but does not consider how this encounter might have made her feel.

At one point, he describes Erica's state of mind as ascetic and compares it to religious fasting (p. 152). While she is retreating into her mind where only her feelings for Chris exist, she is escaping the material or physical realm. The ritual of fasting has a similar function for believers: it is supposed to train the believer in abstaining from material and mundane pleasures in order to better focus on the spiritual experience. Additionally, at an earlier point in the novel, Changez describes Erica's feelings for Chris as a "religion that would not accept me as a convert" (p. 129). Shortly after this, he compares his failed attempts at courting Erica to his relationship to the USA as a country. He feels that he is and always will remain inadequate for Erica and in a similar manner, he feels that the USA will only accept him as a 'convert' as long as he tries to blend in with them. Changez' American Dream was not just to make money, but it was to be accepted as an American as easily as his momentary American Persona (Chris) had been accepted by Erica. But Erica's retreat made him feel that Changez would never suffice and his American Dream disappeared, along with Erica, who wants to accept him but is unable to because she can only love Chris, which is essentially also a narrative that her mind had construed. Her death is the result of the narrative that her happiness was with Chris and there can be no more happiness without him in the future. There is no external, tangible factor which killed Erica, but only the conviction of a constructed narrative in her mind. Changez' forfeiture is also based on a narrative built on the distrust he is shown by strangers, whilst overlooking the candidness of Erica's affection for him and her efforts to establish a relationship with him. Furthermore, he is unable to appreciate the perfectly functional relationships he had with his co-workers, friends, and supervisors. The feeling of being rejected by Erica triggered the construction of the anti-American narratives in his mind.

The comparison of non-religious value systems to religion suggests that Changez also views the USA as a religion which is refusing to accept him as a convert. There is an obvious parallel: the woman he saw himself spending the rest of his life with was disappearing into her nostalgia and the country he wanted to live in was doing the same thing.

> Possibly this was due to my state of mind, but it seemed to me that *America, too,* was increasingly giving itself over to a dangerous nostalgia at that time. There was something undeniably retro about the flags and uniforms, about generals addressing cameras in war rooms and newspaper headlines featuring such words as *duty* and *honor*. I had always thought of America as a nation that looked forward; for the first time I was struck by its determination to look *back.* [...] What your fellow countrymen longed for was unclear to me – a time of unquestioned dominance? of safety? of moral certainty? I did not know – but that they were scrambling to don the costumes of another era was apparent. I felt treacherous for wondering whether that era was fictitious, and whether – if it could indeed be animated – it contained a part written for someone like me. [Emphasis added] (pp. 130-131)

Underwood Samson, the firm which represents the doctrines of capitalism, is actually compared to Islamism rather than Islam by the term *fundamentals.* Jim repeats the words "Focus on just the fundamentals" to Changez like a mantra, and by *fundamentals* he means the numbers signifying monetary value. His decision to abandon his job there explains the title of the novel: *The Reluctant 'Fundamentalist'*. Against my expectations as a reader, I found out that the term fundamentalist in the title does not mean the religious kind. Plus, the repetitiveness of this principle is also imitative of religious mantras or prayers. Prayer and meditation are largely based on ritualistic repetition, instead of questioning, analysis or explanations.

Underwood Samson's capitalist values serve as a bulwark that resisted nostalgia by clinging to its capitalist directives and commandments and keep looking to the future, offering Changez a temporary escape. He started working even more productively and made himself popular among his colleagues but then two men insult him with racial slurs in a car park, to which he responds with a sudden outburst of rage, grabbing a tire iron and feeling ready to wield it. After a while, Jim notices that Changez is always preoccupied. Around the same time, Changez learns that Muslims are being subjected to a wave of discrimination in the workplace since the 9/11 attacks and gets worried about his job. The economy had been negatively affected resulting in a cutting of jobs.

The 9/11 attacks are a turning point in the novel because its immediate aftermath makes Changez feel excluded again: he is colleagues fly back to New York City from Manila on the day after the attacks. Changez is singled out and put through more security checks than all the other passengers. He boards the plane last and the passengers seem to look at him with distrust. He takes hours to get through security in New York and by the time he gets out his colleagues have all left. In short, Changez starts to feel a disparity again, which he had not felt since he had entered the upper class and moved to the cosmopolitan city of New York. He observed a sudden wave of people feeling frightened.

Changez describes his own stoicism as "armor of denial" (p. 108). On his next project in New Jersey, Changez faces misconduct from the employees of the firm, because they knew the result of Changez' research on their business may lead to cuts in human resources. He frequently finds the tire of his car punctured. Even though these actions against him are not related to his race or religion, they provoke him greatly.

Without realizing it – or at least without mentioning it in the narration – Changez becomes nostalgic as well, starting when he decides to visit his family in Pakistan over the Christmas holidays, even though his parents advise him against it for reasons of safety. Upon his arrival, he notices how much things seem different to him. They appear to look more rustic but then he realizes that it is just his view that is changed:

> I was looking about me with the eyes of a foreigner, and not just any foreigner, but that particular type of entitled and unsympathetic American who so annoyed me when I encountered him in the classrooms and workplaces of your country's elite. This realization angered me; staring at my reflection in the speckled glass of my bathroom mirror I resolved to exorcize the unwelcome sensibility by which I had become possessed. (p. 141)

After these thoughts, Changez can see the history and charm of his home and look upon it with humility and affection once again. During his stay, he finds that the people there are living under the looming threat of a war against India. Not expecting any help from the USA, his family and neighbours are stocking up on supplies and bracing themselves for the humanitarian emergency that is war. This confrontation with the threats to his home and family make Changez feel like a coward and a traitor for leaving them. He feels especially guilty when he considers, "And what was I abandoning them for? A well-paying job and a woman whom I longed for but who refused to even see me?" (p. 145) Unwilling to leave them, he returns to the States against his wishes but refuses to shave his beard, even though his mother and later his co-workers insist that he should. Back in New York City, he faces a lot of criticism for his beard and he wonders at how dramatic it appears to be that a beard should evoke such extreme feelings of mistrust, fear and even hatred. Erica is the only one who compliments him on it. Interestingly, beards became very fashionable about a decade later. In the years following the 9/11 attacks, however, it reminded people too much of Osama bin Laden. So, even though Changez was presumably not unattractive with the beard, its association with the enemy of the state triggered a lot of adverse reaction in people. It is important to note, however, that having a beard is considered a religious obligation among orthodox Muslims, Jews, and Christians. According to Islamic teachings, it is a so-called *sunna* because the Prophet Muhammad is known to have kept a beard. The *sunna* is the collection of the Prophet's deeds, mannerisms, personal habits, customs and practices and is supposed to serve as a comprehensive guide to how Muslims should live. It is controversial whether the contents of *sunna* are obligatory or optional. The *sunna* is considered to be a source that complements the Quran, for instance about the prayer ritual. The Quran contains the commandment that Muslims must pray but offers no detailed description of it, which can, however, be found in the *sunna*. Most Muslims pray the way the Prophet Muhammad and his adherents prayed. Some non-Sunni sects of Islam, however, do not consider the *sunna* a primary source of Islam and therefore, their ritual prayers vary. In conclusion, while it is true that some Muslim men may grow a beard because of religious injunction or desire to emulate the Prophet, most of these men probably do not correlate to the Islamist narrative. Therefore, regarding it as an identifier of Islamist extremism is so reductionist that it falls under the category of stereotyping.

After an exchange with the bookstore owner in Chile who compares Changez to the *janissaries* of the Ottoman Empire, his change of heart is complete and he decides to go back to Pakistan. One of the most discernible elements in this development is the fact that the return to Pakistan was not generated by an external source but by an impulse from within Changez' own mind. The Chilean manager's comment did not include any instruction, but it was merely an observation: he had been watching Changez' inner crisis for some time and finally offered him a diagnosis of his malady since Changez himself was too confused and distracted to recognize it. The decision to act upon his change of heart by going back was initiated by Changez alone. Choosing to drop everything and return to the country of his origin because of a sudden wave of national pride was the ultimate manifestation of nostalgia on his part. Additionally, it was certainly not Erica's disappearance that caused him to give up his life in America since he learns of her disappearance only after he returns to New York to quit his job, fully aware that this will cost him his visa. Her death clearly played no part in the act of mental suicide of his American persona. Thus, Changez' character arc is simply from a young man who aspires to become an American to a hot-headed patriotic Pakistani who wants to fight the US influence in Pakistani politics.

Whilst recounting this change of attitude the protagonist makes a point of noting that in his memory of this change of heart occurred not long after the night he and Erica had tried in vain to make love – even though he does not remember exactly, he feels it was only a day or two afterwards. He also mentions that his sudden wave of emotion against America surprised Changez himself. The rage that suddenly erupted in him was not easy to overcome for a while:

> [...] sometimes I would find myself walking the streets, flaunting my beard as a provocation, craving conflict with anyone foolhardy enough to antagonize me. Affronts were everywhere; the rhetoric emerging from your country at that moment in history – not just from the government, but from the media and supposedly critical journalists as well – provided a ready and constant fuel for my anger.
>
> It seemed to me then – and to be honest, sir, seems to me still – that America was engaged only in posturing. As a society, you were unwilling to reflect upon the shared pain that united you with those who attacked you. You retreated into myths of your own difference, assumptions of your own superiority. And you acted out these beliefs on the stage of the world so that the entire planet was rocked by the repercussions of your tantrums, not least my family, now facing war thousands of miles away. Such an America had to be stopped in the interests not only of the rest of humanity but also in your own.
>
> I resolved to do so, as best I could. But first I had to depart. (pp. 190-191)

Changez then reflects on how his life continued in Pakistan after the grave decision of giving up his career and a future of great wealth. He had given up claims to an American identity but found himself unable to shed off all of its remnants in his personality. He continued to picture himself in a married life with Erica but in a Pakistani setting this time:

> Such journeys have convinced me that it is not always possible to restore one's boundaries after they have been blurred and made permeable by a relationship: try as we might, we cannot reconstitute ourselves as the autonomous beings we previously imagined ourselves to be. Something of us is now outside, and something of the outside is now within us. Perhaps you have had no comparable experience, for you are gazing at me as though at a raving madman. I do not mean to say that we are all *one,* and indeed – as will soon become evident to you – I am not opposed to the building of walls to shield oneself from harm; I merely wished to explain certain aspects of my behavior upon my return. (p. 197)

Even though he is speaking about the process of getting over Erica it is emblematic for his relationship with the USA as well. Both had become part of his present, his identity, and future aspirations. While he seems to have found it fairly easy to map out a new future without America, he did not succeed in mapping out one without Erica. Perhaps the reason for this was that Erica had rejected him while he had rejected America. His and Erica's relationship was based on mutual respect, admiration, and trust, while his relationship with America was based on an imbalance of power. Changez' relationship with Erica did not end because of inadequacies on his part, and yet since she broke up with him, Changez perceived it differently. In his narration, he describes Erica's state of mind as an exclusivist religion which would not let him in. Thus, what Changez is comparing to a religion is a mental illness. Erica is a patient of severe depression and thus unable to function in the real world, which is why she prefers to live in the clinic. The nurse describes her to Changez, saying that she cannot handle reality anymore and that Changez is the most real thing in her life. Changez clearly does not see, even after four years, that no one can be blamed for the falling apart of their relationship. His relationship with America failed because it began with him as a submissive subject who did not question the inferiority of his own country to the USA, but after the 9/11 attacks his attitude changed due to two factors: a) the moment when a so-called Muslim entity stepped into the ring to challenge the USA as an opponent on an equal footing, his worldview where all non-Americans must look up to them and struggle to become part of them became obsolete; and b) after the attacks the atmosphere in the USA and especially in NYC, a place where he previously had felt at home, made him feel like a foreigner again and further, it made him feel like an enemy. In the beginning, his identity crisis had been subtle which he felt during his stay in Indonesia. At that time, he could not put his finger on what was bothering him. At the very end of that stay, 9/11 happened and his crisis surfaced. By the end of the story, he was no longer able or willing to subordinate himself to the US-American people, never realizing that no one had ever actually asked him to subordinate himself to any people. This is the narrative of disparity that Changez' insecure, narcissistic, hypocritical and egocentric subconscious had designed, and as a result, the desire to live in the USA or become a US-American faded away. Had Changez not felt inferior to Americans in the first place, then he may not have been obsessed with his ethnic background. Perhaps then he would have been able to practice empathy for Erica, instead of tracing her problems back to him. His preoccupation with his post-colonial and orientalist experience made him unable to understand that what Erica was going through had begun a year before she even met Changez.

To sum up: in a re-evaluation of the post-colonial experience, the post-9/11 events in Hamid's novel have inverted the idea of religion causing a disparity between Islam and the West. In this novel, a young Pakistani man falls in love with a young US-American girl, and it is not his parents, his culture, or Islam which get in their way, but her preference for a dead white man – even though, objectively speaking, it was her mental illness that got in their way, that is not the way Changez sees it. This principle also applies for every other social encounter that Changez had: Changez is given the chance to live in the USA, is offered the opportunity to make a great career and not once does his religious or ethnic background interfere with his professional and social progress at work. There is no clash of values or incompatibilities due to a lack of tolerance on the Americans' part or because of any unwillingness to assimilate on Changez' part. And yet in Changez' perception, the US-American capacity for tolerance and acceptance ends when he grows a beard. A beard is only a change of looks which does not in any way adversely detract a social encounter until it is viewed with hostility and fear. He could only have been accepted, had he been willing to subordinate himself to the others by shaving his beard. And finally, Changez departs from the USA, because he decides he cannot accept the doctrine of capitalism, and not because he felt restricted in practicing his religion. Therefore, the disparity in this literary narrative happens to be caused by inflexibilities in the narratives of the secular side and by a sudden outbreak of cultural vanity in Changez. Since Islam or traditionalism often plays the role of the divisive element in stories, the comparison of the inflexible elements of secularism with religion makes perfect sense. Arguably, this lack of tolerance for religious eccentricities – at least in the present dimensions – is also a result of the rise of religious extremism in the post-9/11 years. Thus, even if it is not Islam, it is the exclusivism which is best known from the religion of Islam (even if other religions have exclusivist variants as well) which causes friction between Muslims and the people of the West. I mentioned earlier that Hamid chose the dramatic monologue as a mode to deliver the narrative in order to stress the influence of the narrator's psychosis on the literary narrative. And by the logic of this story world, a strong commitment to any ideology or value system – religious or not – can have an inhibiting effect on the mind and result in a fractional worldview in the form of divisive narratives. The novel demonstrates how personality disorders like narcissism and hypocrisy are practically a prerequisite for the construction of narratives of disparity. They also explain why the process of this construction does not have to be intentional, even though lobbies, think tanks and news media (Fox News, for instance) have certainly taken the skill of constructing and distributing narratives of disparity to a new level in the post-9/11 era.

The inflexibility in the secular value systems causing the friction between Changez and his US-American persona are not the systems themselves, but the narratives of disparity that were suddenly omnipresent after the 9/11 attacks. This is evidenced by the fact that Changez is not made to leave, but leaves on his own account. Even though he is "a lover of America" (as he introduces himself to the US-American soldier at the very beginning of the frame narrative) he gets caught up pondering different narratives defining his duties as an American on the one hand, and separate narratives defining his duties towards his family and his country as a Pakistani on the other hand. The final stab is one narrative based on a historic reference to *janissaries* in the Ottoman Empire which causes him to give up his life in the USA as if he could not possibly continue to live there. He was not compelled to leave by an external force but by the force of narratives: historiographical and political narratives of disparity. Thus, this novel is distinct from the trope seen in Nadeem Aslam's *Maps for Lost Lovers* – to name one – as it shows how commitment to non-religious ideas can be equally divisive as religious dogmatism.

I will now summarize the narratives of disparity vis-à-vis Islam in the West that are constructed in this novel, starting with the kind that came up most strongly after 9/11: the narratives of mutual distrust. Before his departure from JFK airport in New York, Changez remembers Erica and how she left her clothes behind before she disappeared. Thinking of how cold she must have been in those moments, he feels compelled to do something about it, and so, as a symbolic offering for Erica, he removes his Jacket and leaves it on a bench outside JFK airport. It is a natural impulse to make such a rite of passage in order to get closure because even though such acts are often irrational in their nature, they can help with a transition. Similar to religious rituals, some acts seem irrational but can still be helpful to a person in a way that only he or she can understand. Shortly after, Changez witnesses with irritation from the terminal that his abandoned jacket on the bench had caused a security alert.

NARRATIVES OF MUTUAL DISTRUST IN HAMID'S *TRF*

> [One of his friends] went around the table and asked each of us to reveal our dream for what we would most like to be. When my turn came, I said I hoped one day to be the dictator of an Islamic republic with nuclear capability; the others appeared shocked, and I was forced to explain that I had been joking. (pp. 32-33)

People are used to being around strangers today, especially in big cities. This is why we generally do not feel frightened in the proximity of even large numbers of strangers in public. Despite the dangers that may come with being alone with people we do not know, we routinely spend a part of everyday life in their proximity: in restaurants, buses, trains, waiting areas, parks, etc. However, a feeling of fear may arise in response to a stimulus: e.g. if a stranger looks suspicious or behaves in a suspicious manner (like trailing us) or if we feel vulnerable or defenceless (in darkness or in some remote area). The respective situations in this novel describe very regular everyday situations, where random people see Changez as a possible threat, for instance, while walking the streets in New York City, or boarding a plane. Psychological studies on trust or fear often state that the opposite of fear is not courage but trust; or conversely that the opposite of trust is not distrust but fear. In this context, distrust is meant as a lack of trust mixed with fear. Nevertheless, I chose the word "distrust" for the classification of these narratives over "fear" because fear is: (a) a reflex which cannot be unlearned, and (b) an impulse that is necessary for survival, unlike learned distrust. Being frightened of a stranger of a certain ethnicity solely because of his or her resemblance to a famed mass murderer of that ethnic group is a feeling as unyielding as fear and as harmful to society as lack of trust is to a relationship. It is also rather irrational because it is based only on prejudice. Therefore, distrust is more than just a lack of trust; it is the presence of suspicion and doubt based on insufficient grounds. Thus, if one extreme is to blindly trust a perfect stranger, and the second extreme is to suspect strangers of wanting to inflict harm on you based on the association of a dark-haired beard with Osama bin Laden, the norm would be located between these two positions: neither trusting a stranger blindly, nor giving in to paranoia. The example with the association of a beard with Islamist terrorism demonstrates that such a distinct deviation from the norm does not happen entirely without reason. The culprits from the 9/11 attacks were of Middle Eastern ethnicity; their leader and public spokesman became the most recognized bearded Arab Muslim in the world. Therefore, the distrust towards young men of Middle Eastern ethnicity with a beard arose when the 9/11 attackers became a stereotype of terrorists. Up to here, we can certainly speak of a natural reaction to a real threat that the people of the West found themselves facing repeatedly, with more terrorist attacks in other Western countries in the years to follow. However, such stereotypes can obviously not serve in any serious discourse as they are unable to stand against the apt censure of racism. But with the Western interventions and armed conflicts in the Middle East that were in the making, it was helpful to maintain an enemy stereotype in the collective mind of the people of the West. Wars are much easier to justify and execute when the population feels threatened by the opponent. This is one of the reasons why narratives of distrust are sometimes fabricated and circulated intentionally.

Narratives of distrust construct stimuli that trigger feelings of distrust against certain groups, thus making irrational fear based on nothing but stereotypical associations seem like a rational concern based on facts, however self-styled. In May 2014, comedian and author Bill Maher hosted a panel on his show *Real Time with Bill Maher* discussing the question, whether Xenophobia/Islamophobia really is a phobia "if you have something to be afraid of". Central to their discussion was the notion that the threat of Islam was real enough, and so a fear of it should not be disparaged as irrational or politically incorrect. On the one hand, the narrative of distrust was initiated by the likes of bin Laden: they spoke and acted not only in the name of their respective organizations but in the name of 'Muslims' and in the name of 'Islam'. Thus, bin Laden became the originator of the narrative that Islam and Muslims are now at war with the West, willing and ready to do a lot of harm to its people. On the other hand, these narratives are adopted and spread by people of the West (politicians, authors, journalists, think-tanks, etc.) by refusing to distinguish between Islamism and Islam. Islamists themselves never distinguish between the two either. Narratives of distrust are constructed on both sides of a conflict. They sound like echoes of each other: *"Muslims hate us. I have a reason to hate Muslims: 9/11. They hate us for our freedom."* And "*Americans hate us. I hate Americans for all the wars they have waged and for the occupation of Palestine, but they hate us just for being different.*"

Such narratives of mutual distrust are a driving force in the plot of the novel *The Reluctant Fundamentalist.* As already indicated in the previous section, both the plot and the character arc of Changez were driven by narratives rather than external forces or circumstances. When strangers on the street make Changez feel that they distrust him, and when he is singled out at the airport for security check-ups, Changez feels that he is now under constant suspicion. This damages his relationship with "his American Dream": America suspects him of treason, and Changez refuses to try and win her trust. Partly out of disappointment and partly out of a sudden wave of nationalistic pride, Changez insists Americans must prove him guilty, rather than Changez having to prove he is innocent. Changez grows a beard and does not consider looking more trustworthy to US-Americans a good enough reason to shave it. The Muslims (or Pakistanis and Indians) of Changez' acquaintance tell him rumours about Muslims in the USA losing their jobs, or disappearing into interrogation centers of the CIA, etc. Changez even begins to fear for his own position as well, even though his co-workers or superior officers at Underwood Samson never subject him to any stereotyping because of his ethnic and religious affiliation. So, Changez suspects his superior officers of intending to discriminate against him without any proper reason to base this suspicion on. Instead of focusing on the trust he is given by his mentor who sends him to Chile to take on a project with no backup, Changez gives in to narratives that make him distrust his boss. He spends hours on the internet following the escalation of the conflict between Pakistan and India instead of working. And soon Changez concludes that the USA and Pakistan cannot be allies because the former is not helping the latter. This leads to a polarized view in which Changez feels there are only two options: to side either for Pakistan or against it. And since he works in the USA, he begins to feel he is like a *janissary*, working for his enemy against his own people. Thus, one of the reasons for Changez' departure and his commitment to the anti-American activism in Pakistan is the emergence of narratives of distrust on both sides which then fed on each other.

The frame narrative of the novel is in its entirety a narrative of mutual distrust. What begins as a casual conversation over tea is actually a battle of wits between two warriors: a soldier or possibly an army officer of the USA against an anti-American activist fighting for the Pakistan:

> A common strand appeared to unite these conflicts, and that was the advancement of a small coterie's concept of American interests in the guise of the fight against terrorism, which was defined to refer only to the organized and politically motivated killing of civilians by killers *not* wearing the uniforms of soldiers. (p. 202)

The two are civil to each other but tense and ever ready for attack. They both also seem to be very observant of each other, and the environment. Changez notices many details about his American guest, like his clothes and bearing as well as his responses to external stimuli in their immediate environment. Since the American is described as a tall man of physical strength, Changez guesses he might either be a soldier or a professional athlete. He even estimates how much weight the American might be able to bench-press. He notices that the man chooses to sit with his back against the wall and refuses to remove his jacket. At this point, the reader wonders if his choice of seats is a form of professional precaution and whether his jacket might have to remain in place because it conceals a weapon. Additionally, the American's nervous demeanour seems suspicious as he is alarmed upon the arrival of the waiter. The narrator notices his hand moving toward the inside of his jacket. While we suspect that this movement indicates toward retrieving a gun, the narrator waves it off to placate him and to show him that he (the narrator) did not suspect that his guest was carrying a gun under his jacket: "You seem worried. Do not be; this burly fellow is merely our waiter, and there is no need to reach under your jacket, I assume to grasp your wallet, as we will pay him later when we are done." (p. 6) There is reason to assume that Changez was only pretending to think he was reaching for his wallet. Having lived in the USA for several years where, like most other places, it is customary to pay the bill at a restaurant after being served, makes it rather unlikely that Changez could have really thought that his guest was reaching for his wallet. So, it seems that Changez may be hiding his true motives, much like the American who discloses no information about his. Changez introduces himself as a lover of America but later declares himself to be an anti-American activist, which is possibly an indication of deception rather than hypocrisy. It is possible that Changez knows more about his American guest than he lets on and, in conclusion, it seems likely that their paths did not cross by mere chance. He seems to either know or suspect him to be a US spy or secret service agent who came for him because of his comment that got aired in the News. Changez is possibly trying to keep the soldier distracted without revealing his intentions. Meanwhile, the American seems equally conspicuous for his unwillingness to share anything about himself and for being visibly nervous and tense the whole time.

In the case of this novel, there is no definite way of knowing what is going on and the reader can only speculate. The information we are given through the narrative and by its subtext is such that we can only say that it is unlikely that either party does not have ulterior motives. It remains impossible to decisively assign the roles of 'protagonist', 'villain', or 'victim'. Unlike in historical or nationalist narratives, in politics, there is no good or evil. Most nations always present themselves as 'the good guys' vs. 'the bad guys'. Nations fighting the war on terrorism portray themselves as the good guys. Terrorist organizations would also refer to themselves as the good guys while in fact, both sides are responsible for civilian deaths. The death toll of some actions of NATO members is many times larger than most terrorist organizations. Obviously, this does not mean the terrorists must be 'good' or at least 'better'. This level of ambiguity and complexity epitomizes the conflict between Islam and the West. A narrative consists of a series of carefully selected and concatenated information, deliberately omitting facts that might weaken the narrative. The frame narrative of the novel follows this pattern.

The aura of suspicion is continued throughout the frame narrative. While they are waiting for their tea, the nested narrative begins as Changez starts to tell the American guest about his time at Princeton. When the tea arrives it is apparent that the guest is hesitant about drinking it which indicates that for some reason he is suspicious. Changez jokes it off, reassuring him that the tea will neither give him diarrhea nor will it poison him. After having made this comment Changez even switches their teas so as to reassure his guest. While at first the reader feels that it is the American who seems to distrust and be wary of the narrator and the reader is under the impression that the narrator is only a person who has been deeply affected by his stay in the USA and wants to share his feelings and experiences with someone from that country; gradually the monologue begins to indicate this wariness and suspicion is mutual. Changez is watching his companion very closely and he notices every anomaly and atypical behaviour. He seems to be perfectly able to guess the thought, motivation or emotion beneath each of his guest's conspicuous mannerisms which would reveal him as a spy, yet Changez can always give another explanation which, if true, would be perfectly natural for a regular tourist. Alas, Changez knows that he is not a tourist but an army soldier. The guest is also watching his companion very carefully and notices a scar on Changez' forearm. Again, Changez' response is smooth, yet conspicuous:

> I see that you have noticed a scar on my forearm, here, where the skin is both darker and smoother than that which surrounds it. I have been told that it looks like a rope burn; my more active friends say it is not dissimilar to marks on the bodies of those who have taken up rappelling – or mountain climbing, for that matter. Perhaps a thought of this nature is passing through *your* mind, for I detect a certain seriousness in your expression, as though you are wondering what sort of training camp could have given a fellow from the plains such as myself cause to engage in these activities!
>
> Allow me, then, to reassure you that the source of my injury was rather prosaic. [...] In America, this would have been the start, in all likelihood, of a protracted bout of litigation with the manufacturer for using candle-wax with such a high, and unsafe, melting point; here, it resulted merely in an evening of crying and the rather faint, if oddly linear, scar you see today. (pp. 53–54)

Before their time in the café comes to an end, Changez makes one more attempt to win the American's trust in vain:

> And lest you think that I am one of *those* instructors, in cahoots with young criminals who have no interest in education and who run their campus factions like marauding gangs, I should point out that the students I tend to attract are bright, idealistic scholars possessed of both civility and ambition. We call each other comrades – as, indeed, we do all those we consider like-minded – but I would not hesitate to use the term *well-wishers* instead. So it was with immense consternation that I learned recently that one of them had been arrested for planning to assassinate the coordinator of your country's effort to deliver development assistance to our rural poor. (pp. 205 - 206)

Here, the innuendo is complete. The description of campus factions can be a terrorist training camp as viewed by an idealistic instructor or it may be a respectable, proper educational institution. Thereafter the soldier and Changez lock horns over this point in his narration where one of Changez' students has disappeared. While Changez vows that he had no inside knowledge of such a plan he also believes the boy to be innocent. This implies an injustice on the prosecutor's part, which makes the American uneasy. He becomes suspicious of Changez for being so certain of the boy's innocence while claiming to have no inside knowledge. Changez is irritated by the soldier's accusatory tone and refuses to try hard to convince him of his innocence. At the same time, he does take the time to accuse the American side of detaining the boy on false pretences: "In any case, it was impossible to ask the boy himself about the matter, as he had disappeared – whisked away to a secret detention facility, no doubt, in some lawless limbo between your country and mine." Shortly after his student's disappearance, Changez happened to be interviewed for a comment:

> When the international television news networks came to our campus, I stated to them among other things that no country inflicts death so readily upon the inhabitants of other countries, frightens so many people so far away, as America. I was perhaps more forceful on this topic than I intended. (p. 207)

This comment on the boy's disappearance was rerun a few times on the Pakistani news channel, leaving Changez paranoid that America might now act against him, but also hopeful that Erica might see him on TV and then decide to find him. Changez obviously fails to see how low the joint probability would be that Erica was alive and watching a Pakistani News Channel.

At this point, the readers begin to wonder whether the purpose of the American soldier's visit to Lahore might be to investigate this assassination by tracking down the arrested boy's teacher for interrogation. Unlike a regular interrogation setting, where the person being questioned is usually detained and made to feel as helpless as possible, this situation resembles more the everyday encounter of people of Islam and the West. We meet, we socialize, we work together, and we converse about politics without restraint on an equal footing. Unlike in an interrogation, Changez seems entirely unafraid of the American, who in turn is very much afraid of Changez and the waiter. Changez has the home field advantage which puts the American in a position where he cannot practice limitless and unquestioned power over anyone. A position Changez would not have in the States shortly after 9/11 when distrust was indeed very prevalent:

> I ignored as best I could the rumours I overheard at the Pak-Punjab Deli: Pakistani cabdrivers being beaten to within an inch of their lives; the FBI was raiding mosques, shops, and even people's houses; Muslim men were disappearing, perhaps into shadowy detention centers for questioning or worse. (p. 107)

He convinced himself that his financial status was likely to protect him from the discrimination and suspicion that Muslims were subjected to at that time. It is remarkable, however, that he seems to have never questioned the truth of the rumours. Even so, he had no confidence in his co-workers and superiors who had been very kind and fair to him thus far, to shield him from discrimination. His lack of confidence is based on nothing but rumours he heard from people he did not know. Such distrust is mutual because narratives of disparity are often responded to by counter-narratives. Someone must be blamed and to make sure it is not 'us' it must be 'them'; but first, these two hypothetical entities must be identified.

NARRATIVES OF DISTINCTIVE IDENTITY IN HAMID'S *TRF*

It is in human nature to respond to feelings of distrust by making efforts to ensure safety. Every living creature relies on the quickness of instinct, rather than on intellect which requires a longer reaction time, when faced with real or imagined danger. One way to brace oneself against danger is to identify the source of a potential threat and to find backup in order to defend your position. The 9/11 attacks revealed that there were organizations threatening Western civilization and everything it stood for. The people in the West immediately reacted by identifying an 'in-group' and the hostile 'out-group'. Hence, the world became divided in a hypothetical '*we*' and a hypothetical '*they*'. Everyone can have individual standards by which to decide who belongs to which bloc. The result of these efforts can be subsumed under the term Narratives of Distinctive Identity.

Narratives of Distinctive Identity serve to create identities that are deliberately distinct from each other, drawing tangible lines between 'in-group' and 'out-group' members. In order to outline this distinctive identity, markers are drawn from different sources: nationalism, patriotism, history (collective memory), present ideology, political orientation, code of ethics, code of law (constitution), etc. There are several ways in which narratives of distinctive identities manifest themselves – in other words, divide the world into 'we' and 'they' – in social encounters, some of which are used in this novel.

Changez' character arc begins as a young man who moves to the USA hoping to be accepted and to become an American. During his first international project in Manila, his identity crisis begins to surface when he finds himself regretting that he tried to adopt American mannerisms so as to be at the top of the chain of command. His uneasiness stems from instances where he went against values which he had been taught by his family – like respecting elders. The narratives of disparity were already in his mind when he assigned certain attributes to the Pakistani culture and others to the American culture based on his own experience. He is oblivious to the fact that his own experience is limited to only the Pakistani and American people he has known or met personally and that he cannot make sweeping statements about an entire people based on that. The fact that his parents taught him to respect elders does not mean that all Pakistani people teach their children this particular value, and the fact that some of his American fellow students have not internalised this value does not mean that all Americans are the same way. This manner of assigning attributes and qualities to a group of people known as stereotyping is a common basis for narratives of distinctive identity. The 'self' (we) and the 'other' (they) are identified by stereotypical attributes and qualities. The element of distinction in the composition of such narratives is most obvious in one particular example from the novel: within the frame narrative, Changez' takes great pride in Pakistani cuisine, but not without making a negative comparison to American food habits:

> These, sir, are *predatory* delicacies, delicacies imbued with a hint of luxury, of wanton abandon. Not for us the vegetarian recipes one finds across the border to the east, not the sanitized, sterilized, processed meats so common in your homeland! (p. 115)

Actually, there are reasons for the Pakistani disregard of the mannerisms he lists in the above quote, from simple ignorance to a habituated immunity, as well as a preoccupation with far greater problems of subsistence level and the poverty line. It is a common adage in Pakistan that less fancy places serve tastier food. In fact, Changez had introduced the *Old Anarkali* café by stating that even though the place does not look very fancy they served exquisite tea. The above quote is followed by one more claim: "Here we are not squeamish when it comes to facing the consequences of our desire" unless it is sexual desire, one might add. Changez, however, fails to see this fault in his proclamation. He evades any inconsequential argument in regard to Pakistani sexual morals, by offering a different logic in order to make them better when compared to the prevailing sexual morals in the USA:

> But you must understand that in Lahore [...] relationships were often conducted over fleeting phone calls, messages through friends, and promises of encounters that never happened. Many parents were strict, and sometimes weeks would pass without us being able to meet those we thought of as our girlfriends. So we learned to *savour* the denial of gratification – that most un-American of pleasures! – and I for one could subsist quite happily on a diet of emails such as that which I have just described. (p. 79)

Changez frequently makes distinctions between ethnic groups in the embedded and the frame narrative by using collective pronouns, making each person of his acquaintance a synecdoche for their ethnic group. Changez notices, for instance, that the waiter of the *Old Anarkali* seems to intimidate his US-American listener he responds thusly:

> And if you [addressing the US-American soldier] should sense that he [the waiter] has taken a disliking to you, I would ask you to be so kind as to ignore it; *his tribe* merely spans both sides of *our* border with neighbouring Afghanistan, and has suffered during offensives conducted by *your countrymen*. [Emphasis added] (p. 123)

After the 9/11 attacks which happened on his last day in Manila, his identity crisis begins to surface with a vengeance. This is in part due to the fact that after the attacks, Changez is met with a display of the narratives of distinctive identity in the public sphere of the USA upon his return. In the mourning and the patriotic symbolism that are displayed in New York after the attacks, Changez sees a reproach against his initial lack of sympathy when he first heard of the attacks in the news.

> Your country's flag invaded New York after the attacks; it was everywhere. Small flags struck on toothpicks featured in the shrine; stickers of flags adorned windshields and windows; large flags fluttered from buildings. They all seemed to proclaim: *We are America* – not New York, which, in my opinion, means something quite different – *the mightiest civilization the world has ever known; you have slighted us; beware of our wrath.* Gazing up at the soaring towers of the city, I wondered what manner of host would sally forth from so grand a castle.
>
> It was against this backdrop that I saw Erica again. (p. 90)

When he does see Erica again shortly after the attacks and about six weeks after their last encounter before he went to Manila, she tells him that because of the attacks old feelings have surfaced, which she had been unaware of before. This makes Changez wonder if the same is true for him. While Erica meant that her lingering feeling for her deceased boyfriend had resurfaced, Changez seems to be implying that his buried dislike of American Imperialism had emerged after the attacks: he used to love America but after the attacks his immediate reaction to them and his emotional response to the display of patriotic mourning makes him question whether his admiration and fondness for America was real. Further on in the narration, he reflects if he ever believed in his American Dream at all:

> I wonder now, sir, whether I believed at all in the firmness of the foundations of the new life I was attempting to construct for myself in New York. Certainly, I

> wanted to believe; at least I wanted not to disbelieve with such an intensity that I prevented myself as much as was possible from making the obvious connection between the crumbling of the world around me and the impending destruction of my personal American dream. The power of my blinders shocks me, looking back – so stark in retrospect were the portents of coming disaster in the news, on the streets, and in the state of the woman with whom I had become enamoured. (p. 106)

In order to create a disparity between the 'self' and the 'other', it is essential to make sure that the differences are clearly visible. Thus, the resulting image of the 'self' is not necessarily based on reality but on a depiction deliberately distorted in order to fulfil the distinction requirement. The resulting narratives are deceptive, but they are also easily believed due to a bias in perception. A narcissist, for instance, is very likely to easily believe any compliment, no matter how far-fetched. Hypocrisy and narcissism provide the necessary bias in order to construct such images of the 'self' and the 'other'. The standards composed by a hypocritical narcissist can be fatuous but still efficient in their divisiveness. Narratives of distinctive identity have the purpose of dividing the world into two sides, like Islam and the West, and its demography into 'us' against 'them', the 'good' against the 'bad', heroes against villains, soldiers against terrorists, etc. This brings us to the next kind of narratives of disparity: the narratives of inadequacy, which serve to perpetuate an image of the other which is less deserving of every right that the 'in-group' claims for itself. These are essential in the case of an actual confrontation or when a conflict is being carried out in the form of a battle of any kind. Whether in a fight to the death or a simple argument, the dehumanization or denigration of an enemy goes a long way to justify all actions taken against them.

NARRATIVES OF INADEQUACY IN HAMID'S *TRF*

The plot of the frame narrative unfolds largely in a Lahori bistro named *Old Anarkali*. Changez makes only one brief reference to Anarkali very early in his narration: "Surely, at this time of day, only one thing could have brought you to the district of Old Anarkali – named, as you may be aware, after a courtesan immured for loving a prince – and that is the quest for the perfect cup of tea." (p. 2)

Thus, Changez summed up the story of Anarkali in one narrative of inadequacy: she was immured because she was deemed unworthy of a prince. Anarkali's existence is not confirmed, but she is said to have lived while Saleem (later known as the Emperor Jahangir, whose son Shah Jahan built the Taj Mahal) was the crown prince and his father Akbar was king. *Anarkali* means pomegranate blossom; it was a title given to her by her superiors as an act of validation. Her tale has been depicted in literature, art and cinema, which all end in Anarkali's being either exiled or killed as punishment for her transgression. In different versions of the story, the King was opposed to Anarkali's affair with his son out of jealousy and not because of social boundaries; and in the movie version she was not killed at all, but secretly sent into exile with her mother. Changez does not specify which version of the story he is referencing. Additionally, it seems he is referring to Anarkali as a historical figure. He is implying that there is only one version in which she was killed (and not exiled) for crossing social boundaries. Changez is insinuating that (a) Anarkali existed and (b) that she was undoubtedly immured because she was considered not good enough to love a prince. Both points are historically undetermined which Changez conveniently fails to mention. This concealed vagueness makes Changez' version a narrative of inadequacy.

The version referenced in this novel is closest to the movie version titled *Mughal-e-Azam* (1960) in which Anarkali was indeed immured but not killed: she is secretly saved through a tunnel and sent to exile with her mother and sister. In the beginning of the movie, she is thrown into the dungeon for her audacity to fall in love with the crown-prince. While it would have been acceptable for Anarkali to be just another one of the prince's mistresses, marrying him and thus being elevated to the rank of a future queen was considered unthinkable. The next morning, the emperor offers her a chance to be freed from the dungeon if she declares that her affection for the prince had been fake. She appeals to the emperor's sense of justice, but to no avail. Anarkali reluctantly agrees but shortly before she fulfils her part of the bargain with the king, Saleem comes to see her. He questions the truthfulness of a love that gets scared away so easily. His main grievance to Anarkali is that now their daring and defiant love, which they should have been proud of, will be reduced to the disgrace of a shady dalliance. Shortly afterwards, Anarkali appears before the royal household where she is supposed to declare that she never had any true feelings for the prince. Instead, she declares her love for him without fear of punishment or respect for social boundaries, singing "*why be afraid of being in love? I have loved someone and not stolen anything. So, why should I hide my feelings?*" While singing these verses she dances towards the prince, removes a dagger from his holster and gracefully places it in front of the emperor, daring him to use it to punish her. One of her final verses in the song is, "*When there is nothing hidden from the eyes of God, why should I hide something from men.*" Interestingly, being addressed as a human being is an insult to the emperor who is used to being formally addressed as *zilleh ilahi* (meaning shadow of God on earth). She was reminding the emperor of his station before God as a human being just like herself. Inevitably, Anarkali is imprisoned again after this performance but this time she does not beg or waiver. In the remaining part of the movie she never tries to renegotiate with the King to save her life, but at the end, she trades him her life in exchange for Saleem's. Anarkali is considered a figure representing the stand taken by a lower-class person against the ruling class. She embodies courage and a claim for equality.

Even though Anarkali's narrative of inadequacy is not discussed at length in the novel, it is mirrored in Changez' own life story. Much like Anarkali in the movie performing a renowned song – defying the powerful emperor, refusing to be intimidated – Changez confronts his co-workers and boss in order to declare that he refuses to work for them any longer. While he does indeed feel sadness, he does not mention feeling any sort of fear while making this choice. Changez refuses to accept his subordinate role to the *fundamentals* which Jim keeps asking him to focus on. He is specifically not allowed to feel compassion or even to be distracted by concern for his family at home, just so he can function according to the standards of the company. He is expected to work with complete disregard for his home country. While his concept of the American Dream 'invited him in' for his abilities and talents, so that he could work like a slave or a *janissary* to America's advantage and Pakistan's disadvantage, his love for an American woman, who embodied the emotional side of his American Dream, was doomed to failure because she continued to love someone else. On an emotional level, Changez competes against a white American rival and cannot win, even though the rival is deceased. Though Erica rejects Changez against her own wishes, he loses her before he can gain the courage and strength that Anarkali could draw from love. Instead, Changez submits himself to pretending to be his American rival to make love to Erica. Changez is overcome by shame and eventually realizes that by impersonating a dead man, he proved that his love was not strong enough for Erica in its own right. Afterwards, he shares a realization of these feelings with Erica in an email, hoping for a chance to mend this mistake, but by this time Erica is caught up in her depression and probably never received that email. We know that Erica disappeared two weeks after Changez' last visit, and it is likely that more than two weeks had passed by the time Changez sent her this email from Chile. When he announces that he will not work any further, he knows he will be losing his job and his visa. The thought of leaving the USA means losing the last hope of ever being with Erica but he consciously refuses to link this decision to his romantic sensibilities, because they are superseded by his new-found post-colonial super-ego by now. The fact that he continues to dream of a married life with Erica in Pakistan indicates that up to that point he thought he still had a chance to win her over. With the last email he wrote to her, he was trying to save their relationship by resolving to be true to himself. Ultimately, he was shedding off his American alter ego and replacing it with a Pakistani identity, hoping that this would make him strong enough for Erica to lean on. Anarkali gave her life to save Saleem, and Changez gave the life of his American persona hoping to save Erica.

Apart from Anarkali, there are many other examples of such narratives in the novel. Erica's father sums up the situation in Pakistan with a condescending tone that annoys and provokes Changez:

> 'Economy's falling apart though, no? Corruption, dictatorship, the living like princes while everyone else suffers. Solid people, don't get me wrong. I like Pakistanis. But the elite has raped that place well and good, right? And fundamentalism. You guys have got some serious problems with fundamentalism.'
>
> I felt myself bridle. There was nothing overtly objectionable in what he had said; indeed, his was a summary with some knowledge, much like the short news items on the front page of *The Wall Street Journal*, which I had recently begun to read. But his tone – with, if you will forgive me, its typically *American* undercurrent of condescension – struck a negative chord with me [...]. (p. 62-63)

In this last sentence, Changez is already responding to his narrative of inadequacy with a counter-narrative of inadequacy. By the time Changez has decided to leave the USA, his personal narrative of inadequacy for the USA has been finalized:

> I reflected that I had always resented the manner in which America conducted itself in the world; your country's constant interference in the affairs of others was insufferable. Vietnam, Korea, the straits of Taiwan, the Middle East, and now Afghanistan: in each of the major conflicts of Asia, America played a central role. Moreover, I knew from my experience as a Pakistani – of alternating periods of American aid and sanctions – that finance was a primary means by which the American empire exercised its power. It was right for me to refuse to participate any longer in facilitating this project of domination; the only surprise was that I had required so much time to arrive at my decision. (p. 177)

Narratives of inadequacy produce reasons and justification for prosecution, conflict or battle. Starting with negative stereotypes and clichés, narratives of inadequacy compose a line of reasoning which can blame almost any targeted 'out-group' for almost any chosen problem. Extreme examples from history of ethnic cleansing like the holocaust demonstrate how effective narratives of inadequacy can be in justifying almost any inhumane behaviour towards others. The holocaust did not arise out of thin air since anti-Semitism existed in Europe as early as the Middle Ages. Even though the Nazis did not invent anti-Semitic sentiments, they did enhance the use of this scape-goat principle by circulating narratives of inadequacy about Jewish people: the group of Jewish people was made synonymous with 'the source of all our problems' and soon after, the removal of Jewish people emerged as a solution to eliminate these problems – a scheme which began with the relegation of Jewish people from certain circles and professions; then took the form of a radical segregation and isolation of the Jewish people and ultimately ended with a refined machinery for ethnic cleansing killing over 6 million people within 4 years. This steep climb in the curve that suddenly brought about such a horrid apex of anti-Semitism in the form of concentration camps was due to a calculated process of systematic dehumanization of the Jewish people and of blaming them for economic breakdowns and other critical developments.

This example shows how useful the blaming of one group for something is for the justification of persecution. The failings cited to the denigrate a group of people or a nation in order to compose a narrative of inadequacy can have a basis in reality, but the inspiration usually comes from isolated examples. The narratives are especially evasive of the fact, that the chosen failing cannot be conclusively linked to all members of that 'out-group'. In fact, upon a closer look, the same failings are often found in the 'in-group' as well, but they are either overlooked or deliberately concealed. The alleged inadequacies of the 'out-group' justify not only the conflict itself but also – if necessary – any action however unfair or immoral that must be taken to win the battle.

Narratives of inadequacy are balanced out by narratives of superiority. In fact, all the four kinds of narratives of disparity often blend into each other. This is because every narrative of disparity must be counterbalanced in order to make them easily digestible. These narratives are meant to trigger intuitive and sentimental responses by appealing to very basic human fears and needs. This is why they work best when they are accepted immediately and without question. The idea of the 'out-group's' inadequacy is balanced out with the idea of the 'in-group's' superiority which any member of the 'in-group' will be ready to believe. If a narrative of disparity is well balanced, in that it offers reasons to look down on others along with a sense of elevation, then the recipients will not only see the need to look down on others but also feel entitled to do so. Nevertheless, narratives of superiority perform another task: after the means of a battle have been justified, there is still the need to recruit enough people for an unfair fight against the distrusted and distinctively inadequate 'other'. Narratives of superiority which are especially attractive for young people have proven very effective to that end.

NARRATIVES OF SUPERIORITY IN HAMID'S *TRF*

Narratives of distinctive identity help divide the world into terrorists and soldiers or oppressors and the oppressed Then the narratives of inadequacy perpetuate reasons to hate the 'other' enough to justify their persecution and elimination. All NoDs help overlook the fact that Soldiers and terrorists have one thing in common: their self-image of being altruistic, superhuman and heroic.

The profession of both soldiers and terrorists entail grave dangers and consequently require a great deal of commitment to the respective cause. Making the distinction between 'we' and 'they' clearly visible will not be enough to invoke the willingness of people risking their lives in a fight. Therefore, it will be necessary to construct an image of the 'self' which must not only have nothing in common with the 'other' but must also be better. No similarities mean less risk of feelings of empathy and feelings of superiority mean less risk of inhibitions for ethical or moral reasons. The resulting image of the 'self' is largely compounded with ideals and values which are then signposted on battlefronts in order to recruit people for this greater cause. For soldiers, that ideal can be freedom, nation, religion, etc. And for terrorists, the ideal they can be very much the same as most of them do not call themselves 'terrorists'. Members of the Hamas, for instance, would describe themselves as freedom fighters, whereas al-Qaeda members were bound by the idea of a theocracy penned by Sayyid Qutb (1906-1966). The term 'terrorist' is an external classification which dictates how people should feel about certain groups or organizations irrespective of what they are actually fighting for. We may not that even animal rights activists can be persecuted as terrorists under the US federal law known as the Animal Enterprise Terrorism Act (AETA) from 1992. This law gives the US Department of Justice a large scope of action against activists if they become a threat to large animal enterprises. Even though these activists have committed themselves to a good and altruistic cause of fighting for animal rights, this law does not only criminalize their efforts but also marks them with a label as revoltingly malevolent as 'terrorism'. This example is meant to demonstrate not only the objective of labeling any endeavour as terrorism but also the discrepancy between the external and internal signposting of a fight. Obviously, I do not intend to deny that most organizations classified as 'terrorist' probably deserve this title. The intention was to point out that due to a Eurocentric view on global politics we tend to see only the external classification of so-called terrorist groups and pay little regard to what they believe they are fighting for. Terrorist groups also have a battle agenda just like governments do before going to war. However, the ideals that are signposted by either in their war efforts are not always the real objectives and motives behind the scene, yet they are labeled as the ultimate cause which fighters are willing to die for. This cause consists of narratives of superiority which certify the respective ideals' primacy over any other ideal in order to make the fight worthwhile.

The presence of narratives of superiority in *The Reluctant Fundamentalist* portrays the interactions in the frame narrative as a battle, as opposed to their being a social encounter. The earlier example of Pakistani cooking might also be interpreted as a narrative of superiority, even though its superiority is only implied and refers merely to personal preferences But of course, the definition of narratives of superiority goes much further this. They have to have an unequivocal claim of superiority. Narratives of superiority are sources of inspiration and motivation for battle and sacrifice. Thus, they are often based on philosophical, religious, political, or historical entities (figures, ideas, events, etc.). Also, they may be based on transcendental ideas, images or idolized figures.

Nationalism is one which explains most of the names chosen for the characters in this novel; which by the way have been interpreted repeatedly – sometimes wrongly – in most analyses of this novel to date. Delphine Munos notes in her paper that "the English-speaking western readership" associated an English-centred interpretation of the protagonist's name *Changez* referring to the English homophone *changes*.[175] To correct this, Munos reads from an interview with the author Hamid himself in which he states that Changez Khan is the Urdu version of the historic Genghis Khan, "the warlord who conquered territories ranging from the edges of present-day Europe to China"[176] – a connection which could seem obvious to a non-Eurocentric audience. Other than

---

[175] Munos, '*Possessed by Whiteness*', p. 404
[176] Ibid.

the protagonist, there are several references hidden in the names which have been spotted by most literary theorists over and over again: Juan Bautista, Am/Erica, and Chris/topher Columbus.

Even art can be a source of inspiration for narratives of superiority, like the Anarkali trope used by Changez. Apart from the previously described narrative of inadequacy regarding his romance, the legend of Anarkali contains a narrative of superiority in the epic love story it comprises. It is a popular trope in Indian literature and cinema wherein the heroism of male figures lies in their superhuman capabilities like strength, resilience, and willpower, the heroism of female figures – like the heroine or any mother or sister figure – is her superhuman ability to love boundlessly. This ability to love is exhibited by her courage to profess it before anyone and also in her selflessness, faithfulness and – of course – a willingness to make the ultimate sacrifice if necessary. Anarkali's narrative of superiority is her love story, which is weighed against the love of another courtesan, Bahar, who sabotages Anarkali out of jealousy. In every version of the story, there is one character who drives the plot with his or her jealousy and thus poses the antithesis of the self-sacrificing love of Anarkali and Saleem. The movie *Mughal e Azam* even contains a singing battle between Anarkali and Bahar, in which Anarkali contends that her love is of a superior kind, especially if she loses her life for it because that would ensure that her story will be remembered forever. Anarkali does not mind dying for love as long as it makes her story a source of inspiration for future generations. Thus, she composes this narrative of superiority herself and Changez' reference to her suggests that she inspires him.

Changez' personal narratives of superiority did not surface until the 9/11 attacks. Before the attacks, Changez had been very receptive to the US-American narratives of superiority and sought access to their different sources, namely money, accomplishment, efficiency, professionalism, etc. The following excerpt of his first day at Underwood Samson and Company exposes that Changez had previously accepted the US-American narrative of its superiority over other countries, including Pakistan; and Changez was eager to become part of that narrative, willing and ready to shed off all previous affiliations:

> I remember my sense of wonder of the day I reported for duty. Their offices were perched on the forty-first and forty-second floors of a building in midtown [...] and while I had previously flown in airplanes and visited the Himalayas, nothing had prepared me for the drama, the power of the view from their lobby. This, I realized, was another world from Pakistan; supporting my feet were the achievements of the most technologically advanced civilization our species had ever known.

> Often, during my stay in your country, such comparisons troubled me. In fact, they did more than trouble me: they made me resentful. Four thousand years ago, we, the people of the Indus River basin, had cities that were laid out on grids and boasted underground sewers, while the ancestors of those who would invade and colonize America were illiterate barbarians. Now our cities were largely unplanned, unsanitary affairs, and America had universities with individual endowments greater than our national budget for education. To be reminded of this vast disparity was, for me, to be ashamed.
>
> But not on that day. On that day, I did not think of myself as a Pakistani, but as an Underwood Samson trainee, and my firm's impressive offices made me *proud.* (pp. 37–38)

Changez is given a clear plan of action, as to how to achieve that, when the vice president lays out what Changez calls the "ethos" of their company to him.

> "We're a meritocracy," he said. "We believe in being the best. You were the best candidates at the best schools in the country. That's what got you here. But meritocracy doesn't stop with recruiting. We'll rank you every six months. You'll know your rankings. Your bonuses and staffing will depend on them. If you do well, you'll be rewarded. If you don't, you'll be out the door. It's that simple. You'll have your first rankings at the end of this training program." (p. 39)

He is one of six trainees and together they go through a four-week training covering the contents of one year of business school, as well as workshops in computer programs and a soft skill training which Changez describes as "a form of mental judo for business". (pp. 40–41) After the first four weeks of extensive training by the company, the six of them are ranked with Changez at the top.

Narratives of superiority make an appealing offer, suggesting that anyone can have access to some elevated rank in the hierarchy of all life on earth, but they are tied to a set of standards which can be arbitrary. In religious value systems, for instance, the claim of superiority is usually linked to conditions like belief in its creed and adherence to its tenets. Extremists tend to simplify a faith in order to appeal to the masses so that a religion consists only of constantly asking oneself what is 'permissible' and what is 'prohibited'. Most religions have a lot to offer in terms of philosophical, theological or even psychological explanations for life, its ups and downs, God, the universe and the individual. This does not appeal to the masses, however, and it offers no claims for superiority but 'only' inspiration and orientation. Extremists or dogmatists set the bar for righteousness so low that it becomes especially easy for adherents to distinguish believers from non-believers even though ethically speaking it should be almost impossible for anyone to make such a judgement about someone else. It is the standards that make an exclusivist system. Within a meritocracy, for instance, it is fairly easy to exclude someone by setting them up for failure: the standards are designed by the 'in-group' in such a way that its members can easily fulfil them – by means of faking them if necessary. Hypocrisy makes it especially easy to fulfil these contrived and arbitrary standards and to use them for exclusion. They can be adjusted and readjusted in order to rate anyone as a failure because they could not meet those standards. Not only does the 'in-group' decide who fares well in the test, but the standards that are set up dictate the rules and priorities of the assessment process. Changez sums up the priorities and rules of living in a meritocracy in the following manner:

> I see you are impressed by the thoroughness of our training. I was as well. It was a testament to the systematic pragmatism – call it *professionalism* – that underpins your country's success in so many fields. At Princeton, learning was imbued with an aura of creativity; at Underwood Samson, creativity was not excised – it was still present and valued – but it ceded its primacy to *efficiency*. Maximum return was the maxim to which we returned, time and again. We learned to prioritize – to determine the axis on which advancement would be most beneficial – and then to apply ourselves single-mindedly to the achievement of that objective. (p. 41)

These were the rules that Changez seemed to have no trouble abiding by until the 9/11 attacks changed the way he viewed both the country he was living in and the religion of his ancestors. He watched the attacks and they made him smile because that was the moment he learned that Muslims can compete with the USA over the position of global hegemony:

> The following evening was supposed to be our last in Manila. I was in my room, packing my things. I turned on the television and saw what at first I took to be a film. But as I continued to watch, I realized that it was not fiction but news. I stared as one – and then the other – of the twin towers of New York's World Trade Centre collapsed. And then I *smiled*. Yes, despicable as it may sound, my initial reaction was to be remarkably pleased.
>
> Your disgust is evident; indeed, your large hand has, perhaps without your noticing, clenched into a fist. But please believe me when I tell you that I am no sociopath; I am not indifferent to the suffering of others. [...]
>
> But at that moment, my thoughts were not with the *victims* of the attack – death on television moves me most when it is fictitious and happens to characters with whom I have built up relationships over multiple episodes – no, I was caught up in the *symbolism* of it all, the fact that someone had so visibly brought America to her knees. (pp. 82–83)

While the 'smiling' is probably a way to highlight this key moment, the underlying issue is that the significance of the World Trade Center was extremely high in the minds of Americans as a symbol of their invincibility/superiority. This concept was not present in Changez' mind. He was almost a dispassionate observer not particularly emotionally affected by this event which shocked Americans and other Westerners. This stark difference in his reaction betrayed how superficial his connection with his newfound American life had been. This started the process of his disenfranchisement of the American dream.

As Changez describes the stages of mourning and later the resolve which the people of the USA evinced after the attacks, he uses the rhetoric of distinctive identity of 'you' against a hypothetical 'we'. In a reproachful tone, he describes the phase which he calls America's "self-righteous rage" (p. 106) when collective mourning led to a buildup of hostile emotions against the Islamic world. At the same time, the reader can observe anger building up in Changez over this development, like an echo to the defensive and inimical posture of Americans. The following quote comprises an outburst of animosity and combativeness on Changez' part:

> For we were not always burdened by debt, dependent on foreign aid and handouts; in the stories we tell of ourselves we were not the crazed and destitute radicals you see on your television channels but rather saints and poets and – yes – conquering kings. *We* built the Royal Mosque and the Shalimar Gardens in this city, and *we* built the Lahore Fort with its mighty walls and wide ramps for our battle-elephants. And we did these things when your country was still a collection of thirteen small colonies, gnawing away at the edge of a continent.
>
> But once more I am raising my voice, and making you rather uncomfortable besides. I apologize; it was not my intention to be rude. (pp. 115-116)

This entire passage is an example of a historical basis of a narrative of superiority. Changez is making claims of cultural superiority by dismissing the present situation of his people and substituting the present image with a glorified still-life picture from a time in the past when his ancestors were superior to his guest's ancestors. Changez wants to take credit for historical monuments, only because he happened to be born into the country where they were built centuries ago. In her analysis, Delphine Munos recognized this claim for superiority, which she argued stems from a frustration after failing to reach the ideal of whiteness.[177]

---

[177] Munos, '*Possessed by Whiteness*', p. 397

Munos refers to Changez' thoughts when he compares the grandeur of the New York City skyline to the historical monuments in Pakistan and describes them as "Changez' endorsement of the Aryan myth so as to rationalize the noble genealogy of his people as well as their *superiority* at a time". [178] [Emphasis added]

Interestingly, the narratives of superiority were the ones which proved the most divisive in this particular plot. In general, however, I would argue that all of the above-mentioned categories of NoDs can be equally divisive, depending on how they are composed and circulated.

Since narratives of disparity are partly true, they can be persistent, and they are never helpful in resolving a conflict, as the literary narrative of this novel demonstrates. Many counter-narratives, were disseminated with the intention of deconstructing the narrative that says *Islam is inherently violent and anti-Western as evidenced by the actions of al-Qaeda*, by fashioning its counter declaring *al-Qaeda has nothing to do with Islam*. But the opposite side always responds with new counter-arguments, and the vicious cycle continues. So instead of deconstructing any narrative, a counter-narrative which is composed in the same pattern provides more targets and inspiration for a comeback, thus ensuring a continuation of the narratives and their further perpetuation.

After having demonstrated how NoDs work to keep Islam and the West segregated from each other in the plot of *TRF*, the analysis of the upcoming novel's will demonstrate how the influence of NoDs on well-renowned authors might have changed their outlook after 9/11.

---

[178] Ibid., p. 402

HARM (2007) BY BRIAN WILSON ALDISS

ISLAM AND NARRATIVES OF DISPARITY IN ALDISS' *HARM*

HARM is the tale of Paul Fadhil Abbas Ali– a 21-year-old British author of Indian descent – who is arrested and tortured by a government department of the UK called the Hostile Activities Research Ministry (HARM) on suspicion of Islamist terrorism based on a passage in a novel he wrote. Paul's imprisonment is mostly spent in solitary confinement in the uninhabitable ruins of a mansion, with several routine disruptions for beatings and interrogations each day. The rooms are permanently dimmed, infested with vermin, extremely filthy and damp. There is no bed, bunk or blanket and Paul suffers so much from the cold that he becomes feverish. He does not even know where the prison is located. This ordeal triggers a psychopathic identity crisis in him which forms the basis of this dark, science fiction novel. there are two main interrogators at the HARM facility: Gibbs, the British prison director who insists that the prisoners never see his face, and Ramson, the US-American official who supervises and counsels the former.

Due to the physical deprivations in custody, the psychological strains of isolation and the constant fear of more beatings, Paul begins to hallucinate. He suffers from a dissociative disorder; a mental illness that causes him to develop multiple personalities. Paul shows his interrogators a note from a psychiatrist, stating that his mental illness increases when he is left in isolation or when he is unclear of the time or his whereabouts. The interrogators show no interest in the note, and it seems that they are already aware of this information and using it to make their torture more effective. Paul does not find out that the HARM facility is actually in England until he is released towards the end of the novel. Upon Paul's repeated inquiries about their whereabouts, one prison-guard yells that they were in "fucking Syria". Shortly afterwards, Paul starts to hallucinate that he is on a planet called Stygia "where men are free".[179] It seems Paul's mind associated the phonetic resemblance of Syria to 'Stygia', which he recalls from John Milton's *Paradise Lost*. Stygia is another name of

---

[179] Aldiss, *HARM*, p. 5

the river Styx, sometimes called Acheron: the melancholy river in Greek mythology that leads to the underworld 'Hades'. Hades is of course associated with hell. The name of Stygia's ruler is Astaroth, like the demon known in Gothic mythology as the Duke of Hell – one member of the so-called unholy or evil trinity with Lucifer and Beelzebub. In *HARM* Astaroth rules the planet Stygia, which is equated with hell.

Whenever Paul falls asleep or passes out he adopts the personality of Fremant, a resident of Stygia where human settlers from earth have landed. They had arrived in a spaceship called *New Worlds* to escape a hydrogen bomb, which was launched in the USA. The journey from earth to Stygia took hundreds of years. During this long period, the travelers were dismantled into their "essence" while the ship was steered by androids. Five years before arriving on Stygia the people were "reconstituted from the essence", and then those who showed mental or physical weaknesses were "simply eliminated" (p. 97). Fremant is a human male but did not arrive there with the settlers; he has no recollection of how he got there. By the time the settlers reached the planet they had lost an immense part of the knowledge possessed on earth, including any knowledge about husbandry or economy. (p. 18) Therefore, Fremant can observe their endeavours at settling and establishing a just society from the position of intellectual high ground. Large parts of the knowledge from the earth was lost because the initial plan was of this trip included that all memories of organizations, relations, and ties were to be obliterated because these had caused all conflicts on earth. That is why the people chosen to be brought to Stygia had no relations amongst each other. Nevertheless, during the last five years of the journey, the people on the ship found themselves split into two rival sects: one led by Astaroth, the other by Captain Calex. The captain was killed by Astaroth shortly after they all landed on Stygia. As a result, Astaroth became their leader while Captain Calex' adherents slowly formed a resistance group.

Astaroth believes they had all come to Stygia in order to build a great new civilization with the help of the Western Armed Alliance (WAA). He wants the people of Stygia to unanimously adopt an ideology that he calls the 'faith of Waabee' or 'Waabism'. It is clearly a caricature of the conservative interpretation of Islam known as *Wahhabism*, which – in the protagonist's alternate reality – Ramson had mentioned to Paul shortly before. The key principle of Astaroth's Waabee faith is austerity: "We must live austere lives. Austerity must become our faith." This 'faith' demanded "total commitment to the organization", no alcohol, no electronic equipment, "no sex before marriage, no private ownership, no fun, no reading, no singing, no bourgeois indulgences such as 'kindness' or 'understanding', no affection towards others, including wives" (p. 17). It is remarkable that Astaroth calls his idea of a world order consisting only of a set of commandments and prohibitions, a 'faith'. While speaking of a legal code he uses the word 'faith' when he is probably thinking of 'religion'. Astaroth fears that without imposing restraints on food and other needs the settlers would lose their humanity and become like wild animals. This is because the soil on the new planet is poor and offers no abundance of food. The rival view to this 'faith' has similarities to a Puritan Christian worldview. It was initially advocated by Captain Calex. While on the ship the captain attempted to destroy all weapons they found on board. Astaroth managed to save one knife and stabbed Calex to death with it. Calex' admirers are organized in a group called the Clandestine Order and they later manage to overthrow Astaroth's rule. Calex wanted to destroy all remaining weapons and build "a single gentle culture without the divisions that troubled Earth, with its poisonous history." Unlike Astaroth who had sent out a force to systematically eliminate the dominant species on Stygia, natives called Dogover; Calex believed that their first big effort should have been to make friends with the native peoples. Calex had ordered that there should be no reproduction until they had peace on Stygia. However, the Clandestine Order is (eventually) led by Essanits, who believes the genocide of the natives is part of a divine plan. He also believes that Jesus had walked on Stygia once, but had left because he had found no humans there. Ultimately, a third order forms on Stygia when the scientist Safeltky takes charge. Safeltky is a rationalist and secularist who is incapable of empathy or regret. This allegory of Islamic, Christian and Secular values on earth is depicted in a dystopian setting of a planet called Stygia, a different name for hell. The dystopian plot begins with a focus on the vast differences between these three parties and ends showing how each of these disparate creeds exercises power in the same tyrannical manner. Their ways of running their new home are the same, even though they each cite different reasons for their actions.

Aldiss' *HARM* is a political commentary on his historical time frame, war, terrorism[180], national security, and torture. He uses science fiction as a thought experiment that transcends the boundaries of reality in order to reassemble real ideals in a fictional realm, thus offering possibilities to reflect upon present circumstances.[181] Similar to Hamid's novel, *HARM* does not discuss Islam on a soteriological or theological level, as evidenced by the fact that Islamic tenets

---

180 Hankins, '*Fictional Islam*', p. 81
181 Ibid., p. 76

are never discussed or reflected upon. Instead, it discusses Islam as a marker of identity and as a tool for oppression. Paul is Muslim only by name, in fact, by external designation. And on Stygia, Islam is represented as nothing other than a set of strict rules such as austerity. The key element in the divisiveness of ideals or beliefs even when all national, religious, and organizational affiliations and identities have been eliminated, is power. All three parties manage to take control of Stygia consecutively. None of them prove to be good leaders, not because of the flaws in their values but because they all believe that state leadership means forcing their values on everyone, rather than taking the responsibility to safeguard individual freedom and choice. The radicalism of the three factions on Stygia leaves no room for compromise and accounts for an extremely harsh disparity among them despite their similarities.

Both storylines in the novel are fraught with narratives of disparity, which remain unresolved. Thus, Aldiss' thought experiment paints a rather bleak picture for multicultural and multi-religious communities in the future. The renowned science fiction author was asked about the pessimistic outlook he portrays in *HARM* in an interview because it is notably atypical of him. Since Aldiss has been writing since the early 40s and publishing since the 50s, he can not only boast of a sizeable collection of works – varying between fiction and non-fiction as well as poetry and prose – but also of great international success and recognition. One of his short stories even became the basis for a movie directed by Stephen Spielberg, *A.I. Artificial Intelligence* (2001). The above-mentioned interview ascertains this change in Aldiss' outlook on Europe from optimistic to pessimistic. The interviewer specifically asked Aldiss whether he has become more pessimistic about the world by confronting him with a statement he made seven years earlier, in 2000 after the publication of another science fiction novel titled *White Mars*. At that time, Aldiss, who is known for using the utopian trope for intellectual reflections on various complex issues, had said:

> Perhaps the further evolution of humankind does require some sort of collaboration; at present, almost a quarter of humanity is disenfranchised, starved, exploited. Could we not do better? Why does pity not move us? These are questions worth asking. I have no great faith in utopias ever being established, but questions must be posed now and again. Could we not do better? Is not the West in a position to do better?[182]

After reading this quote back to Aldiss the interviewer asked him: "How do these words resonate for you today? *White Mars* – which, like *HARM*, features

---

[182] Aldiss, *HARM,* p. 224

an attempt to build a utopia on another world – seems a much more hopeful book than this one. Have you become more pessimistic about humanity's future?"[183] Aldiss answers in the affirmative and then draws a link between immigration and the loss of his optimism:

> I have become less optimistic about today. Many people have taken refuge in Britain from dirty, dusty villages in the Middle East. They neither know nor understand the West. Consequently, many would destroy it. They have never heard of that ancient piece of sound advice: 'When in Rome, do as the Romans do.'[184]

In her *Literary Review and Comparative Essay on Islam in Science Fiction and Fantasy* Rebecca Hankins notices an inconsistency between the message of Aldiss' novel *HARM* and the above-quoted statement he made in an interview. She concludes:

> According to Aldiss, leave off your ethnic, religious and cultural identities when you leave your home country. But on the other hand *HARM* reveals that it doesn't matter because you will never be accepted even when you *do as the Romans do* as Paul attempted; he would never be considered a Roman. Unfortunately, Aldiss doesn't have a follow-up response to the dichotomy he poses with *HARM* and the real world advice he quotes.[185]

One year before the tragic events of 9/11 Aldiss was optimistic about the West's abilities to "do better" and he wrote novels that raised questions about possibilities of improvement. A few years after 9/11 Aldiss is pessimistic and cites immigrants' unwillingness to adapt to the ways of the West as the reason for it. Thus, somewhere in the years after the attacks, while the looming threat of Islamist terrorism was being discussed in the West, Aldiss' thinking shows trails of the four kinds of narratives of disparity. The novel, as well as the abovementioned interview, will now be analysed with regard to each kind of narratives of disparity.

NARRATIVES OF DISTINCTIVE IDENTITY IN ALDISS' *HARM*

Paul is the author of a novel titled *The Pied Piper of Hament* in which two figures joke about assassinating the British Prime Minister. On these grounds,

---

[183] Ibid.

[184] Ibid.

[185] Hankins, '*Fictional Islam*', p. 82

Paul is detained for interrogation in a wreckage of what used to be a large mansion. The story is narrated in a third-person voice, with the perspective limited to the protagonist's viewpoint for most of the time. The narrating voice refers to Paul using his several names or with the third person pronoun 'he', and narrates only what can be immediately perceived by Paul. Since Paul remains ignorant of the location until the last part of the novel, the reader remains ignorant with him. The narration often zooms in close and adopts the character's language patterns, recounting his thoughts using free indirect speech and sometimes zooms out to take a more objective view. In very few passages, the focalization point shifts to Algernon Gibbs, the British controller of the facility.

While Paul is tortured and questioned about the novel he wrote, his interrogators claim that the Pakistani anti-terrorist organization ISID accused Paul of being a member of an organization called *Al-Muhajiroun*, which is allegedly "an extremist Islamic group full of evil bastards and suicide bombers" (p. 8). Interestingly, *al-Mu-Ha-Ji-Roun* is actually Arabic for 'migrants'. The terrorist organization, which fought in the historical Soviet-Afghan war, and whose most famous member was Osama bin Laden, was named *al-Mu-Ja-Hi-Deen*. It remains unclear in the novel whether *al-Mu-Ha-Ji-Roun* is simply a mispronunciation of *al-Mu-Ja-Hi-Deen* on the guards' part or a bluff in order to scare Paul. Either way, the use of the Arabic word for 'migrants' as the name of a terrorist group might be a reference to a common fear in the West that every migrant is a potential terrorist. And even though Aldiss does not put refugees under general suspicion of terrorism, he does describe them as a homogenously backward and savage group of people "from dirty, dusty villages [...] who neither know nor understand the West".

Aldiss also implies that things would be easier if all immigrants adhere to the proverb: 'When in Rome, do as the Romans do.' Aldiss calls this an "ancient piece of advice" and yet he does not think it the least bit outdated. This is probably because today's West has constructed an intellectual identity with large parts of the knowledge and ideals of the Romans. Today's West also takes great pride in values of individual freedom and equality. As Hankins pointed out, the author seems unaware of the absurdity of asking people to integrate by blending in and at the same time they must take care not to overstay, because they will never become an integrated part of the West. His idea of the West in this statement is a homogenous one and the exact opposite of the homogenously dirty and dusty Middle East. Unlike the recognized literary genius of pre-9/11-Aldiss, the post-9/11-Aldiss seems oblivious of the plurality of the West and the Middle East, as well as the logical fallacy of expecting immigrants to make efforts at assimilating to the West but also not wanting to stay.

Aldiss happens to be reproducing a generic narrative of distinctive identity, including the classic trope of deflecting blame on one 'out-group' and then offering a simple solution. In this case, the solution is that they must be compelled to blend in with the majority for the duration of their stay so as not to disrupt the implied homogeneity. Furthermore, the stay must be temporary because they can never become members of the 'in-group'. These narratives construct distinctive identities of the 'self' and the 'other' by overemphasizing and enhancing the differences, whilst implying a total lack of similarities. The major characters in *HARM* serve as a synecdoche for a hypothetically homogenous entity or group: Astaroth, Essanits, and Safeltky on Stygia, and Gibbs and Ramson in the HARM facility. These characters are different from each other in their strengths, values, priorities, and ideas. However, they are all the same in their weaknesses: their insecurities, lust for power, sadistic fetishes, xenophobia, megalomania, egocentrism, and narcissism. Their narcissism makes them turn a blind eye to their own weaknesses which is why they are oblivious to their similarities to each other.

Most characters are adamant throughout the novel to maintain the disparity between different affiliations, be they religious, national or ideological. This is obvious in the tripartite division on Stygia, as explained in the previous section. In the frame narrative, this division is between two figures, the British Gibbs and the American Ramson who, like the factions on Stygia, are competing for the position of absolute power. Ramson has come to teach the British all about interrogation under torture and Gibbs is not only annoyed by the fact that he has no authority over Ramson but also by cultural differences in Ramson's US-American business manners (p. 42). It is only Paul, and Fremant respectively, who give an adaptation of new values a chance at all in *HARM*, but all their attempts fail. Paul's self-identification as British is rejected by British government officials. Even though he clearly does not "[adhere] to religious tenets of the Islamic faith" he is "judged based on that identity" throughout the story.[186] Fremant, on the other hand, is susceptible to every leader's worldview on Stygia. He decides to change sides once he gets disillusioned with one but ends up getting disappointed by all three views depicted in the novel.

---

[186] Ibid., p. 84

The fact that the protagonist has so many different names demonstrates the fluidity of his identity throughout the novel. His full birth name consists of four names: Paul Fadhil Abbas Ali. On Stygia his name is Fremant and at the HARM facility, he is known as Prisoner B. Paul is a British citizen born in the UK to an English mother and an Indian father. Even his father was born and raised in British Uganda, which reduces Paul's affiliation with India even further. Because he was mocked for his heritage at school he dropped the second half of his name and changed it to Paul Fadhill (two Ls), which he calls his 'English persona' (p. 133). It is a common trope in contemporary literature dealing with Islamic immigrants that protagonists change their name as a means of distancing themselves "from their Islamic identification where their current names mark their Muslim origins."[187] While the changing of Paul's name was indeed an attempt at distancing himself from Islam and from his genetic heritage, all the other names represent his own confusion about his identity. Instead of forming a complex individual identity, Paul had been evading certain parts of his heritage, and he proves unable to face them. Escape in the form of adopting different personalities or different identities seems to be the intuitive response that Paul is conditioned to when meeting resistance or complications, rather than confronting them. He escaped his father's violent attempts at raising Paul as a pious Muslim by renouncing the faith of Islam and leaving home at a young age. Shortly after, Paul "underwent psychoanalysis for his various insecurities" (p.44) but is still oblivious to these patterns. He created his above mentioned 'English persona' as an escape from mockery at school, and in prison, he creates Stygia and Fremant in order to escape the realities of torture. A possible way of explaining his failure to form a believable identity is because these changes are inspired by fear and evasion rather than actual conviction.

In the course of the story, Paul experiences an unnaturally drastic change of heart in a very short time. The inhumane treatment he suffers causes him to question his life-long attempts at becoming British and leaves him thinking he needs a more spiritual foundation in his life. By the end, Paul rediscovers Islam because he is convinced that it is an inescapable part of his identity. Like Mohsin Hamid's protagonist, Changez, Paul had buried an old identity crisis in his subconscious mind by years of shallow attempts to become Western. Both, Changez and Paul, face rejection, distrust and abuse (verbal in Changez'

---

[187] Ibid.

case, and physical in Paul's) causing their identity crises to resurface and ultimately leading them to restore their Muslim identity. The implication here is that Islam is not a faith that a person might decide to turn away from, but a race, which cannot be cast off. Paul thinks he cannot denounce Islam and that the Muslim identity cannot mingle with any elements of Western identity. The same is true for Fremant on Stygia.

The protagonist incarnates different types of personalities within the two plots, and yet in both plots, he is the misplaced stranger whose attempts to fit in had been doomed to failure from the get-go. Paul tries to cross the boundaries drawn by narratives of distinctive identity between Islam and the West, thus becoming a stranger. "'You, Fremant, you're always asking questions, you'd be the Eternal Stranger.' [Fremant] thought the observation was acute. He was eternally a stranger, even to himself." (p. 64) Based on this passage in *HARM*, Hankins detects a recurring role of what she calls "the *stranger* imagery" in written fiction about Islam and finds a possible explanation in one particular book:

> This echoes the sentiments expressed in Muslim writer Ian Dallas's science fiction novel *The Book of Strangers* (1972). The story describes a librarian's mystical journey of self-discovery in a technologically advanced world. The *strangers* that this book speaks of are those people that seek to find the dedicated and spiritual teachers of Islam; those who selflessly work to perfect their faith. The stranger concept in Islam is from a saying of the Prophet Muhammad that is referenced in Dallas's book, 'Islam began as a strange element and will become thus again, as it was at the beginning. Blessed, therefore, are the strangers.' Paul/Fremant is a stranger in both worlds, searching for his place in Stygia and British society. His journey of self discovery [sic] leads to a tragic end, but in his final words, he finds his Islam.[188]

The 'eternal stranger' is the one looking for the perfect version of Islam or of society and will never fit into any community which claims to be perfect already. Since perfection, however, cannot realistically be claimed, most societies or communities make do with a claim of superiority over every other. The claim of superiority over others requires a very flawed entity in place of 'the others' to serve as a negative benchmark. Narratives of inadequacy construct a severely flawed identity of the other and due to the narratives of distinctive identity, the same flaws are overlooked in the self.

---

[188] Ibid.

NARRATIVES OF INADEQUACY IN ALDISS' *HARM*

Narratives of inadequacy about a certain group or organization are constructed with the use of recurring tropes. Western narratives of inadequacy about Islam often consist of one trope which dates back to the 18th century: the odd sexuality of Muslims:

> Islamic sexuality is explored [in *HARM*] but Muslims are viewed as sexually repressed, hypocritical, inhibiting, and often criminal. This is another one of those stereotypes that is advanced, but Islam, in contrast to Christianity has never viewed sexuality as only a means of procreation. On the contrary, sex in Islam, albeit marital sex, is encouraged as a means of mutual pleasure and satisfaction for both partners. There are numerous stories about men and women asking the Prophet Muhammad intimate details regarding sexuality and marriage including a woman who complained that her husband 'was like a limp cloth.' This reality stands in stark contrast to Aldiss' portrayal of Islamic sexuality. In *HARM* Aldiss says that for the women of Stygia 'The protocol was against love and lovemaking.' (21) The only love for these women was through abuse or rape as represented by Aster, the daughter of Astaroth. Aster is sexually abused by her father and raped by Fremant, but neither man is punished for their crime.[189]

The reason why Aldiss' discussion of Islamic sexuality and gender roles fails lies not only in the inaccuracy of the portrayal of Islamic sexuality but also in *HARM*'s failure to mend the most common flaw in religious narratives regarding gender roles: Hankins points out that the female characters in *HARM* are no more than sexual partners, whose character arcs and story outcomes are entirely dependent on the men. Their ultimate fates are not even revealed as they simply disappear after serving their role in the plot centred on men. Quoting Howard Eilberg-Schwartz in *Off With Her Head: The Denial of Women's Identity in Myth, Religion, and Culture,* Hankins concludes that Aldiss did not even try to overcome gender stereotypes in his own writing.[190]

In conclusion, Aldiss has composed a narrative of the inadequacy of Islam with regard to gender roles, whilst failing to see that his own novel reproduces the traditional tropes for female characters serving only as love interests or sexual partners for male characters. Hankins identifies Aldiss' use of another trope at the cost of women, which is often used in order to depict a flawed image of Islam:

---

[189] Ibid., p. 85

[190] Ibid., p. 86

> Another side issue that is always beneath the surface in Western writings on Islam about Muslim women is the headscarf. For many writers the headscarf is a symbol of oppression and degradation. In *HARM* the women on Stygia 'went hooded and masked outside their home...' (21). Aldiss also has Paul hooded during his torture in prison, another bid to the oppressive symbol that the veil signifies. In *HARM* the women had no choice but to wear the veil [...]. Aldiss continues the mindset of those writers that see the veil as something that women wear out of duress and at the behest of men; it couldn't possibly be something that women would choose to do. Covering women's hair is used repeatedly and consistently to demonize and stereotype Muslims and Aldiss continues that narrative. [...] Covering the hair is a practice of women in many societies and faith traditions, but it is those Muslim women who veil that are stigmatized, stereotyped, and labelled as backward, oppressed or ignorant.[191]

Narratives of Inadequacy are useful when ill-treatment of the 'out-group' requires the breaking of any rule. The inadequacies of the victim can help deflect from the hypocrisy or injustice or even serve as a justification for any action against them. The invaders of Stygia, for instance, wipe out the entire population of (what they believe to be) the dominant species. Astaroth orders their systematic obliteration based on his assessment of them as being primitive in comparison to humans. His narrative is that since the humans were there now, the so-called Dogovers no longer deserved to live because humans were more advanced. He also claims that the indigenous species might have carried diseases which are unknown and dangerous to humans.

In the same manner, Astaroth decides which members of the humans under him "deserve" to survive, which is why he forbids help of any kind. For instance, he is infuriated when he sees someone donating food in order to help some settlers survive 'the shawl', which is like a long night. Recurring every ten days the Shawl is a time when the planet is covered in darkness, forcing people to stay indoors and store food for the duration of this time:

> 'Why give away food? Men must earn their living, their very bread. That is a basic law of life.'
>
> 'Without food they might have died, sir, and had no law.' [...]
>
> 'Then they should have died. Those who would die are the ones who have no sense, who would not store food.'
>
> Essanits, standing by, [...] said mildly, 'Some of the poor are unable to afford to buy anything ahead of time, sir. They have to live from hand to mouth, if I may remind you.'

---

[191] Ibid., p. 87

> 'You may, Soldier Essanits,' replied Astaroth, controlling his anger, 'and I will remind you that such men are worth nothing to our community. The days of the egalitarian society we had on the ship after LPR[192] in its final years are long over. Here we must fight for our living.' (p. 65-66)

Essanits goes on to become the leader of the Christian sect, the Clandestine Order, which eventually gains power. Even though Essanits resents the genocide of the natives and tries to make amends for it, he also manages to come up with a narrative of inadequacy of his own. When his attempt at saving the last surviving Dogover fails, he concludes that this must have been part of the divine plan:

> [Essanits:] 'The day will come when we see that it was necessary to destroy the autochthonous race in order to establish God's will on the planet.'
>
> [Fremant:] 'Really? Then I don't think much of your God.' (p. 169)

Since Essanits and the Clandestine Order believe that they were brought to Stygia by God himself and that they were ordained to rule over it because of their superiority, his narrative of inadequacy for the others is based on their lack of guidance by God.

Meanwhile, Paul and Fremant were susceptible to all narratives of inadequacy that were presented to them:

> Paul and his alter ego Fremant viewed Islam as the source of his problems and he felt the need to distance himself from that identity. Fremant's alternate reality views any religion as seriously flawed as represented by first an oppressive Islamic government that is overthrown by a Christian sect that becomes just as intolerant as the previous system.[193]

However, Paul's character arc eventually shifts towards the construction of a counter-narrative about an inadequacy of the West. Initially, he shares the narrative of inadequate Muslims deserving to be mistrusted: In response to an interrogator's statement about Muslims wanting to destroy their culture, Paul corrects him but then his mind starts to wander:

> 'Muslims, no. Only a few terrorists...'
>
> Yet he thought to himself [...] that many Muslims had made the mistake of living apart, emphasizing their difference by insisting on dressing differently, on living tribally, on remaining woefully ill-educated, as many had lived for generations in dusty distant villages. Little had changed in two thousand years. Unlike the Hindus, who slipped successfully into British life, many men he knew kept their

---

[192] LPR stands for Life Process Reservoirs, which is where the essence of people was stored. The PR was the Process of Reconstitution (p. 97).

[193] Hankins, '*Fictional Islam*', p. 85

> wives imprisoned in their houses, unable to speak a word of English. He had integrated, had naïvely thought himself English; now he was being disabused. (p. 136-137)

Immediately, after this post-colonial thought about his own failed attempts to be accepted into western society, it occurs to him that refusing to do so might have been better. However, his acceptance of this conclusion is not based on the futility of adapting to Western ways because immigrants still end up being treated the same way by Western countries. His acceptance of is because he now finds the West flawed in a way that Islam allegedly could not be:

> And yet ... all prejudice aside, Muslims were right, surely, to disapprove of the behaviour of many young English men, the binge-drinkers of both sexes, the young women dressed as if ready for immediate promiscuous sex. The display of female navels. The disrespect shown to their seniors. (p. 137)

By the end of the novel, he finds himself disoriented because he sheds off all his former core-markers of identity. And yet he is certain of his hatred of the British nation:

> [Paul's] feelings were muddied and unclear. At least he knew he now hated the British, the nation he had once greatly admired. His uncle, who had been a lawyer in his Uganda days, had read much English literature, with a particular affection for such works as De Quincey's *Confessions of an English Opium Eater*, with its masterly and elaborate prose, and the learned and abstruse *Anatomy of Melancholy* by Robert Burton.
>
> Some such books had accompanied his father on his escape to England and formed his [Paul's] own early reading matter. Only later did he realize that he had learned of an impoverished yet dignified England which had passed away. A wave of materialism had overtaken England. A disgraceful hedonism was all, a hedonism often taking the form of riots at football matches, binge-drinking and street violence, vomiting and urinating on pavements, sporadic racism. There was no – or next to no – spiritual life remaining. The *Decline and Fall of the Roman Empire* was being repeated – in a minor key. ...
>
> It was for spiritual life he yearned. He longed to leave the sordid England that had imprisoned him. But where to go for refuge? (p. 157-158)

Thus, Paul had reached the point where he could no longer hold on to the same narrative because he was stripped of his right to assign himself to it when his interrogators repeatedly refer to him as "you Muslims". He becomes their opponent and immediately after losing his share in the British narrative he adopts the Islamic counter-narrative of Islamic spirituality over Western materialism. The underlying train of logic beneath both narratives is identical: a number of stereotypical attributes – sometimes in the form of tropes – are randomly listed (binge-drinking in the West; circumcision of women by Muslims, etc.) disregarding the statistical and rational validity of linking such problems to a race, religion, or nationality. In the next step this list of negative stereotypes becomes the projected identity of the respective other, and finally, the own position is juxtaposed against it, concluding its superiority over the other.

NARRATIVES OF SUPERIORITY IN ALDISS' *HARM*

The first two kinds of NoDs lay the groundwork for narratives of superiority: narratives of inadequacy assign selected flaws to the members of the 'out-group', whilst narratives of distinctive identity infer that the 'in-group' cannot be inflicted with those flaws because it has nothing in common with the 'out-group'. In the next stage, the narratives of superiority elevate the 'self' by exaggerating the strengths and bolstering them with heroic, virtuous and superlative attributes that are unsurpassable and often even claim divine ordination or preference.

The protagonist of the novel undergoes a development from a patriotic British young man who blames Muslims for his current torment to a disillusioned and confused boy who begins to understand Muslims and their refusal to adopt the Western lifestyle. Narratives of distinctive identity are one reason why Paul does not even try to find a compromise between these two positions. Another reason for this is that after he had convinced himself that Islam can also claim superiority Paul went from one identity claiming global superiority to another one. Paul is insecure and weak, which is why he needs an affiliation with a strong group. He is not looking for an identity but for a source from which to draw a sense of security and strength.

Narratives of superiority are constructions of self-images of apotheosis, which the reality of the 'self' does not actually live up to. They inevitably depict an unrealistic picture of the 'self' by deflecting certain failings to the 'out-group', completely oblivious to the fact that the same flaws can also be found in the 'in-group'. Narratives of superiority often have an anchor in an entity or concept, which surpasses the boundaries of time and space: like a religious entity, an idea taken from history and/or mythology or any other concept, which is presented as the ultimate and final truth. Astaroth uses the Western Armed Alliance (WAA), the organization that sent them to Stygia, as a reference. Since the WAA is responsible for their survival and their existence and has been left behind on earth, it cannot be challenged. Astaroth uses the language of a religion but does not produce a godlike entity, because he obviously hopes to impersonate that authority himself. The Clandestine Order, however, does use God – or "the Divine Plan" – as an anchor for their narrative of superiority. Finally, there is Safeltky who uses science as an anchor by refusing to believe anything which cannot be established by scientific methods, even though he knows that the knowledge of humans on Stygia is very limited.

Additionally, narratives of superiority work on the weak because they satisfy primal needs in people with inferiority complexes, which are most obvious in Algernon Gibbs. Chapter five opens with a focalization on him. Gibbs feels humiliated by Ramson because he found fault in Gibbs' work. Ramson described the British means of interrogation as amateurish compared to the US-American ones and then left in a stretch limousine. We learn that Gibbs also resents his secretary, Agnes, for being two inches taller than him. Evidently, Gibbs suffers from several insecurities including the so-called Napoleon-Complex. Then, while Gibbs is watching a video, which Ramson gave him for inspiration, Gibbs becomes jealous of the resources that Americans get for interrogation and torture. Soon he feels aroused and masturbates. Masturbation after watching a violent assertion of power reveals the sadistic tendencies that link violence and oppression to primal sexual urges. Sexual violence as well as common forms of repressed sexual urges (e.g. the Oedipus complex, the Electra complex and the Stockholm Syndrome) come and go in *HARM*. Interestingly, however, no character is ever brought to account for any of the sexual offences committed in the novel. Narratives of superiority do not necessarily have to include – or climax in – violent assertions of power, but when they do, they can be linked to the human libido. In a non-violent and non-sexual context, these narratives can satisfy intellectual or emotional needs of the cultural or collective (super-) ego.

Essentially, both plots depict a community that houses a hierarchy of worldviews, because every party claims superiority over all others. On Stygia all three groups are guilty of this, which is why they all prove to be bad leaders. Paul chooses Islam in a fit to find an equally overbearing source of identity to replace the old one. He needs a strong source in order to compensate his weaknesses and shortcomings, and therefore, ends up clinging to a counter-narrative of superiority. As a result, the encounter of Gibbs and Paul fails and ends in a violent climax, because the two of them claim superiority for the West and for Islam respectively.

Narratives of superiority do not only function as a gratifying fantasy but also serve as a basis for self-righteousness. In the first chapter of *HARM*, Paul is told by the guards that they are "just carrying out EU policy" right before they give him a severe beating (p. 8). Clearly, this information was supposed to be a form of reassurance, because they obviously believe their actions cannot be (morally) wrong if they are based on EU-policy. It is not the claim of superiority alone, however, which makes violations of self-imposed values possible. Torture and oppression in *HARM* are not presented as morally correct by narratives of superiority, even though it can be done. The plot of the novel reveals how moral considerations are overcome by narratives of mutual distrust.

NARRATIVES OF MUTUAL DISTRUST IN ALDISS' *HARM*

> Them as are tortured are the torturers. (p.64)

Even though the story is set in the UK, and the controller of the prison is British, we learn that the *HARM* facility is run jointly by the most important member-states of 'the West': Paul knows that there are "French interrogators and American interrogators, and once there had been a stand-in Polish interrogator." (p. 9) Another person in charge at the prison is the U.S.-American, Abraham Ramson who introduces himself to Paul with the following words:

> I hold the rank of Paramount Government Inspector of the Western Armed Alliance [WAA] and occupy a senior position in the American Punishment Section investigating hostile activities in the world. I am well known on both sides of the Atlantic as a military judge, famed for holding the lives of many villains in my hands. My aim is to function as a terror of the terrorists. I have prosecuted many famous cases and, although justice interests me, over and above justice I value the continued survival of Western civilization as of maximum import for the culture of this world, as the greatest bastion of enlightened law and behavior on this planet, certainly in comparison with the degenerate and superstitious tribalism prevalent in the Middle East. As a Muslim, you will be aware that we in the West [...] have a distaste for Sharia Law as well as for many Islamic rules of behavior, from the circumcision of women to the indoctrination of ignorant youths into a form of religion which is in most respects long obsolete and degrading. [...] Wahhabism [...] is a hateful, archaic creed which destroys relationships and withers everything creative. We must fight it before it destroys us [...] The slaves of Wahhab have the deathwatch habit of infiltrating and endeavouring to destroy the decent and law-abiding cultures into which you have inserted yourselves; together with the cowardly resort of suicide bombing. (p. 36-37)

Clearly, the narratives of mutual distrust at work in *HARM* reproduce the enemy stereotypes of Islamist terrorists and make irrational fear seem rational. The plot reveals how a narrative of this kind can make oppressive and fascist means seem necessary and plausible, even to Paul: the victim of this oppression.

Throughout the novel, Paul is tortured and beaten for being of Muslim heritage, and yet for a while, he fails to see the moral failure of Britain, the country he identifies himself with and admires deeply. This is due to his natural impulse of defending the country he feels affiliated to. Additionally, he too has internalised the Western narratives that rationalize and justify their actions, especially their battle strategies. For instance, Paul initially attempts to exonerate his interrogators and the guards, justifying and explaining their actions against him. "Their [the guard's] duties were just a job for them. They went home at six in the evening to wives and kids, and a bottle of beer with a square meal, innocent of ideology." (p. 9) Later on, however, he actually singles out the guard who looks British and indemnifies his behaviour: "[Paul] felt that the older of the two [guards] was not sadistic, merely doing his job within the cruel machine of interrogation and the dictates of the old CIA 'Kubark Manual'. He supposed this man was English. With the other, it was hard to tell." (p. 25)

Paul composes a narrative in favour of the very people who were inflicting awful emotional and physical pain on him. He believes they are *just doing their job*. This phrase is a classic way of denying moral responsibility by claiming to have no executive authority. While the innocence of the guards might even be accepted as true on face value, Paul's defensive attitude towards his tormentors undeniably becomes a narrative at the point where Paul places the blame entirely on Muslims, whereas he exonerates the officials in charge of the HARM facility because they are only doing what they have to do. Curiously, Paul tells himself:

> [It] was the so-called terrorists, the Muslim suicide bombers – and their tacit support from the silent Muslim community – which had brought this disgrace on Britain. ... A curtain of fear had been drawn over this once moderate and modest island. (p. 14-15)

The story continues with a detailed exploration of the consequences of the interrogation measures being used on him, which are "exaggerated forms of common psychological phenomena, exercised precisely to break down the psychological defences of an individual."[194]

The "CIA's 1963 KUBARK Counterintelligence Interrogation manual" is a historic "document summarizing and implementing [...] material, constructing a comprehensive interrogation program, [...] declassified in 1997 (KUBARK was an alternate in-house name for CIA.)"[195] Another quotation of Kaye's that delineates these abuses to human dignity is as follows:

> Over the past several years, a controversy has arisen over the use of medical and psychological personnel for the purposes of interrogating prisoners in the United States 'war on terror.' Recent revelations, including the release of the CIA Inspector General's 2004 Report on the CIA's interrogation program, led the human rights organization Physicians for Human Rights (PHR) to conclude that doctors, psychologists and other health professionals designed, implemented and helped supervise 'a worldwide torture program' following 9/11. Much of the criticism of this program, and its putative legality or illegality, has focused on dramatically abusive forms of coercive interrogation, such as waterboarding. Less well known, but perhaps just as injurious to its victims, are practices such as long-term isolation, sensory deprivation, sensory overload or over-stimulation, and sleep deprivation. These techniques, along with the use of fear, constitute psychological torture. [...]
>
> [...] [P]sychologists, psychoanalysts, and psychiatrists worked for the CIA and the Pentagon to understand and implement these techniques. As a result of this research, sensory deprivation, prolonged isolation, and later, sensory overload became an integral part of the U.S. coercive interrogation paradigm."[196]

The novel's reference to this historic document is one reason to think of this novel as the author's critical commentary on the so-called Global War on Terror and the security policies that it entailed. However, another look at what Aldiss said in the interview that he gave about this particular novel reveals that Aldiss was not critical of the methods because he believed the threat was real. The interviewer had asked him about issues of national security and the methods of enhanced interrogation: at an early point in the interview, Aldiss comments about the situation he had written in his book:

> Sadly, the national atmosphere has become tainted with suspicion. Paul jokes about assassinating the PM to show how far he is from such actions – fatally, of course. (A new report claims that 1,600 young British Muslims are being radicalized and are under surveillance.)[197]

---

[194] Kaye, *Guild Practitioner,* p. 2
[195] Ibid.
[196] Ibid.
[197] Aldiss, *HARM,* p. 219

A few passages onwards, the interviewer refers to the passage where Aldiss sums up Paul's pitiable situation in the novel and asks the author whether he thinks the threat of Islamist danger acute enough to justify such measures as mentioned in that passage:

> Paul is swept up on the flimsiest of pretexts, then subjected to torture that is made even more abhorrent by the vile racism of his interlocutors. Yet isn't there a real danger to the West from Islamic terrorists? Where should the line be drawn in responding to this threat?

Aldiss replies by putting the 'flimsiness' of the pretext of Paul's arrest to question:

> Paul arrested on the flimsiest of pretexts? But paranoia is the last refuge of a scoundrel; they may have had Paul under surveillance for some while. The novel opens with our knowing nothing about Paul. As I write, in the U.K. it's the day of the lord mayor's show, with many acts and groups on the show (including the formidable Knights of Kazakhstan!) parading through a sunny London, and the sidewalks are crammed with thousands of people. How tempting a target for some mad terrorist with a few pounds of explosives strapped round his chest...
>
> Where indeed should a line be drawn?[198]

Since Aldiss composed this fictional plot around Paul, he decided how much information is divulged to the reader. The plot of the novel contains no reason to suspect Paul of taking part in terrorist activities of any kind. On the contrary, the novel makes clear that Paul is innocent: Ramson and Gibbs read through Paul's detailed records together, containing even the mean nicknames he was given by his classmates in school. Ramson concludes that Paul is of no use to them and should be released while Gibbs merely thinks that "they" should all be nuked. (p. 42-45) But in the interview, Aldiss fills in the blanks he left in the novel, with incriminating innuendos (Paul would have been under surveillance for a long time) and circumstantial evidence (Paul's arrest coincided with a parade). In conclusion, during the interview, Aldiss constructed a narrative of distrust towards Paul, by filling in the blanks with suspicion. As a result, Aldiss does not condemn Paul's arrest and torture but leaves it open for discussion.

However, Aldiss says in a previous interview conducted in the pre-9/11 era that he believes "the West is in a position to do better". This is plausible because the West has access to resources such as knowledge, wealth, technology and talent in a way that the rest of the world does not. Therefore, the West is

---

[198] Ibid.

in a position, which promises the best chances at successfully improving the world. This line of reasoning is not a narrative of superiority but an appeal for constantly making an effort to improve oneself. Narratives of superiority aim to assert that one chosen view is already the best by artificially constructing a perfect image of it. The goal of a narrative of superiority is to be recognized as a positive assertion; the best in comparison to others, rather than just a premise of promoting a genuine struggle for betterment. Therefore, Aldiss' thought experiment in *HARM* may have failed to resolve the pessimism of NoDs because ever since 9/11 he seems to have internalised them himself.

This analysis requires one final note regarding the dangers of equating the author's message with the novel's message: while this reading was certainly focussed on the author's possible bias, it is important to remember that a novel can carry more meanings than the author may have consciously intended. The intention was to demonstrate on Aldiss' long career in writing how his outlook on Islam in the West evidently changed since 9/11. The events of that day carried so much meaning that they practically rewrote a narrative of disparity between Islam and the West all by themselves.

Now, after having discussed the role of the West in the construction of NoDs it is also important to discuss the role of Islam in this scenario; this will be the focus of the upcoming novels' analyses.

Maps for Lost Lovers (2004) by Nadeem Aslam

A Reading of Aslam's *Maps for Lost Lovers*

Similar to the novels analysed in the previous two chapters, *Maps for Lost Lovers* depicts a world in which narratives of disparity between Islam and the West prevail. Like the other two authors, Aslam bases these narratives on historical, fictional, mythical and also theological narratives, as well as politicized tropes such as the stereotypically uneducated immigrants with incestuous forced marriages to first cousins, honour killings and other forms of oppression of women. Perhaps inevitably, this novel triggered a controversy about its political correctness and objectivity among many readers. Unlike the previously discussed novels, *Maps for Lost Lovers* does discuss Islam as a religion rather than as a cultural identity. The novel depicts a very specific image of Islam, which will be examined under narratives of disparity in the upcoming chapters. First, it is important to address the allegation of Aslam's stereotypical depiction of honour crimes.

Set in the UK in a town almost exclusively populated by South-Asian immigrants, the story opens a few weeks after the disappearance of 24-year-old Chanda and 40-year-old Jugnu from their house. Both of them are of Pakistani origin but have largely been socialized and educated in the UK. Jugnu is a well-traveled, Harvard-educated lepidopterist; he is westernized and used to dating non-Muslim women. Chanda's parents are the owners of a local grocery store. They are very conventional and had forced her into three marriages to Pakistani Muslim men of their choosing in the hope of securing a traditional life of piety for her. After Chanda's first two marriages fail, her parents become desperate enough to rush her into a third marriage to an illegal immigrant who disappears after securing his legal status. Some months after this, Chanda and Jugnu fall in love but cannot get married because Chanda never got a divorce from her third husband. After her clandestine affair with Jugnu is discovered and made public, the couple decides to live together out of wedlock; despite the offence it causes with Chanda's family and others who consider it a sin and a disgrace. After their disappearance, the police investigate and as the story unfolds we learn that they were murdered by Chanda's brothers in a drunken rage. In her thorough analysis of the novel, Amina Yaqin sums up its polemic capacities:

> Aslam's novel makes an important literary contribution to this 'clash of cultures' debate in a post-9/11 world. Yet a number of readers have commented on the slightly disorienting experience of reading a novel that seems in many ways to reiterate populist clichés in its story of a pair of ill-fated lovers whose transgression is punished with death, and a closed community who shield and support the murderers. They have expressed uncertainty about whether, in the end, Aslam is challenging or confirming popular images of backward and atavistic Pakistani immigrant behavior. [...] *Maps for Lost Lovers* offers an *uneven and contradictory engagement with honour crime*. On the one hand, it is concerned to provide a forensic, pseudo-documentary analysis of a sociological phenomenon – albeit one already overdetermined by Orientalist moral projections. On the other, the story of two lovers killed for their transgression is complicated by the additional factors of ghettoization and lack of material resources and cultural capital. [...]
>
> *In order to explore this trajectory and understand the implications of the novel's key theme it is important to establish a broader political sense of how honour killings and honour crimes are recognized and discussed in Britain.* Primarily associated with the immigrant Muslim population, the phenomenon of honour crime in modern Britain is immediately taken to affirm the perceived polarization between a secular West and its ethnic and religious minorities. Of course, case studies have shown that honour crimes are not just a Muslim issue, but they are almost always portrayed as such in the press and popular media.[199] [Emphasis added]

Indeed, every young South-Asian girl appearing in the novel is subjected to (sometimes fatal) physical abuse, torture and forced marriages. Readers have criticized it for offering a stereotypical depiction of backward, barbaric and anti-Western immigrants and Muslims. This is certainly problematic if the novel is read and assessed like a journalistic undertaking, which is precisely what Yaqin has done in the above-quoted passage. Her article concludes that the reporting of honour crimes is "dubious" and "self-aggrandizing", because of their "high moral tone" and the implication that reporters [...] are contributing to an enlightened project of saving Asian women from patriarchal oppression".[200] While her review of the journalistic endeavours in question may be apt, she fails to explain the logic of compiling all genres of writing behind this assessment and declaring all of them as intentionally damaging:

> Human rights activism, the judicial and legal system, media representation, fiction and fantasy and anthropological study *all conspire to fix and 'solidify* honour

---

[199] Yaqin, '*Muslims as Multicultural Misfits in Nadeem Aslam's Maps for Lost Lovers*', pp. 101–2

[200] Ibid., p. 103

> crimes as timeless cultural practices' [quoting Lila Abu-Lughod, 2011] affiliated to a particular kind of community at odds with western society. Thus, the public imagination is caught both by the scientific mode of factual reporting in human rights data collection and by imaginative storytelling. What also gets fixed is the female body as a receptacle of honour-based violence and it becomes the carrier of an entire discourse by no means exclusive to women.[201] [Emphasis added]

In conclusion, Yaqin feels that Aslam's "prose style is embedded with a liberalism characteristic of the British left in that it deliberately critiques a conservative Islamic consciousness to underline progressive secular principles and in doing so flattens the complexities of faith based [sic] identities."[202] While it is true that cases of honour killings have often been used as a trope in narratives of inadequacy for all immigrants or Muslims, Yaqin's resulting assessment of the novel's depiction of Islam as "uneven" is inept as long as it is based on a journalistic reading of the novel. The contents of *Maps for Lost Lovers* are enclosed in the code of literary genres like dramatic prose and magical realism and can therefore not be read and interpreted like an article in a magazine. In another article on the same novel, Yaqin writes:

> In the subsequent representations of Pakistan's political failure its lack of progress is often partly attributed to a deep-rooted cultural malaise that comes from a pre modern [sic] feudal society rejecting the call of modernity. Historically literary responses have offered a reflective counterpoint to such stereotypes. Diasporic writers such as Nadeem Aslam play an interesting role with Pakistan themed novels in English for consumption in a globalised [sic] world with their position as speaking subjects, whose narrative voice brings an authentic Pakistani perspective to the international stage with anthropologically styled narratives.[203]

Several passages from the novel – for example, "according to the statistics, in one Pakistani province alone, a woman is murdered every thirty-eight hours solely because her virtue is in doubt"[204] – clearly indicate that the novel's primary concern is "the depleted value system of Pakistani society at home and abroad."[205]

The statistics cited in that quote may or may not have been accurate, but it is true that discrimination and violence against women still prevail in Pakistan, especially in rural areas. Additionally, the Pakistani public tends to resist efforts of raising awareness about gender discrimination in Pakistan because

---

[201] Ibid., p. 104
[202] Ibid., p. 114
[203] Yaqin, '*Cosmopolitan Ventures During Times of Crisis*', p. 1
[204] Aslam, *Maps for Lost Lovers*, p. 136
[205] Yaqin, '*Cosmopolitan Ventures During Times of Crisis*', p. 1

they consider it negative publicity for the international media. This allergic reaction to such criticism is evident in the largely negative response of Pakistani media to the internationally celebrated Nobel Peace Prize laureate, Malala Yousafzai, and Academy Award winner, Sharmeen Obaid Chinoy. The more recent case of notorious social media celebrity, Qandeel Baloch, who was murdered by her own brother, also triggered largely defensive reactions in Pakistan, with very little empathy for the victim.

In another passage of the novel, the structural problem of honour killings in Pakistan is described:

> Chanda's brothers, when they confessed to the murders during the visit to Pakistan, had said: "It was a matter of honour." Everyone present had agreed. Such killings were not uncommon in Pakistan, but the killers usually killed openly and were proud of their deed. Some even presented themselves to the police afterwards and said they had done what needed to be done and were now ready for whatever punishment the law of the land thought they deserved. The law of Pakistan was almost always lenient with them and they were out of jail much sooner than those who had committed other kinds of murder. And in their streets and neighbourhoods, their act gave them a certain nobility in the eyes of those around them. Chanda's brothers, on the other hand, had insisted they hadn't killed her and her lover. They knew the law of this country would not view their crime indulgently. They boasted of having killed her and Jugnu— *but only in Pakistan, where the laws and the religion and the customs reinforced their sense of having acted properly, legitimately, correctly.* The people who learned of their crime patted their backs and said they had fulfilled their obligation, that such sons were born only to men among men and women among women. *They said that he who committed the great dirty sin of sex outside marriage was nothing less than evil*[206]; it would not have surprised anyone if bats flew out of the gashes when such a person was stabbed and slain. The friends in Pakistan told them that they had acted wisely by not telling the truth to the English police:
>
> "They would never understand your reasons. The West is full of hypocrites, who kill our people with impunity and say it's all a matter of principle and justice, but when we do the same thing they say our definition of 'principle' and 'justice' is flawed." [Emphasis added] (pp. 347–348)

A discussion of the real problem of honour killings in Pakistan is not stereotyping, just because such crimes occur in some non-Muslim countries, too.

[206] The two statements in italics will not be discussed in more detail as they require a complex discussion of cultural, structural, religious and educational circumstances of Pakistan, which differ from those in Europe. These quotes from the novel demonstrate the dehumanization of women who claim the right of self-determination, especially in matters of sexuality or marriage. Honour crime in Pakistan is not always about premarital intercourse; girls are often killed for having married by their own choice. It is not possible to transfer the theories formulated about Muslim religiosity in Europe to Muslims in Pakistan.

Describing the novel as stereotypical means that Aslam wanted to imply that all Pakistanis or Muslims condone such crimes. One character of the novel, Shamas, does make such a claim at one point, but his voice is not identical with the author's. In my reading, Aslam offers an in-depth analysis of the dynamics around honour crimes, rather than creating stereotypes. The plot of the novel aptly unfolds all the layers that facilitate these particular acts of violence.

Yaqin notes that while Chanda's brothers had been very hostile towards their sister and her indifference to social and religious dogma, it is clear by the end of the novel that the murder was affect-based and unplanned: shortly before the murder, the younger of the two brothers named Chotta finds his lover Kiran in bed with someone else. In a drunken rage he fetches an old gun from home and sets out in the direction of Kiran's house but somehow finds himself walking to Chanda and Jugnu's instead. Chotta attacks Jugnu while Chanda is still in bed. Unable to shoot him, he hammers the butt of the gun on Jugnu's head in a fit of blind rage until he realizes he might have killed him. Chotta then frantically fetches his brother, Barra, to help him dispose of Jugnu's body. When they run into their sister, the elder brother inadvertently breaks her neck while trying to keep her from crying out loud. Both brothers were recovering from personal misfortunes that day and neither had planned the murder ahead of time. Their impulsive act seemed to "owe less to religious motivation than to personal grievances."[207] Even though they were anything but determined and resolute in committing the murder, they presented a different narrative to their peers afterwards: Chotta and Barra immediately fled to Pakistan, where they told their relatives that they killed their sister and her lover to restore their family's honour and that they were proud of it. Chanda's mother – who is rumoured to be losing her mind over the loss of her daughter – is informed by someone that her own husband had expressed gratitude and pride in his sons' actions. Having trouble believing that her husband could have meant that, Chanda's mother consoles herself in her interior monologue by blaming the social pressure for her husband's heartless statements about their daughter's death.

> [Chanda's mother] has not confronted [her husband] with [the rumour that he said he was proud of his sons' crime]. The neighbourhood is a place of Byzantine intrigue and emotional espionage, where when two people stop to talk on the street their tongues are like the two halves of a scissor coming together, cutting reputations and good names to shreds. And so it is possible that the bus driver had lied, that his wife had, and also that Chanda's father had actually said those

[207] Yaqin, '*Muslims as Multicultural Misfits in Nadeem Aslam's Maps for Lost Lovers*', p. 112

> words or something similar, helplessly, to save face in judgmental or belligerent company, implied these words with expressions or uttered them explicitly with the tongue, feeling himself encircled; 'Yes, yes, what had to be done was done. Now leave me in peace.'
>
> There are times in this life when a person must do or say things he doesn't want to. Human beings and chains, it is the oldest acquaintanceship in the world. (p. 176)

She seemed to have succeeded in giving herself momentary satisfaction by deflecting the blame for Chanda's fate away from herself onto social customs. Not once does she consider that the course of Chanda's tragedy began with the very life choices that they – Chanda's parents – had made for her: three forced marriages doomed to failure. The novel highlights the role that social norms play in honour crimes. The thoughts of some villagers on this subject complete the picture:

> '[The] white police are interested in us Pakistanis only when there is a chance to prove that we are savages who slaughter our sons and daughters, brothers and sisters.'
>
> '[...] I know Chanda's brothers are innocent because those who commit crimes of honour give themselves up proudly, their duty done. They never deny or skulk.'
>
> [...]
>
> 'And as for Chanda: What a shameless girl she was, sister-ji, so brazen. She not only had poor Jugnu killed by moving in with him, she also ruined the lives of her own poor brothers who had to kill them...' (pp. 41–42)

Social norms are enforced in the form of social consequences, like disgrace entailing a lack of access to connections, which are necessary for upward mobility. While no one speaks of the murder as a punishment for Chanda's transgression, the rhetoric of all those who defend the actions suggests it was an attempt at damage control of an impaired social status. Chanda's mother, who evidently does not believe the murder was anything to be proud of, seems to feel that the narrative about honour and pride had to be made up in order to get people to stop pestering them about the murder.

Meanwhile, the one character that represents Islam, Kaukab (who repeatedly reminds herself and others of the fact that she is the daughter of a Muslim cleric), does not condone the murder of the couple, yet she believes they were sinners (p.321). Kaukab is married to Jugnu's brother, Shamas. She had taken initiative to try and resolve the conflict between her religious values and the couple's desire to be together by confronting Chanda's third husband and demanding that he divorce her so that she could marry Jugnu. Kaukab tried to assuage her religious conscience by trying to align her brother-in-law's behaviour with her beliefs, but when Chanda's brothers are proven guilty, she remains unable to extract from her religion the principle and courage to condemn their actions.

Then there is an unnamed Pakistani Muslim woman that voices her contempt for the murderers, yet with a lack of empathy for the victims that mirrors the exclusivist attitude of the conservative society. A wealthy woman from Pakistan talks very loudly in Chanda's family's grocery store and is overheard by Mah-Jabin, who tells Kaukab all about it:

> '[The Pakistani lady] must've heard that somewhere around here two brothers had killed their sister [...]. She said, "People like that are ruining the name of Pakistan abroad." She was visiting from Pakistan, staying with her relatives in the suburbs who had brought her to our neighbourhood for amusement [...] to show her how the poor Pakistanis lived here in England, the factory workers, the bus drivers, the waiters. She couldn't hide her contempt for us. Apparently, she had been called a "darkie bitch" by a white man in the town center during her first week here and was resentful. She said, "The man who called me that name was filthy and stinking. And he would not have called me that name if it had not been for the people in this area, who have so demeaned Pakistan's image in foreign countries. Imagine! He thought he could insult me, I who live in a house in Islamabad the likes of which he'd never see in his life, I who speak better English than him, educated as I was at Cambridge, my sons studying at Harvard right now. And it's all the fault of you lot, you sister-murdering, nose-blowing, mosque-going, cousin-marrying, veil-wearing inbred imbeciles."
>
> Kaukab shakes her head in disappointment. 'We are driven out of our countries because of people like her, the rich and the powerful. We leave because we never have any food or dignity because of their selfish behaviour. And now they resent our being here too.' (pp. 311–312)

The lady from Pakistan was not evaluating the murder from a humane or reformist viewpoint. On the contrary, she was also being selfish in her judgement by making the murderers responsible for her being insulted by a random racist on the street. Evidently, she is not concerned with basic human rights but only with the social consequences she faces from the Western society of being stigmatized as part of an illiterate and backward community.

Aslam demonstrates in this novel how excuses about honour as a motive are spread in a desperate attempt to assuage the censure of a hostile and unforgiving society, by members who never learned to question their subjugation to the same. No one in Dasht-e-Tanhaii, including the murderers, claims that it is *right* to kill someone, but they seem to contend it is sometimes necessary. Those who live in complete surrender to the social norms accept social pressure as a compelling factor in this crime. It cannot be said that the murder itself was an attempt at damage control because it is foreseeable that the killing did not work to this effect: the people in the neighbourhood still continued to spread vicious gossip about Chanda long after her death. The fact is that the brothers committed this violent act against their sister when personal grievances caused the pent-up social pressures inside them to explode in blind rage. Many residents of the neighbourhood blame Chanda herself for her murder. They empathize with the murderers and understand the pressure and provocation they must have felt. Even the Pakistani lady who condemns her compatriots' crime fails to present a better image of Pakistanis in general for two reasons: firstly, the lady's annoyance at the murder is based on selfish reasons, which means she is not provoked by the violation of basic human rights but by the loss of her right to feel superior. Secondly, her speaking up against the injustice is clearly not motivated by a desire to make things better by changing the destructive worldview of the people she addresses. And even if we do give her the benefit of the doubt and assume that she was hoping to make people in the town reconsider their views on honour killing, her argument would have had little chance of achieving anything other than antagonizing and provoking them. The basis of her argument is that the old norms of Pakistani people are bad because they make them all appear unsophisticated in front of Westerners. Therefore, her appeal to them to abandon old norms and replace them with new ones will be offensive to them and is consequently self-defeating. The argument does not offer sufficient motivation to inspire a change of mind-set among conservative Pakistanis. It is very unlikely that they would reconsider their values only for the sake of being accepted by the presented image of a hostile and judgemental West, embodied by a racist on the street shouting insults at strangers.

In summary, *Maps for Lost Lovers* offers a discussion of the social complexities behind honour crimes, rather than stereotypes. In a conversation with Suraya, a woman whose husband has divorced her in a fit of rage, Shamas who is having a clandestine affair with her, ponders that in their society people are not taught "how to think" but only "what to think" (p. 225). Rather than blaming a certain nationality or religion, Aslam discusses other forces behind honour crimes. If the upbringing of members of an exclusivist society is not geared to yield individuality and intellectual autonomy, then they will completely and blindly subordinate themselves to social norms and values. They will not develop a functioning set of personal values which they can exercise independently.

There are several figures in the novel who do stereotype immigrants and Muslims by saying for instance that, "Pakistan is not just a wife-beating country, it's a wife-murdering one" (p. 226). Another figure feels that all Pakistani Muslims have the ability to kill their own kind after seeing her mother swinging a knife at her (p. 114), and these are just two examples out of many. Evidently, *Maps for Lost Lovers* presents a world where stereotyping and marginalization exists, which does not mean, that the author himself is doing the same by writing this novel. It simply means that Aslam believes stereotyping and marginalization of immigrants – in other words, narratives of distinctive identities – as well as problems within diasporic and ghettoized communities are well worth talking about.

Aslam's portrayal of Muslim life in the UK depicts the effects of narratives of disparity without reproducing them in its message. In my reading, *Maps for Lost Lovers* is a critique of NoDs and also offers an antidote against them, rather than promoting a disparity between Islam and the West.

NARRATIVES OF DISTINCTIVE IDENTITY IN *MAPS FOR LOST LOVERS*

Maps for Lost Lovers is Aslam's opus magnum, which apparently took him eleven years to complete. Yaqin's reproach that the novel's discussion of honour killings stereotypes Muslims and immigrants is based on a journalistic reading of it. She is disregarding the fact that this novel is a sophisticated work of fiction, enclosing its message in a range of genres and literary devices. It has many similarities to Gabriel García Márquez' *One Hundred Years of Solitude (Cien Años de Soledad,* 1967*)*, which is not a documentary on the history of Colombia but demonstrably a literary portrayal of it. *Maps for Lost Lovers* belongs to the genre of magical realism – a genre often associated with García Márquez. Aslam's fictional world builds on common narratives of distinctive identities, creating a story world in which people of different races, religions, ethnicities and even castes do not mingle. One of the major characters, a highly religious Muslim woman in her early sixties named Kaukab keeps count of her direct interactions with white people per year: "The 'thank you' [Kaukab] murmurs to the flower-deliveryman is her third exchange with a white person this year; there were five last year; none the year before, if she remembers correctly; three the year before that […].” (p. 69) Kaukab’s son, Charag, married a white woman named Stella, but they get divorced. They have a son, whose name is never mentioned, but even he does not represent a successful mingling of two different identities either because the people around him continue to dissect the two genetic identities within him: “[T]he little boy is ‘half Pakistani and half ... er ... er ... er ... human’ – or so a child on his English mother’s side is reported to have described him in baffled groping innocence.” (p. 10)

It is obvious that the immigrant families try to maintain a pure bloodline by marrying their children forcefully to their first cousins. Mingling among immigrants is not allowed either, as no Punjabi marries a Gujarati, no Pakistani marries a Bengali, and no Muslim marries a Sikh or a Hindu in this novel. Kaukab’s brother wanted to marry Kiran, a Sikh girl but they are separated by his parents and siblings who force him to marry a cousin and stay in Pakistan. Another couple of star-crossed lovers in *Maps for Lost Lovers* are simply referred to as the Muslim girl in love with the Hindu boy. She is also forced to marry her cousin, and when she refuses to comply with the expectations of the family, they order a Muslim cleric to perform a torturous act of exorcism on her to rid her of ‘demons’, killing her in the process. The Hindu boy manages to secretly place a letter in her grave and even that is dug up and extracted from the coffin, shortly after the burial.

It is very important, however, to note that the binary worldview is maintained by both sides in this story. And both sides occasionally use violence to enforce these boundaries. On Kaukab’s side, her inability to mingle reflects in her ignorance: “[Kaukab] didn't know how to deal with strangers: full of apprehension concerning the white race and uncomfortable with people of another Subcontinental religion or grouping. She had had no schooling beyond the age of eleven.” (p. 32) The same reluctance is found on the British side, which Shamas – Kaukab’s apostate husband – describes in a diachronic fashion:

> [B]ack in the 1950s when Shamas had arrived from Pakistan. [...] It was a time in England when the white attitude towards the dark-skinned foreigners was just beginning to go from *I don't want to see them or work next to them to I don't mind working next to them if I'm forced to, as long as I don't have to speak to them*, an attitude that would change again within the next ten years to *I don't mind them socializing in the same place as me if they must, as long as I don't have to live next to them*. By then it was the 1970s and because the immigrant families had to live somewhere and were moving in next door to the whites, there were calls for a ban on immigration and the repatriation of the immigrants who were already here.

> There were violent physical attacks. [...] Something died in the children during those years. (pp. 10–11)

On the one hand, we have immigrant families who do everything in their power to shield their progeny from being contaminated by any foreign influence or by a commingling of their genetic material with different races. On the other hand, there are the British people who also go to extreme and unreasonable lengths to segregate the races. For instance, at one point a dead pig's head is left outside the mosque of the town. The police never find the culprit, but the Muslim community suspects a link to an "English girl [who] had converted to Islam [the same month] and had been given shelter in the mosque because her family was hostile towards her decision to change her faith." (p. 57) One white woman is known to have burnt her Muslim husband's Quran (p. 61). Chanda's parents worry about their sons' safety in prison, because of the number of Black Death's in police custody (p. 127). And, most disturbingly, a human heart is found in the village (p. 87), and it turns out that a "young white man was responsible. It was his dead mother's and he stole it from the hospital just because he didn't want it to be transplanted into a black man's body." (p. 153) White people's racist attitudes also get in the way of love as in one case, which Kiran remembers from her school days:

> There was a white man I had gone to school with and had been terribly in love with as a girl. I was the only Asian in my school, and I used to wonder why no one had ever asked me out on a date. I approached that boy to see if he'd go out with me, but he said no. And when I asked him to explain, he said, "Well, you are a darkie!" The word "Paki" wasn't invented until the 1970s, otherwise he would have used that. When he said that to me, I suddenly realized, "Of course I am a darkie." And because I loved him I didn't want him to be called a darkie-lover, and decided to stay away from him. He said, "It's a pity you are a darkie, because if you were white you'd be really pretty." (p. 283)

These are only a few examples, which show that the interactions between people of different affiliations are almost never peaceful. This disproportionate amount of hate crimes and crimes against humanity in only one village in North England is a deliberate device used by the author to paint an especially gloomy backdrop for the heart-breaking love stories the novel comprises. The cold and gloomy village is set not set in a magical realm, but it does not play in the real world either. Instead, it reads more like someone's vivid dream where the real world is perceived but also contorted. The genre of magical realism depicts a world where the natural laws of physics or of logic can be rescinded boldly, yet carefully: even though the story world of *Maps for Lost Lovers* does not imply the existence of supernatural or metaphysical beings, it contains elements, which defy logic. For instance, one character Jugnu "painted radium dials in a clock factory one winter and it was there that a spillage had left his hands with the ability to glow in the dark, making them irresistible to moths." (p. 27) And the most picturesque idea of the author is the wild peacocks roaming around this fictional village in North England:

> A dozen-strong flock of peacocks had appeared in the neighbourhood a fortnight or so previously: they had escaped from the menagerie of a stately home on the other side of the lake […]. They roamed the streets, scratched the paintwork of the cars and attacked cats and sparrows. How three members of the flock had managed to enter Jugnu's house and how long they had been in there could not be determined. (pp. 59–60)

The peacocks occasionally appear out of nowhere, permeating the plot with their seemingly random appearances. They have a symbolic meaning which will be discussed in the final part of this chapter.

The village itself, in my reading, is not a synecdoche for immigrant communities in the UK, but rather a hyperbolic metaphor representing their dislocation from mainstream society. The segregation from the rest of the country is reflected in the fact that the town has an Urdu name: *Dasht-e-Tanhaii*. We never learn its original English name, but we are given a detailed description of how it was rechristened by its residents:

> As in Lahore, a road in this town is named after Goethe. There is a Park Street here as in Calcutta, a Malabar Hill as in Bombay, and a Naag Tolla Hill as in Dhaka. Because it was difficult to pronounce English names, the men who arrived in this town in the 1950s had re-christened everything they saw before them. They had come from across the Subcontinent, lived together ten to a room, and the name that one of them happened to give to a street or landmark was taken up by the others, regardless of where they themselves were from. But over the decades, as more and more people came, the various nationalities of the Subcontinent have changed the names according to the specific country they themselves are from – Indian, Pakistani, Bangladeshi, Sri Lankan. Only one name has been accepted by every group, remaining unchanged. It's the name of the town itself. *Dasht-e-Tanhaii.*
>
> The Wilderness of Solitude.
>
> The Desert of Loneliness. (p. 28–29)

Dasht-e-Tanhaii is taken from an Urdu poem titled *Yad* (Memory, 1952) by modernist Faiz Ahmad Faiz. *Maps for Lost Lovers* reproduces the nostalgia shared by many since the partition of India and Pakistan. In my reading, this seems very apt, as that moment in history brought about a whole set of narratives of distinctive identity between Muslims and Hindus (Pakistanis and Indians). The shared heritage and history was replaced by two new national identities. Faiz wrote several poems about the disappointed hopes for a progressive life in freedom that people had been given prior to the separation.[208] His poem *Yad* "has at its heart the theme of separation and union and is closely connected to the Sufi expression of an unrequited love and desired [sic] for union."[209]

Aslam's novel has one character serving as an allegory of the nostalgia after the separation of India and Pakistan: Chakor, Shamas' father, described only in absentia by his son. Shamas recounts how the separation had uprooted Chakor, who was a born Hindu. When he was a child, he lost his memory after an explosion and got lost from his sister. He ended up in a family in Pakistan and was raised as a Muslim. When Chakor's memory returned, he went through an intense identity crisis. He insisted on being cremated as per Hindu tradition after his death, a wish that his Muslim family, who struggled with his newfound origin, denied him. Chakor then committed suicide by setting himself on fire in the middle of the night. He had cut out his tongue to keep himself from screaming so as not to wake both his sons who were with him at the time. Shamas saw a crow pick up the tongue and eat it. Chakor's family still decided to bury his remains, but his corpse was dug out in protest by unidentified offenders three times. (pp. 84–85) Shamas himself is not a believer (p. 20), and therefore does not struggle with a choice between Hindu or Muslim beliefs. Yet his nostalgia mirrors the overall confusion that comes with the desire to dissect the Pakistani identity from its Indian roots in order to form a clearly distinctive nationality.

Dasht-e-Tanhaii is a village with very restricted channels of communication to the rest of the country. Even the town's letterbox was mistakenly placed at a height of several feet on its pole so that people had to place a ladder in front of it. Whenever one woman of the village wants to post a letter she has to wait for someone to pass by her house so she can ask that person to climb up the ladder for her. *Dasht-e-Tanhaii,* which seems cut off from the rest of England, is a place where people of different races, religions, and worldviews simply cannot mingle. Even if they try, they will be separated either by violence or by fate.

The segregation of races and religions is a hyperbolic representation of the disparity between people of different cultures. It is clearly not a representation of reality. Every conflict, every resentment and all narratives of distinctive identity are amplified and enclosed in known narratives and myths.

---

[208] Yaqin, '*Cosmopolitan Ventures During Times of Crisis*', pp. 6–10
[209] Ibid., p. 10

Maps for Lost Lovers comprises a world where people can either live in *Dasht-e-Tanhaii,* and follow the rules there, or in England, which means abandoning the rules of the immigrant communities. There is no neutral ground for coexistence where everyone can live by their choice. The individual characters are torn apart, as none of them seems capable of actually living by such a strict segregation of identities. Therefore, in *Maps for Lost Lovers* we find that the distinctive identities of Islam and the West respectively are manifested with actions rather than narratives as seen in *TRF* by Mohsin Hamid. This is partly because the genre that Aslam has chosen requires an amplified, dramatic representation of the disparity between Islam and the West, and partly because this story focuses more on narratives of Islam's inadequacy. Unlike TRF, Aslam's novel discusses Islam as a religion and not just as a marker of identity. This brings us to the kind of narratives of inadequacy which has not been discussed in the previous analyses: a theology-based disparagement of Islam.

NARRATIVES OF INADEQUACY IN ASLAM'S *MAPS FOR LOST LOVERS*

While these narratives of distinctive identity serve to set up the segregated backdrop of the plot, narratives of inadequacy are the starting point for the other two kinds of narratives, which complete the process of disparity and dehumanization of the other. Narratives of inadequacy merely associate negative attributes to a group by inductive generalization. In Aslam's novel, Islam's inadequacy – as well the West's inadequacy – is largely constructed through religious dogmas that are interpreted in an unflattering way. Aslam constructs a very specific version of Islam – other than Sufism – in the novel, by citing *hadiths*, some of which turn out to be from rather dubious sources. There is a vast discrepancy between the scientific reliability of religious knowledge and religious platitudes that are circulated among Muslims without question. I will demonstrate this discrepancy on a few examples from the novel.

A *hadith* is a saying by either the Prophet himself or sayings about the Prophet by his wives or companions. Sunni Muslims consider them the most important primary source of Islam after the Quran. This does not mean that anything called a *hadith* is considered to have full validity on its own. In fact, the study of this source has its own very complex scientific method. Ever since the first *hadith* collections were compiled in the third century of Islam, the scholars had a strict evaluating system in order to categorize them into different levels of authenticity. There are six standardized collections from that time by Bukhari, Muslim, and others, who were renowned experts in this study. Bukhari was considered the one with the strictest standards of authenticity that *hadiths* had to pass to be categorized as *sahih*. Only these were recorded in the *Sahih* Bukhari, which is largely considered the most important primary source after the Quran. However, the categorization of a *hadith* as *sahih* does not infer that it can be traced back to the Prophet with certainty; it only indicates that this *hadith* fulfilled Bukhari's standards for a *sahih* Hadith. Interestingly, there are also different levels of discrediting a *hadith*, because early scholars soon realized that fabricated *hadiths* were being circulated. During their assessments of *hadiths*, many of them turned out to be conclusively fabricated, and the scholars compiled these into so-called *hadith munkar*, or *hadith mawdu* collections (these two expressions are also classifications, given depending on how their falsehood was proven). The result of any scholar's research was never considered to be an absolute fact, but only one scientifically appropriate method of generating knowledge. The scholars were made responsible for the *hadiths* they compiled and the interpretations they offered for them, and not the Prophet or Islam itself. Thus, whenever a *hadith* is quoted by a religious scholar, for instance when giving a sermon, he mentions the source (*isnad*) which the historic *hadith* compilers, like Bukhari, quote for that *hadith.*

On the other hand, Aslam has demonstrated in his novel how *hadiths* are quoted and interpreted in everyday life by Muslims, usually based on hearsay: In *Maps for Lost Lovers*, the highly religious character Suraya remembers the following *hadith* (there is no mention of any source): "Mohammad – peace be upon him, peace be upon him – [...] said, 'He who touches the palm of a woman not legally belonging to him will have red-hot embers put in the palm of his hand on Judgement Day'." (p. 227) I looked it up and found that this *hadith* cannot be found in any collection. There is one *hadith* about touching the hands of women: The Prophet's wife Aisha reportedly said that while it was customary that people gave the Prophet their pledge of allegiance by touching his hand, the Prophet would not touch women's hands for it and accepted their pledges orally.[210] This is a translation of this *hadith* in the Sahih Bukhari and also in other collections and commentaries.

The *hadith* quoted by Suraya in the novel is not in the primary *hadith* collections, but I found it quoted in a Book titled *Why I Am Not a Muslim* by an

---

[210] *Sahih al-Bukhari*, Vol. 6, Book 60, Hadith 414

Islam-critic, well-known by his pen name Ibn Warraq. However, it remains unclear which *hadith* collection it is from since Ibn Warraq cites a French text by one Ghassan Ascha titled *The Inferior Status of Women in Islam* (*Du Status inférieur de la femme en Islam,* Paris 1989) as his source for this *hadith.* A search through the canon of primary *hadith* -sources reveals that several collections include the above-mentioned *hadith*, which says that the Prophet may have never touched a strange woman's hand. However, the version found in the novel and in Ibn Warraq's book, suggesting that the Prophet added anything along the lines of being burned in hell for it, cannot be found in any canonized *hadith* collection.

Ibn Warraq, who is not a theologian, interprets selected *hadith* offering neither a clarification on the standards by which he selected them nor a discussion on the *hadith's* classification (level of authenticity); nor any commentary by noted theologians. A theological endeavour would include a critical examination of the primary sources and not just an interpretation of them. Ibn Warraq's book offers an interpretation based on a line of reasoning which is evasive and incomplete in a way that it resembles a narrative of disparity. I will demonstrate this briefly on this example from Ibn Warraq's book.

In a chapter dedicated to proving women's inferior status in Islam, Ibn Warraq lists several *hadiths* in succession, including the one already discussed, as well as the following one: "Three things can interrupt prayers if they pass in front of someone praying: a black dog, a woman, and an ass." [211] In a procataleptic reflex, Ibn Warraq immediately adds:

> Liberal Muslims may wish to dismiss these hadiths as inauthentic but what will they say to the Koran which also says: 'Draw not near unto prayer when ye are drunken, till ye know that which ye utter, nor when ye are polluted, save when journeying on the road, till ye have bathed. And if ye be ill, or on a journey, or one of you cometh from the closet, or ye have touched a woman, and ye find not water, then go to high clean soil and rub your faces and your hands' (sura 4.43; see also sura 5,6 [sic]).[212]

Firstly, even though it is true that the *hadith* regarding prayers being interrupted is recorded in the canonized collections, Ibn Warraq fails to mention that the compilers have also recorded the controversy it caused in its day. The Prophet's wife Aisha had doubted this *hadith's* truthfulness, as reported in the following *sahih hadith*:

[211] Warraq, *Why I Am Not a Muslim,* p. 301

[212] Ibid.

> Narrated by 'Aisha: The things which annul the prayers were mentioned before me. They said, 'Prayer is annulled by a dog, a donkey and a woman (if they pass in front of the praying people).' I said, 'You have made us (i.e. women) dogs. I saw the Prophet (['peace be upon him' in Arabic]) praying while I used to lie in my bed between him and the *Qibla* [the direction of prayer]. Whenever I was in need of something, I would slip away, for I disliked to face him.'[213]

The scholars did not eliminate *hadith* if they were refuted, but recorded all of them, including the basis of refutation. All *hadiths* in circulation were collected by certain requirements and organized by standardized classifications. Some of the *sahih hadiths* from canonized collections have since been criticized and reclassified into different categories of unreliability or weakness.[214] All these scholarly endeavours are predicated on the awareness that neither the authenticity nor the falsehood of a *hadith*, nor its intended meaning can ever be fully proven or disproven. *Hadiths*, their commentaries, and classifications by scholars, their chains of transmission, as well as their refutations are all recorded and, therefore, must be included in a discussion about their interpretations.

Secondly, Ibn Warraq concedes that the above-quoted *hadith* is inauthentic. However, he glosses over this fact by disparaging it as being the opinion of "liberal Muslims", instead of scholars, and he offers a Quranic verse in support of his interpretation of the *hadith*. Also, the verse he quotes does not actually support the contents of the *hadith*, and is misinterpreted by Ibn Warraq: he fails to mention that the Arabic expression for "have touched a woman" used in this verse is translated by most scholars as "have cohabited with a woman"[215] Even though some scholars do take "touched a woman" literally, the majority does not. Ibn Warraq uses this verse to support the claim that "[i]n general Islam treats women as intellectually, morally, and physically inferior." It is noteworthy that he speaks in absolutes.

This analysis of a representation of a *hadith* shows that, unlike Aslam's novel, Ibn Warraq's text follows the pattern of many narratives of inadequacy about Islam, in that it comprises:

- One or more negative stereotypes about Islam presented as absolute facts based on an interpretation of randomly selected theological sources by means of non-theological methods. It is easy to attribute

---

[213] *Sahih al-Bukhari,* Vol. 1, Book 9, Hadith 490

[214] Sarikaya, '*Die Authentizität des al-Ğāmiʿ aṣ-ṣaḥīḥ: Eine Skizze der klassischen Ḥadīṯ Kritik an dem Ṣaḥīḥ von al-Buḫārī*', pp. 20–7

[215] Asad and Moustafa, *The Message of the Qur'ān,* 4:43; 5:6

certain failings to Islam with this approach, which might be called pseudo-theology.

- Procataleptic dismissals of potential counter-arguments, which indicates that Ibn Warraq is probably aware that the truth is more complex than his text suggests.
- A line of reasoning consisting of a string of half-truths as 'evidence' and rhetorical devices (e.g. a rhetorical question, like "But what will they say to the Koran which also says…") that can cover up omissions and logical fallacies.

We have seen a fraction of the way a theologian would have to go about such an endeavour, for which, like Ibn Warraq, I am not qualified. Therefore, I will not offer an alternative interpretation of the primary sources based on my comparatively cursory reading of selected *hadiths* and verses. But even theologians hardly ever conclusively stipulate what Islam "in general" does or does not say about, for instance, the ablution requirements after intercourse. Legitimate scholarship of Islamic theology is a scientific discipline, and as such, does not produce absolutes. The point of this discussion was to mark the discrepancy between theological and non-theological uses of *hadiths*, and the consequence of disregarding the difference.

On the one hand, Aslam's sources about the teachings of Islam seem undeserving. On the other hand, it is true that too often Muslims share beliefs based on unscientific interpretation of primary sources, like the ones mentioned in the novel. Not only do Islam-critics believe in a misogynistic and misanthropic version of Islam, but also many Muslims. Religious illiteracy accounts for many misconceptions about Islam among Muslims who blindly follow the interpretations of their clerics, some of which can be downright baseless. It is easy to circulate fabricated *hadiths* because in most cases neither the source nor the classification of their authenticity is quoted or checked. *Maps for Lost Lovers* has depicted Muslims whose beliefs are built on pseudo-theological interpretations as well as a blind-following of the same. As Suraya reminds herself: "Allah's law is Allah's law and cannot be questioned." (p. 160)

When critics of Islam use pseudo-theological evidence to prove Islam's faults, apologetics can easily counter these attacks by offering their own interpretation of sources, thus diverting the fault from Islam. So, on the one hand, we have narratives of Islam's inadequacy by Islam-critics, who work with blurring the lines between theology and pseudo-theology. On the other hand, we have counter-narratives by defensive Muslims – so-called 'apologetics' (the term will be discussed in the next chapter) – who blur the lines between religion and religiosity. Exonerating Islam from these allegations has little chance of solving a problem like forced marriages: regardless of the question whether it can be conclusively linked to the teachings of Islam or not, the focus of discussions should be how to make conservative parents understand that they must accept their adult children's choices, even if they disagree with them. Aslam's novel does not offer absolute facts about Islam or the West because it is offering a deliberately exaggerated reflection of reality by zooming in on the extremes on both sides.

Narratives of inadequacy go further than to infer just an incompatibility of Islam and the West. They are formed to conclusively link selected failings to one of these identities, rendering the other undeserving of the right to be accepted as an equal partner for social interactions. While Ibn Warraq's text is an example of narratives of Islam's inadequacy, the novel offers examples of the narratives of inadequacy constructed by exclusivist Muslims about the West. These are structured differently, even though they are also partly based on pseudo-theology, as well as hypocrisy.

Shamas is perhaps the most obvious hypocrite in reproducing narratives of Islam's inadequacy in an attempt to convince himself and others of the fact that he is completely westernized. In general, Shamas is very concerned about what the British people think of him. Kaukab notices this on several occasions. For instance, when Shamas has to take Kaukab to the doctor, who points out that it was Kaukab's birthday that day. "Shamas didn't know it was Kaukab's birthday and Kaukab assumes that the only response of Shamas is probably embarrassment in front of the doctor, rather than feeling badly about forgetting it for Kaukab's sake." (p. 65) In another example, Shamas refuses to help Suraya by marrying her temporarily so she can remarry her husband and return to him and her son in Pakistan because he believes Pakistan is a bad place for women. But when Suraya asks him why he let his daughter marry someone in Pakistan and move there, Shamas has no answer but to say: "It's complicated ... She wanted to go ..." (p. 229) His other reason for refusing to marry Suraya is "principle": "I won't marry you on principle: one of the things I find repulsive about Islam is the idea of a man being allowed four wives." (p. 226) Even though Shamas is married to Kaukab, he could marry Suraya under Islamic law to help her out. Therefore, even though Shamas is already having an affair with Suraya, he refuses to marry her because he does not wish to support a concept that he considers Islam's inadequacy. It is hypocritical of Shamas to be denouncing the concept of polygamy and judging Suraya for asking to be his second wife (albeit temporarily) while, at the same time, indulging in adultery with her. He knows that she is having this affair, because she is secretly counting on his help, and Shamas, takes advantage of her desperate situation.

He does not inform her right away that he will not marry her but continues the affair until she asks for his help, which he refuses.

One example of hypocrisy in narratives of inadequacy vis-à-vis the West is a quote from Chanda's father who remarks upon seeing Shamas on a bus with Suraya:

> "[Shamas and Jugnu] can do what they like with white women – we all know the morals they have – but at least leave our own women alone. You would think it was their mission to corrupt every Pakistani woman they come across." And he adds decisively, "In my opinion, they are still infected with their father's Hinduism. Lord Krishna and his thousand girlfriends, indeed! And they jeer at our Prophet, peace be upon him, for having just nine wives!" (p. 177)

"They can do what they like with white women" means that different the codes of morality apply towards women belonging to the 'in-group' and women of the 'out-group'. In other words, while Pakistani men do not have to observe the rules of decency with western women, Pakistani women must be left alone entirely. According to this statement, Chanda's father considers Shamas and Jugnu to be 'inadequate' (used in the sense of narratives of inadequacy) because they do follow the proper custom of leaving Pakistani women alone, and also because their identity is not purely Muslim or Pakistani. And Chanda's father also refers to Hinduism as being 'inadequate' because Lord Krishna cavorted with too many women, even though the Prophet Muhammad also lived in polygamy.

Kaukab represents a conservative anti-Western Islam in *Maps for Lost Lovers*. She is not only convinced that Islam and the West are incompatible, but Kaukab feels genuine contempt for everything Western. She has convinced herself that no good can come from the West, and thus she takes great care to keep the two cultures apart. She believes the "decadent and corrupt West" was responsible for Chanda and Jugnu's transgression because it "had made them forget piety and restraint". (p. 63) Kaukab blames her husband for her predicament because they moved to England at his behest.

Since both sides in the novel are dedicated to maintaining the disparity between Islam and the West, one discussion that occurred in Shamas' house seven years prior to the events of the novel shows the efforts of representatives of both parties to convince themselves of the inadequacy of the 'other': Jugnu and Shamas represent the westernized anti-Islamic parties while Kaukab represents Islamic values. Kaukab recollects this discussion on a night they had invited Jugnu and a white girlfriend of his over for dinner. That evening they happened to have an electricity blackout. Jugnu and Shamas talked about the poor capacities of religious belief to explain the universe as compared to those of science. They cited electricity as a tangible or visible accomplishment of science. Jugnu concludes, "I cannot be expected to believe what an illiterate merchant-turned-opportunistic-preacher – for he was no systematic theologian – in seventh-century Arabian dessert had to say about the origin of life." Interestingly, Jugnu's white girlfriend, who was also present, did not take part in these narratives of inadequacy at all. On the contrary, she (unnamed) argued that science has also produced only fractions of explanations, some of which have been proven to be false. Kaukab's reaction to what she considers a contamination of her home with western influence is extremely dramatic. She did not even realize that she had hit herself because of their discussion that night until she saw herself in a mirror and found her face and eyes swollen and her hair messed up. However, she took care not to let her family see the result of her private outburst. Kaukab was filled with abhorrence at hearing Jugnu's comments about the Prophet but did not reply out loud. In her mind, however, she refuted their narrative by constructing an equally demeaning counter-narrative: "Praising things like electricity: the very thing that's failed this evening, she had fumed inwardly, making you all sit in darkness!" (pp. 38–39)

Other theology-based narratives of inadequacy about the West in Kaukab's mind are largely founded on the idea that people of the West do not fear God. Other inadequacies of "white people" in her eyes include their alleged lack of cleanliness. Since most Muslims believe that Islam requires people to cleanse themselves after any form of excretion and to bathe after intercourse, Kaukab imagines with disgust that non-Muslims do not. This is why she was reluctant to even touch her own daughter-in-law, Stella. Kaukab's resistance to such "contaminations" of her Pakistani Muslim home mostly manifests itself in physical responses like disgust or nausea – possibly because she is unable to engage in a discussion. She nearly fainted when Jugnu made the above-quoted statement, and other times she responds with clandestine actions to set things right, like confronting Chanda's third husband and asking him to divorce her. Furthermore, while trying to purify her children from influences of the West, she took measures that ended up hurting them and ultimately driving them away. Her treatment of her children in this regard is based on a combination of narratives of inadequacy and narratives of mutual distrust, and these are necessary for her to justify her actions. This will be discussed in the upcoming section.

NARRATIVES OF MUTUAL DISTRUST IN ASLAM'S *MAPS FOR LOST LOVERS*

Narratives of mutual distrust seek to demonstrate that Islam and the West, respectively, have the intention and the means to inflict harm on each other. These narratives link one or the other of these identities to feelings of distrust using different stimuli as triggers. Something random like a headscarf or a certain haircut can be defined as a symbol of a misogynistic Islam or violent racism. They can trigger enough distrust to make people demand legal measures against items of apparel that they consider a symbol of their fears. These narratives give a basis to irrational fear, thereby making it seem like a rational concern. One example from the novel is Chanda's brothers distrusting a taxi driver they knew just because he was a Bangladeshi[216]:

> Although they were given the information casually and in passing, they had both wondered whether there was a malicious intent: this was a taxi firm run by Bangladeshis, and they were a treacherous and wicked people, having broken away from Pakistan to found their own country, the treachery and betrayal of their race going back even further to the time in the eighteenth century when, just before the battle of Plassey, Mir Jafar, the commander-in-chief of Saraj-ud-daullah, had signed a secret pact with the Englishman Robert Clive, and ensured him a victory over the good Siraj, a victory that marked the beginning of the British Raj in India and the beginning of the end of the Muslim rule. (p. 349)

In other words, the reason to distrust Bangladeshis is the fact that they share a heritage with a man, who made a deal with the British over four centuries ago. The hypocrisy in this matter is that the two brothers do not resent the British for the history of their oppressive rule. This might be because they have chosen to live in Britain and are benefitting from the services the country provides. Their remarkable knowledge of the history of Bangladeshis offers reasons to deflect their hatred to another 'out-group'. Interestingly though, they do not remember the history of the devastating consequences of this hatred for Bengalis.

In general, historical narratives play a great role in this novel, not only as a basis in NoDs between ethnicities or nationalities, but also in the NoDs between Islam and the West. While most of the narratives of mutual distrust are

---

[216] The word Bangladeshi refers to people from Bangladesh, a country that used to be part of India and then of Pakistan until it gained independence in 1971. Bengali is an ethnicity and Bangladeshi is a national identity.

derivatives of narratives of inadequacy, others are based on the classic scapegoat principle of deflecting all blame on one party. While all narratives of disparity together justify efforts at maintaining the disparity and segregation between Islam and the West, narratives of mutual distrust justify the escalation of the efforts of segregation into violent enforcement, because they deactivate feelings of empathy for members of the 'out-group' and suggest that there is real threat. Neither Kaukab nor Chanda's parents seem to empathize with Chanda. Many even blame her for her brothers' horrendous crime against her. A lack of empathy is so unnatural that it is often viewed as a symptom of mental illness, which is well-represented in the fictional world of *Maps for Lost Lovers*. Shamas is shocked "by the desperation of most people's lives here, family life frequently reduced to nothing more than legalized brutality. He counted nineteen mentally ill people in his own street [...]." (p. 210)

Kaukab's capacity to harm her own children is far from normal behaviour: when her son was just a new-born baby she deliberately kept him hungry during Ramadan. Since Ujala was born without a foreskin, Kaukab was convinced that he was destined to live in piety even as a baby. So, she forced him to fast and – without a shred of doubt that she was doing the right thing – listened to her own baby crying for hours. Kaukab probably never doubts her decisions because she always finds someone else to blame. When her oldest son, Charag, informs her that he has had a vasectomy, she blames everyone in a chain:

> [Kaukab] could find no one other than the old culprits for this new disaster [=Charag's vasectomy] that had befallen her. Shamas. Jugnu. England. The white race. The vasectomy was a Christian conspiracy to stop the number of Muslims from increasing. Her parents were responsible for marrying her to an infidel. Her in-laws were Godless. ... (pp. 58–59)

This interior monologue not only reveals her paranoia and distrust against the West, but its magnitude reveals delusions of persecution, bordering on an egomaniacal worldview: she literally believes the whole world has conspired against her. Kaukab tries so hard to shield her children from the West that she ends up inflicting harm on them because she is using considerable force in her fight against an illusion. It has turned her own children against her. The youngest, Ujala, left home as a teenager and did not return until eight years later. He is so convinced that his mother is responsible for Chanda and Jugnu's deaths, that he told a police officer and a reporter that,

> it was all the fault of his cunt of a mother who had decided not to speak to Jugnu because he was offending her religion and that his fucking spineless father must've just gone along with what she said because she was a poor immigrant woman in a hostile white environment who deserved everyone's compassion,

> what with her sons and daughter away, leading their own lives, and to cap it all she was also going through the menopause. (p. 72)

Ujala puts words into his mother's mouth, claiming she believes they were "dirty unclean sinners" (p 323). Ujala's reason to be this distrustful towards his mother is the same reason he had decided to leave home a few years prior to the plot: during his pubescent phase, Kaukab got so annoyed by his rebellion and disobedience that she asked a cleric for a remedy. The cleric gave her something he called "magic salt," which she secretly mixed into his food. Kaukab did not realize that Ujala had found out about the "magic salt" and decided to have it checked. When Ujala learned that it was bromide that his mother had been putting in his food, he simply left without confronting her and did not return until many years later. He may not have been aware that Kaukab genuinely believed it to be nothing but "magic salt". The eldest son, Charag, was forced by Kaukab to repeat his final year of A-levels to qualify for medical school. When she found out that he wanted to be an artist, she suspected another conspiracy of the British to keep immigrants from succeeding. And Mah-Jabin as a teen was refused a visit to the gynaecologist when needed. These are only very few examples that caused all of Kaukab's children to distrust her.

Distrust of the West is the reason why the people of Dasht-e-Tanhaii marry their children off to their cousins in Pakistan. Mah-Jabin's first love interest was married like this before he went to college. His parents were afraid they could not protect him anymore once he was out of the house, so they married him off before he could 'be contaminated' in college. Heartbroken Mah-Jabin then agreed to marry her first cousin, as well. Ironically, all the failed marriages of young girls and boys in Dasht-e-Tanhaii do not cause other parents to question or distrust this method of marrying their children. Narratives of distrust are not based on experience but only on prejudice based on racial, religious or national affiliations. Mah-Jabin argues with her mother about her failed marriage and asks Kaukab why she did not protect her from making a mistake. Kaukab insists that it was a good idea to marry Mah-Jabin to her cousin, and uses Suraya as an example of a successful arranged marriage (p. 114). Even though Suraya's husband divorced her in a fit of drunken rage and was now keeping her son away from her in order to force her to find a temporary husband, so she could remarry her first husband afterwards. Therefore, Suraya's case is not an apt example for a successful arranged marriage. Furthermore, Kaukab is completely ignoring other examples where this method clearly failed, like in Chanda's case or in that of the unnamed Muslim girl who loves the unnamed Hindu boy.

It was stipulated earlier that Aslam is not stereotyping Muslims as murderers, just as he is not stereotyping the British as racists. In an interview about *Maps for Lost Lovers*, Aslam made clear, that his novel "has no message". He explains "that each shocking incident in the book is based on a true case. There's even abuse by a paedophile [sic] cleric [in the novel], which [really] happened, he says, in a Midlands town. 'The guys from the mosque pulled a gun on the family that was going to the police.'"[217] Even though the novel itself plays in the year 1997, Aslam has made clear that it still comprises a response to the 9/11 events:

> "In a way, the book is about September 11," says Aslam. On visiting Ground Zero, he felt disappointed and angry. "I asked myself whether in my personal life and as a writer I had been rigorous enough to condemn the small scale [sic] September 11s that go on every day." He adds that "Jugnu and Chanda are the September 11 of this book".
>
> Aslam explains further: "Most ordinary Muslims say, 'We just want to get on with our lives. Don't identify us with the fundamentalists.' But it's a luxury. We moderate Muslims have to stand up. As a child I was really frightened of the game Hangman. I was terrified that my not knowing the answer was going to get somebody killed. As a grown-up, I feel that a game of Hangman is being played on an enormous scale in the world, and that sooner or later I'm going to be asked certain questions, and if I don't give the right answer somebody is going to get hurt. [...] America is the sole superpower and as such it must be kept an eye on. But Islam is a great religion which means it, too, is open to abuse."[218]

Earlier in the same interview, Aslam described himself as a "non-believer", but in the above-quoted passage he refers to himself as "we moderate Muslims". Obviously, he continues to identify himself culturally as a Muslim. In my reading, Aslam is trying to shake up the conscience of Muslims all over the world, though he does not specify what exactly he believes they must or should do. His novel is no active appeal or "message" to Muslims, but it is a passive attempt to confront them with the problems existing in Muslim communities, including the accompanying spiral of silence, which Aslam reports to have witnessed himself. He calls the honour crime of the novel a 9/11 of everyday life. The 9/11-attacks were the actions of self-proclaimed Muslims, who acted in the name of their perverted version of Islam. These attacks had started many narratives of mutual distrust between Islam and the West, and Aslam believes moderate Muslims must take responsibility to protect their re-

---

[217] Brace, '*Nadeem Aslam: A Question of Honour*'
[218] Ibid.

ligion from such abuse. The 9/11-attacks, like honour killings, are used as conclusive proof of the destructive capacity of Islam by the West. Many Muslims then responded to these with counter-narratives that essentially diverted the responsibility to colonialists, imperialists, Islamists or sometimes to illusive Islamophobes. In my reading, Aslam wrote a novel about the 9/11s of everyday life because he wants Muslims to concede that – like the 9/11 attacks – honour crimes are often committed by people affiliated to Islam and it is the responsibility of Muslim communities to teach a better understanding of Islam not just to non-Muslims and Islam critics, but also to Muslims themselves. This task is made difficult by one thing – among many – which is not just depicted but amplified in this novel: the averseness of some Muslims to take criticism due to narratives of superiority.

NARRATIVES OF SUPERIORITY IN ASLAM'S *MAPS FOR LOST LOVERS*

Narratives of superiority are not just a last resort for those incapable of finding arguments. On the contrary, these narratives give the illusion that such claims of superiority are justified. In Hamid's novel, *The Reluctant Fundamentalist*, the narratives of superiority were made attractive to young romantics in order to inspire a willingness to sacrifice themselves for the interests of the 'in-group'. At this point, the difference between literature from the pre-9/11 era and the post-9/11 decade becomes visible: before 9/11 young Muslim characters in novels always attempted to become westernized, and be part of the Western narrative of superiority. After 9/11 Islam offered narratives of superiority to attract the young generation. *Maps for Lost Lovers* was written in the 90s and published in 2004. It unveils the outdated narratives the older generation had imported to the West in the form of religious and cultural dogma. Some of these narratives of superiority are still being circulated, and they are much more convincing to youngsters today than they were before the paradigm-shifting attacks of 11 September 2001.

Narratives of superiority invoke incontestable entities or ideals. The local cleric is shown to invoke either God or the Prophet so that no one will dare to disagree with him. By suggesting that the Prophet himself appeared in his dream, he convinces the people of the mosque that the president of the United

States will convert to Islam on his calling. The cleric writes a letter to the president but dies before he receives the polite decline. The villagers then vow not to disclose his dream to the rest of the village because it would prove the Prophet wrong; something they all consider blasphemy. Blasphemy is a very common trope in religious narratives of superiority: almost anything, any person, any creed, any commandment can be declared sacred and then the crime of blasphemy can act as a protective shield around it. It does not occur to the people of the mosque that it could also mean that the cleric had been lying.

Kaukab invokes superiority in matters of piety over everyone else because she is the daughter of a cleric – even though, she often blames her parents for marrying her to Shamas who turned out to be a Hindu after their marriage. Also, Kaukab explains the Islamic dress code to her daughter by invoking the principle of modesty (p. 95), even though Kaukab herself is the most overbearing character in the novel. In comparison, Chanda's brother, Chotta, explained the difference between his sin and his sister's sin by calling her an apostate:

> Some people in the Muslim community were aware of the clandestine love-affair and hoped that Chotta would do the right thing and ask Kiran to convert to Islam and marry her. They—and Chotta himself—saw nothing in common between his secret nights with a woman he was not married to and Chanda setting up home with Jugnu. "I am a sinner," Chotta had said in the past, regarding his fondness for alcohol, "but I am not an apostate. I know I am sinning. That's the difference." (p. 346)

This is a distinction without a difference because apostasy is also considered a sin. And if Chotta's fondness for alcohol and a Sikh woman he is not married to makes him a sinner, then his judging of Chanda and Jugnu makes him a hypocrite. In comparison, Kaukab's lack of self-awareness, her egomania, and authoritarianism indicate that her behaviour goes further than hypocrisy towards pathological narcissism. When things do not go her way, she either faints or reacts with aggression:

> The hard, open palm of Kaukab's hand lunges at Mah-Jabin and in striking her face takes away her breath. This is something Kaukab has longed to do whenever she has thought about the girl in her absence and really isn't a response to what she has just said: she simply happened to be within reach as the need overtook Kaukab and the moment chose itself. The force of the impact knocks Mah-Jabin off the chair, while Kaukab's rosary—looped double at the back of the chair—snaps and the beads clatter to the floor. Kaukab's hand alights and grips the girl's soggy gritty hair like a claw and slams the head many times against the wall with all her strength, the red stain of henna growing richer and larger on the wall, Mah-Jabin crooking her elbow against the side of the head until Kaukab finally lets go and moves to the sink at the other side of the kitchen [...] her back turned towards the girl. (p.112)

Her three children are reluctant to visit their parents because they find it difficult to talk to Kaukab. They all remain traumatized by their young adulthood when they could never be honest with their parents. Kaukab's intellectual restrictions render her unable to defend her views or argue against differing views of others. She is used to invoking her authority as a parent rather than engaging in a discussion. When Mah-Jabin tries to correct one of the neighbours "Kaukab—breath pulled in in disapproval—gives Mah-Jabin a look of reproof for interrupting and trying to enlighten a grown-up." (p. 107) When scientific knowledge of religion was lacking in the older generation, it became difficult for the younger generation to communicate with them. Combined with a pathological superiority complex, this religious illiteracy rendered the generation-gap almost insurmountable. When all efforts for improvement or amendments are blocked out, there is no hope for betterment. Mah-Jabin becomes aware of this vicious cycle when she remembers something after being slapped by her mother: Kaukab used to share her regrets with Mah-Jabin about the things she was refused in her childhood, like education or learning to ride a bicycle. She then asks why Kaukab did not try to do better for her own children:

> You [Kaukab] must be a moral cripple if you think what you did to me [Mah-Jabin] wasn't wrong. Didn't you once tell me that a woman's life is hard because you have to run the house during the day and listen to your husband's demands in bed at night? So why didn't you make sure I avoided such a life? Answer me ... Answer me ... Why do you people keep doing the same things over and over again expecting a different result? [...]
>
> What was it you said to me once, Mother, that the first two decades of marriage belong to the husband, the rest to the wife because she can turn her children against the husband while she's bringing them up, so when they are grown up they'll make him eat dirt while she reigns over them all for the rest of her days. [...]
>
> How fucking wise you are, Mother, such wisdom! Victory awaits all the beleaguered Pakistani women but what a price, Mother, two decades of your life wasted ... What a waste when instead of conniving for all these years you could just walk away... (pp. 113–114)

Kaukab responds by calling Mah-Jabin a "bitch" and swinging a knife at her, claiming afterwards that she did not realize that she had still been holding it. Kaukab firmly believes that parents have a right to hurt their children, as she explains to her son Charag: "Parents are *supposed* to hit children, disciplining them. The Prophet, peace be upon him, said that when you send a camel out to graze, make sure one of its legs is doubled up and tied securely with a rope, so it can't wander too far. Too much freedom isn't good for anyone or anything." (p. 58) The interpretation of this *hadith* is also usually a very different one, but even without a theological discussion it is obvious that it does not say anything about hitting children. Kaukab's understanding of up-bringing was very simple: she expected everyone to behave as she imagined and she either invoked religion or used violence to enforce it. Mah-Jabin's ex-husband uses the same narrative in the letter he sent her, which Kaukab finds by the end of the novel: he reminds Mah-Jabin of the pain she felt when he tortured her and then warns her about the tortures of hell that await all non-believers. At one point in the novel, the Pakistani expression "Earthly God" for husband was used, which gives men the authority to treat women in any way that they see fit. All these narratives seem to claim superiority of parents over children or husband over wife. The fact is, that the roles are not carved in stone: these narratives claim superiority for whoever is superior in matters of religion. Dogmatic religious views serve to satisfy the ego with feelings of superiority rather than serving as an inspiration for a struggle to become a better person.

Ujala questions his mother for reading a Muslim women's magazine from Pakistan but Mah-Jabin tries to defend her mother:

> 'It doesn't do any harm,' Mah-Jabin whispers: she had seen the distaste on his face when he picked up the magazine full of orthodox rants and strictures, apocalyptic visions and prophecies.
>
> 'I think it does.'
>
> She looks away. 'It makes her happy.'
>
> 'I don't think it does. I have never seen more misery and guilt on her face than when she has just finished reading something printed in there. It's turned her into a selfish monster. *She* is the reason why father won't openly condemn the idiocies of Islam. He thought it would hurt her. She and her like don't do any harm? She has harmed every one of us. She won't allow reason to enter this house.' Mah-Jabin leaves the room and he stands looking at the verses on the wall. For millions of people, religion was often another torture in addition to the fact that their lives were not what they should be. (pp. 301–302)

Kaukab's ideas of religion were so restrictive that they were painful to her, too. She learned that religion must be painful, otherwise it is not the right kind. This is why Kaukab inflicted pain on her own children with such ease. The diasporic experience made her delusional about life in Pakistan, which she had not seen first-hand for decades. Kaukab fantasizes that a visit to Pakistan could have instilled the old values into Jugnu and Chanda:

> The decadent and corrupt West had made [Chanda and Jugnu] forget piety and restraint, but the countless examples in Pakistan had brought home to them the

> importance and beauty of a life decorously lived according to His rules and injunctions, Pakistan being a country of the pious and devout, a place where boundaries are respected. (p. 63)

This narrative of Pakistan's superiority is as common as it is illogical: if all people in Pakistan respect boundaries, as Kaukab imagines, then the phenomenon of honour crime would not exist there at all. If all social boundaries would always be respected in Pakistan, then there would be no need for honour crimes. The fact is, that these boundaries are abstract and arbitrary. And according to Kaukab's own idea of religion, the boundaries had to be painful, in order to lead to a happy life – or at least the kind of happiness that a feeling of superiority over every other mortal can bestow. When Kaukab learns the truth about the salt she gave to Ujala, and the pain Mah-Jabin endured in her marriage, she finds herself confronted with the fact that her religious values did not act out the way she had wanted or expected. Kaukab then attempts to commit suicide because she is unable and unwilling to accept that her religious efforts were all in vain.

After having addressed the concerns of those with religious sensitivities, the counter-example of the upcoming novel will show the secular sensitivities about Islam. While *Maps for Lost Lovers* was reproached for being overly critical of Islam, *Minaret* has been criticized for being too favourable about it. The NoDs in this last novel will not be described in the same detailed manner as in the previous examples. Instead, this upcoming analysis will serve to complement the previous discussions around literary depictions of the segregation of Islam and the West.

MINARET (2005) BY LEILA ABOULELA

AN ALTERNATIVE READING OF ABOULELA'S *MINARET*

Minaret by Leila Aboulela is the story of how the protagonist, Najwa, finds solace and hope in a religious community after suddenly finding herself all alone in a foreign country. Najwa fled to London from Sudan with her mother and twin brother, Omar, after her father's government was taken over by a communist group. Shortly thereafter Najwa's father was executed and the family could not go back to Sudan anymore. Having been raised in luxury, the twin siblings – at that time only nineteen years old – struggle to come to terms with the trauma of their loss; in the almost immediate aftermath, both fail to qualify for university. Within the five years after their father's execution, their financial means continue to deteriorate, especially when their mother is diagnosed with leukaemia and requires special treatment. Already deprived of their accustomed standard of living, because the new regime seizes many of their assets, Omar's drug addiction – which had started in Sudan – leads him to sell their remaining valuables and attack his sick mother when she confronts him. By the time the twins are in their mid-twenties, their mother is deceased, and Omar is imprisoned for 15 years, leaving Najwa to care for herself with no qualification, ambition or guidance.

Like *The Reluctant Fundamentalist,* the plot of *Minaret* unfolds in different time periods of the protagonist's life: the framing plot which opens and closes the novel unfolds between 2003 and 2004 in London. At this point, Najwa and her twin brother are in their late thirties. The plot is intermeshed with the chronological narration of two different time periods from their past: one subplot begins in Sudan in 1984 when she and her brother were 19-year-old students of Economics at Khartoum University. This plot ends a year later in London – where the twins and their mother fled to after their father was overthrown and imprisoned – when the exiled family learns that Najwa's father has been executed in Sudan. The interruptions of the framing plot sequence continue with another sub-plot which is set in the years from 1989 to 1991 when the twins were in their mid-twenties. The years in-between these three sequences are omitted (from 1986 to 1988 and from 1992 to 2002).

The story is delivered from Najwa's perspective through homodiegetic narration, but unlike *TRF*, *Minaret* does not comprise a narrating situation or a narratee, and – most noticeably – there is no self-conscious process of narration. She can only offer peripheral comments on her past like in the following sentence: "[Doctora Zeinab] must be no more than ten years older than me – even though I feel she is older. If I feel young, it is because I have done so little. What happened stunted me."[219] Doctora Zeinab is the mother of Lamya and Tamer. Lamya is doing her Ph.D. whilst raising her a two-year-old daughter alone because her husband lives abroad. Lamya meets Najwa at the local mosque and hires her as a maid. Najwa does not elaborate on the above-quoted sentence or contemplate it any further. She knows that the sudden loss of her home and the subsequent loss of her entire family and friends stunted her which is why she ended up becoming a maid, but she has obviously never mentally processed her experiences in order to grasp and overcome her feelings of loss and abandonment, and thus continues to feel that way more than a decade later, as evidenced in the following passage where she is comparing her life to that of Lamya's friend whom she observes at a gathering in her house:

> "I am touched by her life, how it moves forward, pulses and springs. There is no fragmentation, nothing stunted or wedged. I circle back, I regress; the past doesn't let go. It might as well be a malfunction, a scene repeating itself, a scratched vinyl record, a stutter." (p. 216)

She does not feel older because she never matured emotionally or mentally. The fragmented narration of the plot, which reflects the halts in Najwa's development and her resulting inability to contemplate over her life choices from a position of moral or intellectual high ground over her past selves, are crucial in this analysis.

This literary analysis is a critical discussion of other readings of the novel *Minaret*. Sadia Abbas classifies *Minaret* as an apologetic religious novel. Lindsey Moore's and Eva Hunter's reproaches to Aboulela include that *Minaret* is not feminist enough; not progressive enough; not kind enough to the West; not critical enough of Islam and that it is neither Western nor modernist enough. Moore classifies it as a spiritual *Bildungsroman* because in its plot "love is eventually subordinated to personal transformation" toward a pious self.[220]

---

[219] Aboulela, *Minaret,* p. 71
[220] Moore, '*Voyages Out and In*', p. 76

The assigned genre of a novel directs its interpretation. In my reading, the above-mentioned interpretations, which are focused on the absence of specified content based on Moore's and Abbas' expectations from the generic frameworks they determined, fail to do justice to the many layers of meaning which *Minaret* contains. The intention of my alternative interpretation of the same novel is not to question the validity of other scholars' readings of the novel, but to pinpoint where their interpretations seem biased by NoDs between Islam and the West. This does not mean, however, that the novel itself is innocent of reproducing or building on NoDs on its part. This will become obvious in this chapter.

In my view, Moore's, Abbas' and Hunter's interpretations are based on the following two projections into the novel: firstly, they all conceive that Aboulela's views are identical to Najwa's, and secondly, that Aboulela intended the readers to view Najwa as an ideal. In contrast, I believe that *Minaret* is not intended to instigate a desire to emulate Najwa because she is clearly not a heroic figure. The progression of her life from riches to rags, as well as the sudden loss of her entire family, is hardly acknowledged in the abovementioned readings, perhaps because Aboulela delivers Najwa's tragic life story without sinking into a dramatic depiction of her misery. Instead, the story's narration focusses on Najwa's self-inflicted apathy while facing emotional and material deprivation, as well as social and financial decline. Even though she is neither lazy nor paralyzed, she has convinced herself that she cannot accomplish anything on her own. So, Najwa invests all her hopes for a 'better' life into a romantic attachment. After having waited for more than a decade, she finally meets someone who reciprocates her feelings and shares her ideas and values, but then she loses him as well. Najwa's inaction is self-inflicted because she has convinced herself that only unconditional love can salvage her from every burden and thus never considers taking her life into her own hands. Najwa never strives for progress or success; she does or thinks or feels nothing that might inspire readers to admire, envy or emulate her. Consequently, she fails to achieve anything. Najwa only desires to find love that requires no merit – modelled on the love she received from her parents until they died. She is no seeker of superiority; she is a seeker of empathy and love. Najwa is the personification of every human being's insecurities and feelings of insignificance. Aboulela's fictional character inspires compassion in the readers by reminding them of the most vulnerable part of their being which makes one feel too inadequate to deserve something as natural and vital as love.

GENDER NORMS AND FEMALE SEXUAL AUTONOMY IN ABOULELA'S *MINARET*

In my reading, gender plays no key role in the plot of *Minaret*; Najwa's gender does not compel her to be inadequate, helpless or unsuccessful. Her twin brother functions as a male control group to vouch for this because his story, which is almost identical to hers, has essentially the same outcome: both, Najwa and Omar are confronted with the same losses and traumas in the beginning. In response, they both start to throw their money into a bottomless pit – Najwa gives practically all her money to her boyfriend Anwar hoping that he will marry her, and Omar spends all his money on drugs. After this, they are both prevented from making poor choices by a fifteen-year period of isolated austerity in the form of religious piety for Najwa and incarceration for Omar. By the end of this period, neither of them has made any progress.

During the narration, we find many hints towards the unity of the two siblings. Even though, genetically, fraternal twins are no more alike than regular siblings, Najwa seems extremely hung up on the time when they were together in their mother's womb: "'What's wrong, Nana?' How did [Omar] know? Once long ago we were asleep inside Mama's stomach together, facing each other, twisting and kicking. I would like to go back to that time." (p. 38) Najwa has obviously failed to detach from him or her parents. In one passage of the earliest narrated period of their lives, Najwa goes to wake her brother and he pleads with her to put the air conditioner back on by addressing her with her childhood nickname "Nana". Najwa's response is significant: "The empathy of twins gripped me and for a moment I was the one who was hot and unbearably sleepy. I switched on the air conditioner and marched out of the room." (p. 10) After graduating from school she made no choices but simply took the same path as Omar: "Accounting, my least favourite subject, but my father wanted Omar to study Business and, after years in a girls' school, I wanted to be with Omar." (p. 11) Najwa and Omar often spoke or responded in unison, for instance, when Najwa's best friend, Randa, announces her departure (p. 26) and when their father explains his future (p. 52). Even though Najwa and Omar are different people, Najwa does not want to see it that way. This is possibly the reason why Najwa refrained from making independent decisions because that would have risked differing from Omar. One example of when she and Omar had different inclinations was when Omar pleaded with his parents for a chance to study abroad: Omar wanted to, but Najwa wanted to stay with her mother. “The Blue Nile poured from the Highlands of Ethiopia and the Sahara encroached, but neither was able to conquer the other. Omar wanted to leave. All the time Omar wanted to leave and I, his twin, wanted to stay.” (p. 16) She mentions the fact that they are twins as if this should make it impossible for them to want different things. She still supports Omar’s wish in front of their parents because she still had her mother. “I smiled at Mama and she smiled back. We were too close for me to leave her and go study abroad.” (p. 17) After their parents’ demise and Omar’s imprisonment, Najwa’s aunt and uncle offer her to move to Canada with them but she firmly refuses to leave Omar. The two are presented as Siamese twins in a still image on a Polaroid that Najwa remembers. It was taken at a picnic on the day before their father was arrested and their whole lives changed:

> It rarely happened but today Omar and I were dressed in identical colours. We were both wearing Wrangler jeans and I was wearing a beige polo neck and he had on a long-sleeved beige shirt. Mama came and took a photo of us. [...] Omar and I smiling [...], his back against my arm [...]. Everything started to fall that night [...]. (pp. 52–53)

Najwa and her twin brother Omar function as one person, albeit a still incomplete one; rather than each being a *yin* and a *yang* with the ability to complete each other, the two of these are just one half of a *yin* each, while their parents were the *yang* that used to complete them. *Minaret* is the story of a young woman and a young man who feel too inadequate to accomplish anything. They are not paralyzed, but simply never learned to move independently.

Moore stipulates that *Minaret* “[champions] *feminine* rather than *feminist* values”.[221] Moore’s primary criticism is that “[n]owhere in *Minaret* do we find a structural critique of gender norms, for example in the conception of public space as normatively masculine that hijab partly reflects.”[222] It is true that *Minaret* does not offer a structural critique but only subtle discussions of gender norms; for instance, in one paragraph Najwa ponders over gender norms while watching a stranger praying over a grave: “There was no way of knowing if his deceased relative was a man or a woman. All through life there were distinctions – toilets for men, toilets for women; clothes for men, clothes for women – then, at the end, the graves were identical.” (p. 158)

---

[221] Moore, ‘*Voyages Out and In*’, p. 79
[222] Ibid.

Moore concludes that Aboulela's views on feminism are apparent from the inadequacies she portrays in Najwa, without considering that (a) her limitations are not due to her gender, as evidenced by the fact that almost all the other female characters in the novel are obviously not inflicted with Najwa's incapacities, and (b) that two of the male characters in the novel share Najwa's weaknesses. Moore based her reproaches exclusively on Najwa's priorities, desires, and feelings. Even though Najwa does not believe being emancipated and independent as a woman is wrong or bad. On the contrary, she is very much aware of the fact that women should strive to achieve more than just matrimony:

> I wished I could feel like an emancipated young student, driving her own car with confidence. Was I not an emancipated young woman driving her own car to university? In Khartoum, only a minority of women drove cars and in university less than thirty percent of students were girls – that should make me feel good about myself. But I preferred it when Omar was with me, when Omar was driving. I missed him. (p. 10)

She knows that she should feel good about being independent. But since she never had to fight for her independence she could take it for granted. It is not an issue for her; she knows no one will stop her from being independent. All she wants is to be surrounded by people she loves and trusts, so that she can delegate all her decisions to them. Najwa's lack of ambition probably resulted from the lack of interest that her father took in building her career:

> I don't know if I ever told my father how much I loved the university he chose for me. I don't think I spoke to him much. I know he didn't think a lot about me, not because he didn't love me but because I was a girl and Mama's responsibility. He had detailed, specific plans for Omar's future, while I was going to get married to someone who would determine how the rest of my life flowed. I am glad Baba didn't live to see what happened to Omar. Or even to me. (p. 78)

In contrast to her brother Omar, Najwa never had to struggle for her father's approval for anything. Najwa does not mention whether her parents specifically told her to await marriage. Najwa's immaturity suggests that her childhood fantasies of connubial felicity (Barbie and Ken in a dollhouse) persisted until the time in young adulthood when her mental development stopped entirely because of the losses she suffered. Even though she never mentions having played with dolls in her childhood, this seems logical, simply because she repeatedly implies that she has hoped to get married for as long as she remembers. She even recalls being surprised when she realized her female fellow students did not dream as small as she did:

> I was in university to kill time until I got married and had children. I thought that was why all the girls were there too, but they surprised me by caring about their education, forging ahead with jobs and careers. I surprised myself by never getting married. (p. 102)

When 19-year-old Tamer asks Najwa in her late thirties about her past, her response is still lacking a reflected self-awareness: "When I was your age, I imagined I would get married, have children, the usual things. I didn't imagine anything different. I had friends who wanted to be doctors, diplomats but I never had these ambitions." (p. 198)

Najwa's lack of reflection about her underperforming is important because it shows that she does not have regressive or traditional views regarding women's role in society. She knows that she should feel emancipated and that it is something to be proud of. She knows it is a privilege and a merit and she feels humbled by the fact that she does not find herself coveting it. In her late thirties, Najwa even feels envious of what other women have: her employer Lamya's independence, Lamya's friend's perspectives in life, and Doctora Zeinab's sovereignty. When she sees a happy and energetic Lamya returning home from work she thinks: "Is this how a young affluent woman feels, fulfilled in her work, coming home to a young child? I owe myself an absence of envy; I owe myself a heart free of grudges." (p. 73)

Najwa's incapacities are not due to gender norms or regressive values that she has internalised. When Doctora Zeinab, makes a comment on gender norms it is obvious that Najwa disagrees even if she remains quiet: "[Doctora Zeinab to Najwa:] 'Lamya's always been a bit stiff. She sees things in black and white, no compromises for her. I often used to wish that she was the boy and Tamer the girl.' I smile at what I regard as a humorous remark, but she does not smile back." (p. 261). While Zeinab does not believe in the subordination of women to men, she knows the ways of the world and that strong-minded women find it difficult to get settled in family lives. Zeinab's views on her daughter's marital problems are not regressive, as she does not believe that her daughter must sacrifice everything, including her career, for her marriage; Zeinab simply believes that if Lamya plays it well, then she can have both. She mentions this to Najwa: "Lamya has to be diplomatic – please him and please herself. That way she can both keep her husband and get her PhD." (p. 262)

Doctora Zeinab is clearly the matriarch of the family who pays off Najwa so that she would end the relationship with Tamer. These female figures clearly play driving roles in the plot of the novel. Yet, the analyses of Abbas, Moore, and Hunter have reduced the novel's views on feminism to the flawed and diffident character of Najwa unequipped to face the world, which is what Aboulela is actually portraying.

It is obvious that her mother did not try to teach her to be weak, since she trusted her more than she trusted Omar: "When I was young my mother said, 'Look after Omar, you're the girl, you're the quiet, sensible one. Look after Omar.' And year in, year out, I covered for Omar. I sensed his weakness and looked out for Omar." (p. 13) At no point in the novel do we learn that Najwa was brought up in a patriarchy or raised to think well of it, yet Eva Hunter censures Aboulela for having stated in an interview that *Minaret* is a feminist critique of Sudanese patriarchy because all the men in Najwa's life who were obligated to protect her and provide for her according to Islamic tradition fail to do so. Her father dies, her brother is imprisoned, and her uncle emigrates. Her boyfriend Anwar did not care about her enough to want to protect her from his roommate's molestations. In a passage quoted by Hunter, Aboulela says:

> The men in Najwa's family [...] fail to protect her and protection is a woman's right from an Islamic point of view. When this happens, the customary qualities of an attractive Sudanese woman [such as docility and modesty] become ... characteristics that expose her to exploitations by other men.[223]

Hunter finds this insufficient because she feels that "[r]ather than criticising [sic] patriarchy, Aboulela is criticising [sic] the fact that it does not work as it should."[224] The logic behind this sentence seems flawed to me because criticizing patriarchy by pointing out its impracticality is still criticism. Additionally, the novel demonstrates that the theory of patriarchy does not consider the dangers that women are exposed to if they happen to be under the charge of selfish, perverted men with no moral compass. The fact is that in the development of the plot and what it tacitly evinces *Minaret* is doing more than criticizing patriarchy by pondering the risks of raising girls to rely on men, as it incapacitates them to question men's intentions and consequently to protect themselves from exploitation. Interestingly, neither Hunter nor Abbas or Moore discuss the exploitations that Aboulela was referring to in the above-quoted passage.

Anwar exploits Najwa financially, emotionally and sexually. Throughout their intimate relationship, which must have lasted a few weeks, Anwar disregards her feelings entirely and even expects her to tolerate his roommate's attempts to molest her. Both Hunter and Moore notice Najwa's sexual guilt

---

223 Hunter, '*The Muslim "Who Has Faith" in Leila Aboulela's Novels Minaret (2005) And Lyrics Alley (2009)*', p. 93

224 Ibid.

depicted in *Minaret* and use it to imply that the novel tries to make a clear statement against extramarital sex.

> Najwa's self-loathing is exacerbated when she succumbs to the sexual pleasure of Anwar, a secular nationalist forced into exile once the forces that destroyed Najwa's father fall, in turn, to an Islamist coup. Looking in the mirror after sleeping with him, Najwa recalls also being distracted by her own image while her father was being arrested: as these narcissistic moments in the past and the present conflate, she vomits.[225]

Najwa does feel guilty and dissatisfied by her intimate relationship with Anwar, and silently pines over the fact that it happened out of wedlock. Interestingly though, her post-coital interior monologue is not concerned with punishment from God but almost exclusively with the discrepancy between her fantasies about her 'first time' and the disappointing reality. She had imagined a wedding night in a clean and comfortable hotel "with its glow of approval" (p. 176) which makes Anwar's bedroom appear gloomy and uninviting. Her regret features a lack of approval instead of imaginary disapproval by her late parents. Najwa had imagined that her mother would call her the morning after her wedding night out of concern for her, which indicates that Najwa wishes to share her experience with someone who cares about her wellbeing. Anwar's coldness towards Najwa makes her miss her mother's genuine concern. Najwa does not see it as a religious transgression. At that time, she had not yet discovered religion for herself, but even after her religious transformation, she believes in God's mercy, rather than his punishment. After having given the relationship a chance to give her stability and a sense of direction in life, she finds herself retreating from Anwar as he continuously disappoints her expectations. In my reading, Najwa loses interest in Anwar because he leaves her emotionally unsatisfied and not just because he refuses to get engaged.

Even though Najwa reflects that it was "inevitable" that they would get physical eventually, it is unclear whether Najwa had given explicit consent before they engage in sexual intercourse for the first time. All we know is that Anwar takes initiative after deciding out loud that she had "teased [him] enough" (p. 172). After some time in this relationship, Najwa does express her disinclination towards sex, but Anwar shoves it aside as guilt. Anwar's response is a classic narrative of trying to render consent obsolete by referring to the pleasure of the act:

---

225 Moore, '*Voyages Out and In*', p. 77

> Anwar said: 'You can't still be feeling guilty, you're enjoying yourself too much.' He laughed and said, 'If your conscience was troubling you, you wouldn't be so eager now.' So, I kept my thoughts to myself. [...] 'You have become quiet,' he said, 'you have become dreamy.' I dreamed of nothing, no happy dreams and no sad dreams. (p. 177)

Anwar implies that the body's natural response of arousal to physical touch renders getting the partner's sexual consent unnecessary. He dismisses Najwa's hesitations by implying that her body has made a choice that she must accept. Najwa's religious awakening came after her feelings of guilt and shame surfaced. She initially feels ashamed for having an intimate relationship, probably because it merely serves as physical relief and offers neither the security of a marital bond that she was seeking nor the companionship and compassion that she was aching for. Najwa feels overwhelmed with this conundrum and withdraws into herself without knowing why.

The fact that there is no one in her life who might be scandalized if she were to become pregnant actually makes her nostalgic. The people who most undoubtedly loved Najwa and cared about her are no longer there to weigh in on her choices, which is a grave loss to a young woman who has trouble making independent decisions. Anwar feels no affection or even empathy for her and is only concerned about himself. So, Najwa slowly begins to doubt the decisions that Anwar makes for her because they only serve his own needs whilst disregarding hers entirely.

Right from the beginning of their intimate relations, Anwar shows little concern for her hesitations and tells her that he believes that since they are living in London they must live like Londoners. Anwar convinces Najwa that in the UK it is not normal for a woman to be a virgin at her age, which makes Najwa comply temporarily. Even though Eva Hunter concedes in her criticism that it may be "unfair to burden this novel with expectations the writer has not set out to satisfy"[226] she still concludes that "it does not seem unfair to wish that [Aboulela] showed some understanding of the intensity of the anger and suffering that animates Muslim women who are active in the cause of women's emancipation."[227] Though Hunter, Moore, and Abbas imply that women should not be forced into sexual austerity by religious guilt because it is a marker of patriarchy, they do not see the converse that women should not be forced into having sex by someone's interpretation of Western values. It might

---

226 Hunter, '*The Muslim "Who Has Faith" in Leila Aboulela's Novels Minaret (2005) And Lyrics Alley (2009)*', p. 93

227 Ibid., p. 97

be an indicator of the influence of the narratives of inadequacy in Hunter's reading to demand more feminism from Aboulela, whilst overlooking the fact that Anwar used the narrative of the superiority of Western sexual morals over Sudanese values to seize Najwa's right to refuse extramarital sex. I think it is fair to expect from a feminist to acknowledge a woman's right to refuse sex for any reason that she wishes, even if it is for religious or cultural reasons even though they might seem traditionalist or regressive from a 'western' point of view.

Najwa lacks the mental independence to make decisions like terminating the relationship with Anwar, so she starts avoiding him instead. On the lookout for someone to replace him as her warden and as her hope for salvation, she turns to the only person who had kept reaching out to her since her mother's funeral: a young Muslim woman from the local mosque who had repeatedly called Najwa to ask how she was doing and to invite her to the mosque.

MINARET – RELIGIOUS CONDUCT BOOK OR SPIRITUAL LOVE STORY?

The generic framework of any literary work of fiction should help understand the content and unfold all its layers of meaning. Categorizing it as a spiritual *Bildungsroman*, as Hunter did, insinuates that the author followed a specific intention: Hunter believes Aboulela is "preaching" an ethics of personal cultivation over political interests to women.[228] While it is true that Najwa is a woman with no interest in politics, there are also female figures in the novel who are interested in it as well as male figures who are equally disinterested in them, like her twin brother, Omar, and her love interest, Tamer.

Hunter has categorized *Minaret* as a spiritual *Bildungsroman* by tracing the following spiritual development of Najwa,

> the narrator-protagonist of *Minaret* sheds several shards of identity that pose obstacles to her spiritual growth. These include the formative influences of her childhood and young adulthood in Khartoum. Her family belonged to the Sudanese elite, who welcomed the seeming progressiveness of Western Europe. [...] In exile in London, Najwa will deplore the superficial gestures towards religion made by her family of origin. She will also reject secularism, political activism,

[228] Ibid., p. 91

> and sexual attachment – in the person of her lover Anwar, a Marxist who is also Sudanese and so incarnates affiliations with her country of origin. Najwa increasingly turns to the emotional and psychological security that she gains from her faith and her visits to a mosque (the dominant architectural feature of which gives the novel its title) where she enjoys the friendship of, and the fostering of her spirituality by, a multi-ethnic group of women.[229]

However, in my reading, neither Omar nor Najwa seem to have a character arc: their financial situation changes but their mental capacities remain the same throughout the novel. Even though Hunter suggests that Najwa's movement toward religion is a character arc, it is rather obvious that there is no development in the form of growth, movement or transition towards piety. When Najwa lives alone, she stops listening to music but only because she realizes that she never liked it anyway but only listened to it with Omar. Najwa does not become more religious, she just begins to practice religion more. This factor is more due to nostalgia than to a spiritual awakening. Her piety begins with contacting the woman who gave her mother the Islamic cleaning ritual before burial – a woman she remembers as "the woman who shrouded my mother" (p. 240) – and it peaks with her decision to cover her hair with her dead mother's clothes. Her reversion to religion reads like an attempt to be closer to her late mother.

> Wafaa taught me a specific prayer – asking Allah to wash my mother's sins with water and ice. I forgot the exact wording but the image of ice remained and the feeling she imparted that my mother needed me still. Everyone else seemed to think that my mother didn't need me anymore, that I was free. (p. 135)

Najwa had grown up with religion and always identified herself as a Muslim, but in her youth, she was lazy in her practice of the tenets. Najwa had never abdicated from Islam and can therefore not revert to it. Most importantly, Najwa's commitment to religion was not initiated by her retreat from Anwar but by her bond with Wafaa. Since she did not have the strength of will to break up with him by asking him to stop visiting her, she used the hijab in order to push him away from her. It is noteworthy that people drive her towards religion, and not some divine calling.

Abbas, on the other hand, suggests that *Minaret* is a religious novel, building on plotting devices of religious conduct books in order to promote selected religious values as offering inner fulfilment to the protagonists. Religion is obviously important to Najwa but her counterpart, Omar, does not take the religious path to deal with the same predicament and yet Najwa is neither more

---

[229] Ibid.

nor less successful in her quest than Omar. While religion may have given Najwa some direction on her path, the novel does not conclude that religion saved her life or made things objectively better for her. A religious conduct book would have tried to persuade the readers that religion solves every problem, or at least that the protagonists deserve – after having walked the path of virtue and passed the tests of temptation – to have what they desire.

Moore describes the ending of *Minaret* in an interesting way: "While romance is foreclosed, the spiritual journey is further enabled."[230] Even though Najwa informs the reader that she intends to go on Hajj with the money she received from Tamer's mother, the novel ends with Najwa mourning so severely that her friend had to come and check on her. She seems to be in a state of apathy, and as she falls asleep and dreams of being a sick child resting in bed between her loving parents, it is unclear whether she will be able to pick herself up again in the morning. Moore believes that "Najwa's reversion to Islam" was "at the heart of the text",[231] but to me, it seems it revolves around the sad love story between Tamer and Najwa because the romance plot frames the entire literary narrative: the novel opens with their first encounter and ends with their separation.

Najwa was convinced that love would be her salvation and not religion. As the title suggests, Islam does play a key role in Najwa's life by serving as the compass that steers her through the circumstances of her life, which she tries hard to convince herself are only temporary. Religion keeps her headed somewhere safely. She finds tenets in Islam which give her the hope that she can do something to help her parents even after their demise. Islam is also not her new decision maker: Najwa gives up Tamer for his own sake and not for the sake of her spiritual growth. She does not choose to leave Tamer to go to Hajj. She chooses to leave him, so he will not be punished by God – as she believes Omar had been punished for hurting his mother. The decision to go to Hajj to start her life anew comes later. Just like her brother Omar, Najwa wants redemption for herself and her family. While Omar decides to seek it legally, by going to Sudan and trying to exonerate his father, Najwa tries to do it with prayers.

> I remember how Omar and my father used to argue. Yet now Omar is his staunchest defender. "I want to clear his name," he says.

---

230 Moore, '*Voyages Out and In*', p. 77
231 Ibid.

> And what do I want for my father? Every day I pray that Allah will forgive him; every day I ask mercy for his soul. But I am not motivated to clear his name. A sentence was passed and we have to live with the consequences.
>
> I ask Omar, "What good will it do him to clear his name?"
>
> "It will do us good. We might get back some of our inheritance that the government took [...]."
>
> "Maybe." I imagine a long bitter fight and little gain.
>
> Omar insists. "Just to prove that it was all lies against him, all motivated by malice and politics."
>
> "But for him, where he is now, it is better if we pray, if we give money to the poor. That's what matters when you're dead."
>
> "When you're dead, you're dead, Najwa, and nothing else matters." He sits back in his chair and a world separates us in spite of genes and love. (p. 195)

However, the description of the novel as "spiritual" seems accurate because *Minaret* does advocate a clear preference of spiritual directives over mundane goals. This is obvious in Aboulela's unnecessary efforts of composing Anwar's secular character as vastly inferior to the religious and non-political Tamer. Additionally, the mosque is depicted as the only place where Najwa encounters people who believe in mercy. She recalls an excerpt from a lecture she had heard at the mosque: "The mercy of Allah is an ocean. Our sins are a lump of clay clenched between the beak of a pigeon. The pigeon is perched on the branch of a tree at the edge of that ocean. It only has to open its beak." (p. 4)

In comparison, Anwar shows neither mercy nor any concern for justice for Najwa's father, simply because he disliked his political views. The novel does not discuss – for example – theological dissent or religious exclusivist attitudes which can be equally divisive and even violent. Instead, the readers are kept within Najwa's comfort zone, where there is nothing but consensus among Muslims:

> The Tajweed class is my favourite. I learn how to pronounce the letters correctly [...]. This concentration on technique soothes me; it makes me forget everything around me. Um Waleed is a qualified teacher, with a degree in Sharia Law. Many of the sisters say that her other classes on Law and History are more interesting – they generate a lot of discussion and the sisters, especially the young British-born ones and the converts, like to discuss and give their opinions. *But I become fragmented and deflated in discussions; I never know which point of view I support.* I find myself agreeing with whoever is speaking or with the one I like best. And I become anxious that someone's feelings will get hurt, or worse take serious offence, *as sometimes happens*, and stop coming to the mosque. Here in the

> Tajweed class, all is calm and peaceful. We practice and practice until we can get the words right. I want to read the Qur'an in a beautiful way.
>
> After the class, I have a new energy. [Emphasis added] (pp. 78–79)

It is important to note, however, that *Minaret* does not assert a practical superiority of Islam over Western values. When Najwa and Omar lose their home and their parents, one sibling chooses the religious path to cope with the hardships, the other does not. Both of them go through a phase of poor choices which impedes their progress on their different ways: Omar stabs a policeman and ends up in prison, and Najwa spends all of her money on her boyfriend Anwar and realizes that he neither loves nor respects her. Since Omar started at a disadvantage of already having been addicted to drugs – a condition dating back to the time when their family was privileged – his lot is naturally worse than Najwa's. But Najwa also experiences a deep fall from being a privileged young adult, with the prospect of earning a university degree, to being a middle-aged single woman with no degree or qualification, who has to work as a maid to sustain herself. By the end of the novel, both Omar and Najwa end up just where they started off: Najwa receives the money that she had spent on Anwar, which means she is back to the same financial status that her mother had left her with, and Omar will come out of prison and start over exactly where his mother had left him. Religion in the form of her hijab helped Najwa push Anwar away because she was unable to terminate the relationship herself. It may be noted that her faith did not help her to make progress in her life. Most significantly, neither Omar nor Najwa mature mentally. One example of Najwa's lack of maturity is the fact that she remains unable to meet people like Doctora Zeinab eye to eye: near the end of the novel, when Doctora Zeinab gets into the taxi, she hands Najwa a ten pound note in Tamer's presence, probably to remind her of her inferior station, and Najwa in still unable to decline. In the same fashion, when Omar and Najwa discuss the last fight that Omar had had with his mother before her death, his comments reveal that even after a decade and a half, he has not matured enough to show regret. Instead, he looks down and says:

> 'I didn't hurt her.'
>
> 'You pushed her. She was ill and you pushed her.'
>
> 'I didn't mean to. She wouldn't give me her purse. It was my money. She made me so angry!' (p. 196)

Nearing the end of the novel, the almost forty-year-old Omar utters the same words which the twenty-five-year-old Omar had uttered at that time: while he was shaking his terminally ill mother, he shouted, 'It is my money.' Fifteen years onwards, there is no regret or recognition of the simple fact that he should not have pushed his mother, regardless of the circumstances. So, even though Omar's journey was worse than Najwa's as it was spent almost entirely in prison, they both circle back to their starting point by the end of the novel.

Religion may have helped Najwa to stay away from decisions or temptations that might have meant a decline in her situation and the prison did the same for Omar. Therefore, even though Najwa is convinced that religion is the best way to move forward in life, the novel's plot does not exemplify this notion.

In summary, I would describe *Minaret* as a spiritual love story, rather than a spiritual novel. There are two romance plots at the centre of the novel, narrated in parallel order by means of a fragmentation and realignment of the temporal sequence of the plot. *Minaret* is a spiritual love story because it clearly uses its narrating device in order to highlight the vast superiority of the spiritual love between Tamer and Najwa – depicted as being mutual, affectionate, compassionate, selfless, forgiving, patient, chaste, considerate, etc. – over the profane relationship between Najwa and Anwar – which is depicted as being disproportionate, carnal, passionless, selfish, inconsiderate, incontinent, etc.

The fact that this novel does not discuss the downsides in life is another marker of a romance plot: the denial of ugly realities. This degree of genteelness in *Minaret*'s love story results in a reduction of complexity, which, in my view stifles its spiritual tenor. From the Eurocentric perspective, however, it can seem an indicator of an idealization of Islam. This impression is amplified by the narratives of distinctive identity which *Minaret* builds on.

ISLAM AND NARRATIVES OF DISPARITY IN ABOULELA'S *MINARET*

Minaret's protagonist sees the world and its people as divided into twos: rich and poor, Sudanese and British (mostly referred to as Western), Muslim and non-Muslim, political and non-political, educated and uneducated, among others. She even struggles to understand the motives of converts for accepting Islam:

> I said to Anwar, "It's interesting about converts, isn't it? What would make a Westerner become a Muslim?"

> He made a face.
>
> "I think they're brave."
>
> "You say that because as Muslims our self-esteem is so low that we're desperate for approval. And what greater stamp of approval can there be than a white man's?"
>
> He had fixed ideas about religion. The Islamist government in Khartoum was his enemy. He liked to point out its faults and contradictions. (pp. 159–160)

Yet even after getting to know one convert better, Najwa continues to dissect the two identities within him:

> Ali [Wafaa's husband, a convert] intrigued me. I had got the impression from Anwar that the English were all secular and liberal. Ali was nothing like that, yet he was completely English and had never set foot outside Britain. When I got to know Wafaa better, she told me about his conversion, how he used to be a devout Christian and felt that the Church was not strict enough for him. The more lifts I accepted from them, the more I got to understand him, listening to him complain to Wafaa about the traffic or joke with one of the children. It was not only his accent that I found odd. He was not very bright, but I was touched by his patience with the children, the way he took on life. I thought of Anwar and Ali, how they would never meet, how the existence of one somehow undermined the other. (p. 241)

Other characters in the novel defy these borderlines, like Tamer who falls in love with poor and uneducated Najwa, who is also older than him. Again, Najwa's limitations are not the author's or the novel's limitations, and yet the novel fails to reconcile Islam and the West, as Hunter points out:

> Aboulela does not produce a version of Islam that had been modulated by its experience in Britain [... and instead asserts] difference and foreignness, together with what appears to be a somewhat blinkered understanding of British culture and religion [...].[232]

In *Minaret*, Islam and the West remain two segregated identities, which are occasionally even defined by their differences. For instance, both Tamer and Najwa acknowledge their share in the Western identity, yet they explicitly say that they identify as Muslims because they do not feel Sudanese anymore. (p. 110) It is even more obvious in a conversation between Najwa and Tamer where she says:

> One of the Muslim scholars or maybe even the Khalifa Omar, I'm not sure, said that the Rum [meaning the Romans], the Europeans, are better than us in that

---

[232] Hunter, '*The Muslim "Who Has Faith" in Leila Aboulela's Novels Minaret (2005) And Lyrics Alley (2009)*', p. 97

> when they fall down in battle they quickly get up, dust themselves and fight again. I try to forget the past, to move on but I'm not good at it. I'm not European. (p. 118)

Najwa was told that there is a quality which is characteristically European and that since she is a Muslim and has no share in the European identity she cannot have the said quality. This is a narrative of distinctive identity, assigning oppositional attributes to each side and thus constructing mutually exclusive identities.

When Eva Hunter suggests that "Najwa's limitations [...] reflect Aboulela's own aversion to and misunderstanding of Western culture",[233] she is using a rhetoric that is typical of a defensive and apologetic attitude that is similar to an outdated Muslim narrative that tries to dismiss any inadequate behaviour of Muslim groups (for instance, misogyny, violent enforcement of tenets, even terrorism, etc.) by stating that they have *misunderstood* the teachings of Islam. Hunter's proposition is based on the premise that Western culture is without question better than Aboulela's understanding of it, and that if she failed to see its merit then she must be misinformed or mistaken. Apologetic statements of this kind lack objectivity and expose a wounded ego. While apologetic narratives clearly do exist, the label of apologetics is often applied too generously, or without proper consideration of the line of reasoning. Sadia Abbas, for instance, argues that *Minaret* is a religious novel because of the characteristic "apologetics":

> Let us add another way to write a religious novel to our list: produce an apologetics. Again, Aboulela obliges. She offers up visions of women who seek their own subjection and writes a romance that attempts to dramatize the conditions for what it casts as an ideal Muslim marriage [...]. Add to Aboulela's ode to subordination allegories of the (happy) defeat of the left and we have a perfectly steeped apologetic brew.[234]

As argued earlier, apart from Najwa, all women depicted in *Minaret* are intellectually and often even financially independent. Even Najwa's married friend from the mosque, Wafaa, who had recently had another baby, enrolls at a university by the end of the novel. And although Najwa does not measure up to these superficial standards of female emancipation, the fact that she responds to these women's achievements and prospects with feelings of envy shows that she does not have a regressive, anti-feminist or misogynistic

---

[233] Hunter, '*The Muslim "Who Has Faith" in Leila Aboulela's Novels Minaret (2005) And Lyrics Alley (2009)*', p. 92

[234] Abbas, '*Leila Aboulela, Religion, and the Challenge of the Novel*', p. 443

worldview. Abbas overlooks the fact that Najwa's fantasies about being Tamer's families' concubine bear no similarities to Abbas' idea of what she calls an "ideal Muslim marriage": "I would like to be his family's concubine, like something out of The Arabian Nights, with life-long security and a sense of belonging. But I must settle for freedom in this modern time." (p. 215) Najwa desires a role in a family with a function that is undistinguished, yet permanent.

> I enjoy being in a home rather than cleaning offices and hotels. I like being part of a family, touching their things, knowing what they ate, what they threw in the bin. I know them in intimate ways while they hardly know me, as if I am invisible. It still takes me by surprise how natural I am in this servant role. (p. 83)

She says she wants to be invisible in a home, so she can be part of a family without the pressure of having to fulfil the expectations that social commitments usually entail. She has no ambition to impress, but neither does she want to disappoint. Najwa wants to be useful but not indispensable; taken care of but not subjected to constant attention. This is why she considered marrying Anwar, and even her cousin, Nabil – neither of whom she seemed to love – just for the stability. She does not seek subordination in a partnership, as evidenced by her romantic attachment to a 19-year-old whose immaturity or innocence she finds attractive:

> "I feel sorry for you," [Tamer] says [to Najwa]. I need this from him. It feels right, nourishing. Then he asks me if Omar has ever tried to escape like prisoners do in films. He flickers between soulful depth and immaturity. This flickering is attractive; it absorbs my attention. (p. 197)

Abbas' line of reasoning demonstrates a common narrative of distrust for any positive account of Islam by labeling it as apologetics. I would argue that this label of apologetics is often used in a derogatory fashion to denote a line of argumentation characterized by 1) a defensive stance, 2) a denial of negative truths about members of the 'in-group', and/or 3) a rhetoric of understating flaws, faults or problems (relativization).

Minaret does seem to offer an exclusively good account of Islam, which makes the novel somewhat subjective and biased. However, Abbas' dismissal of it as apologetics – even though Aboulela is clearly not offering a defence against any prejudices or reproaches – because it gives a positive representation of something that is usually negative in the Western perception is equally biased. *Minaret* seeks to demonstrate how Islamic values can be helpful or useful to individuals in difficult times. The category of a religious novel with apologetics as a characteristic element insinuates that a good representation of

Islam in novels can never be trusted because it seeks to manipulate or persuade, rather than to discuss. While I denounce Abbas's case for its assumption that a good image of Islam is not to be trusted, I do concede that Aboulela should not have built an image of Islam as warm, safe, merciful and selfless by placing it into a contrasting backdrop of a cold, pragmatic, ruthless and judgemental picture of the West.

In summary, the three analyses by Moore, Hunter, and Abbas use conclusive arguments to prove that *Minaret* promotes an image of the West as the embodiment of all that is materialistic and inhumane, whilst presenting Islam as the remedy against it. I would argue that the novel promotes a preference of spiritual goals over mundane priorities, which is why I agree with the labelling of it as a spiritual novel. It is arguable, however, that the novel is biased, not because it presents a good image of Islam but because it lacks a critical view on it or its adherents. The novel builds on narratives of distinctive identity and thus serves to solidify the gap between the two sides, like in the following passage describing how Najwa and Tamer walk the streets of London:

> I sense the slight unease [Tamer] inspires in the people around us. I turn and look at him through their eyes. Tall, young, Arab-looking, dark eyes and the beard, just like a terrorist. (p. 100)
>
> There are other places in London that aren't safe, where our very presence irks people. Maybe his university is such a place and that is why he is lonely. (p. 111)

Even so, *Minaret* does not establish the superiority of Islam or the West by means of transcendental ideals, images or idols, other than the idea of God's mercy. Religion and pragmatism, represented by Najwa and her twin brother, Omar, respectively, are equals in the novel. Najwa and Omar both believe that their father was not guilty of the charges he was executed for. But unlike Omar, Najwa believes the fall of their family could have been prevented if they had all been devout. She believes she still has the chance to save her brother if she can get him to pray and repent. This is why Omar is the only one Najwa tries to convince to practice religious rituals like prayer. (pp. 95–96) While Najwa tries to persuade her brother to pray and repent so he can be forgiven for his offence against his mother, she does not try to persuade him to change his beliefs; neither does Omar try to dissuade Najwa from being religious: "Najwa, listen, you obviously feel happy being devout – that's your business. But I'm fine as I am." (p. 96)

Since no one is trying to recruit someone for a cause, or wishing to inspire someone for great sacrifice, there is no need for narratives of superiority in *Minaret*. Najwa's sacrifice of her happiness by breaking up with Tamer was inspired by her love for him, and not by some sense of religious duty. In other words, faith in *Minaret* is merely spiritual and has no political agenda. Perhaps the novel promotes the idea that religion must be free from political ambition in order to thrive spiritually, but a less segregated depiction of Muslim life in Britain would have made it more realistic, fair and relatable to everyone.

Result of Literary Analysis

Dastan-e-Ishq: Fiction's Remedy Against NoDs?

The object of the literary analysis was to prove that the binary worldview creating an irreconcilable conflict between Islam and the West is constructed by a perpetuation of NoDs. The protagonist of *The Reluctant Fundamentalist* neither seems to identify as a Muslim, because he is not religious at all, nor does he seem to feel very American because when war breaks out he instinctively sides with Muslims and Pakistanis rather than the US-American forces. Yet somehow he is convinced throughout the novel that he has to be either Muslim or American and that he cannot simply be both or neither. This illusion that there is a chasm between the mutually exclusive identities Islam and the West is a result of NoDs. These NoDs are recognizable by recurring patterns and constituents some of which go way back in history. After recognizing and pinpointing these NoDs, the next question is: what is a possible remedy against these efforts to maintain a disparity between Islam and the West?

Mohsin Hamid has left the ending of the frame story open. His mode of narration activates the reader who is left to judge what happens at the end. Ilott ponders:

> The playfully ambiguous style of *The Reluctant Fundamentalist* works to foreground our role as readers and in so doing encourages an active and engaged method of reading. However, the absence of a satisfying conclusion means that any singular or fixed conclusion that readers might arrive at would have to be based on readers' own inductive leaps. The novella simultaneously encourages interpretations through its ambiguity but also resists the fixing of singular interpretations as a symptom of the fundamentalism that the work persistently deconstructs.[235]

Following this thought, I would offer a new interpretation of the novel using another generic framework. Ilott noticed that the novella applies a "layering of different genres, which means that the reader has to choose what he or she

---

[235] Ilott, '*Generic Frameworks and Active Readership in The Reluctant Fundamentalist*', p. 582

believes to be the most suitable generic framework for understanding the novella."[236] She brilliantly identifies the love story in the novel as a *dastan* "which was originally an oral Persian tale and later became an Urdu literary form."[237] Much like the Arabic tale of Layla and Majnun (Dastan-e-Layla Majnun), or the Indian tale of Anarkali and Saleem, it is a love story in which "the lover is crucially unattainable [...]. If we were to read the tale according to this generic framework we would be aware from the outset that the love affair would be doomed; this would, therefore, place more emphasis on the pursuit of the beloved, or the work required by the lover."[238] What Ilott did not discuss, however, is the fact that this would make the love story of Changez and Am/Erica, and of Erica and Chris, a tale of *ishq* and not of love.

The term *Ishq* must be translated to *love* because the English language does not make this particular distinction. It is originated in Sufism (Islamic Mysticism) as the only kind of relationship of love that human beings can have with God: if the object of love is as transcendental as God, then naturally the lover knows from the beginning that he or she can never obtain the beloved, but still loves him/her. This is not 'just' love, but it is *ishq*, which is a recurring trope in South-Asian fiction, most obviously in Bollywood movies. Even though the *Ishq*-trope does not come up in Aboulela's *Minaret*, it does discuss the love between a believer and God. Yet, Najwa and Tamer's love story could have been remedial of NoDs because the protagonist of *Minaret* is the antithesis of narcissism. Najwa never loved herself as much as she wanted to be loved by others. Her altruism is a remedy for the human weakness of chasing images of superiority to feed one's ego. Najwa and Tamer's love for each other was doomed to failure even without his mother's interference: Najwa was aware that Tamer was still young and would soon outgrow his admiration and attraction towards her: "This is what I'm doing; waiting for the day he will outgrow me, heading towards it like death." (p. 214) Najwa decides to let Tamer go, not for her own sake, and not for his mother's sake either, but only for his sake. She makes a deal with his mother that if Najwa breaks up with Tamer, his mother will not force him to study economics anymore and allow him to study whatever he chooses. Thus, at the end of the novel Najwa does more to ensure Tamer's happiness in the future – which she will have no share in – than she has ever done in pursuit of her own. However, since this is a love story between

---

[236] Ibid., p. 572
[237] Ibid., p. 580
[238] Ibid.

two Muslims who feel equally misplaced in the West, it fails at offering a remedy for the narratives that maintain the disparity between Islam and the West. Najwa falls in love with Tamer because he seems to be the only character who can empathize with her and vice versa. The reason why they can empathize with each other is that they are immensely similar in their values, priorities and interests. So, rather than a love story that overcomes differences and hatred between the explicitly defined 'in-group' and 'out-group', this love story literally suggests that people can empathize with – and consequently love – only those most similar to themselves. Unlike the young and discontented Tamer, Najwa is able to empathize with everyone, even with Tamer's mother who resents their love, and with Anwar who effectively had Najwa's father arrested and executed. So, Aboulela managed to compose an engaging story despite Najwa's seemingly dull character, by placing an otherwise undistinguished protagonist with a remarkable capacity for empathy in a non-compassionate environment. It is a pity that *Minaret* does not feature the star-crossed-lovers-trope – or *ishq* trope – of *Romeo and Juliet* that might have conquered profane boundaries maintained by NoDs.

Ishq is necessarily selfless, destructive, unconditional as well as unrewarded except with *ishq* itself. In contrast, love is a human need and thus linked to the hope of finding happiness with it. It can end the relationships fails to bestow the hoped for contentment or when one of the partners dies, but *ishq* transcends all that is human and profane and is supposed to continue even in the afterlife. While love's fulfilment results in satisfaction of a need, *ishq* offers no satisfaction or reward. Being in love usually entails the desire to be with the beloved and not having to share their affection with someone else. *Ishq* however, is love for its own sake and means a total surrender for no gain at all; instead, it has destructive capacities, which are reflected in the concepts of *fanaa* (destruction for/by love) and self-sacrifice. Erica continued to love Chris long after he had passed away. She had nothing to gain, nothing to receive from him, and yet she continued to love him so much that she willingly let that love destroy her. Changez also continues to love Erica even after she is dead.

In my view, the *Dastan-e-Ishq* in *TRF* provides a powerful remedy against all biases that produce NoDs. A *Dastan-e-Ishq* focuses on the pursuit of love, rather than its seizure and possession because the pursuit of love is considered a form of worship, while love in the form of *ishq* itself is considered a manifestation of the divine. If we read the love story between Changez and Am/Erica in the same way as *Romeo and Juliet*, whose *ishq* defeated hatred between the irreconcilable Capulets and Montagues and established peace in Verona, then perhaps the ending of the frame narrative can be read as the preliminary stage to a reconciliation between the battling Changez and his guest representing the battling forces of the USA.

Similarly, most topics and recurring tropes in *Maps for Lost Lovers* seem to reproduce the NoDs between Islam and the West, but one theme defies them: the theme of love and all the emotions and desires connected to it through a certain choice of tropes.

> Aslam's novel has many intertexts with an intra ethnic [sic] cultural tradition of love that is anti-clerical [sic] deploying the motif of the folk tale [sic] romance known as the *qissa* from Sindhi and Punjabi linguistic traditions such as, the story of Sassi Punnun and Hir Rangha. These stories of unrequited love, family honour, and forced marriages encapsulate some of the themes Nadeem Aslam revisits in his novel. He deploys a genre of devotional Sufi literature, the *qawwali*, usually attached to patron shrines and the internationally recognised figure of Nusrat Fateh Ali Khan, the renowned Pakistani singer/*qawwal*, as a real character in the novel who performs for the community giving them a live rendition of a local aesthetic form of devotional music. Underwriting the universal tragic folk tales [sic] are the realist tragedies of love for ill-fated lovers in the novel from different religions, classes, ethnicities. The folk tales [sic] are used polemically to explicate the tyranny of men toward women and to connect to a Sufi tradition that has traditionally relied on a feminine voice to represent oppression.[239]

Like Mohsin Hamid, Aslam applies the genre of a Persian *Qissa* or *Dastan*, as well as Sufi love poetry. The *Qissa* or *Dastan* also uses the amalgamation of the names of the lovers, as a symbolic union. *Dastan-e-Layla Majnun* (rather than *Dastan* of Layla AND Majnun) is the eastern equivalent to modern western portmanteaus like Brangelina (for Brad and Angelina).

"Faiz' '*Dasht-e-Tanhaii*' has at its heart the theme of separation and union and is closely connected to the Sufi expression of an unrequited love and desired [sic] for union."[240] Aslam used the partition of India and Pakistan as a powerful analogy for the pain of separation with Urdu poetry. Yaqin ponders: "Nadeem Aslam responding to a post 9/11 world turns to a utopian model of cosmopolitanism, looking for the universal theme of love to repair a dysfunctional society."[241]

Aslam's novel arguably does not promote the NoDs between Islam and the West, it rather offers a very critical discussion of this disparity. The novel is a dystopia in which the disparity between Islam and the West – a destructive development visible in some communities all over the world – is enhanced and

---

[239] Yaqin, '*Cosmopolitan Ventures During Times of Crisis*', pp. 8–9
[240] Ibid., p. 10
[241] Ibid., p. 1

exaggerated and then implemented in a fictional society called Dasht-e-Tanhaii. As we noted in the analysis of *Maps for Lost Lovers*, the plot did not once allow two lovers or two ethnicities to mingle or even to communicate. However, even though the hateful societies succeeded in tearing them apart every time, they could never prevent clandestine copulation. In defiance of radical and even violent interference of the people of all the different communities, every couple of star-crossed lovers in *Maps for Lost Lovers* did manage to have intercourse at least once. The fictional concept of *ishq* often builds on either the beauty of transient bliss or the idea of the lovers being united in the afterlife. Either way, in fiction, love always finds a way to triumph over hate. Fictional love is non-political in the way that it does not make demands on what people, communities or identities should be. The lovers in Aslam's novel often have different religious or ethnic backgrounds, like a Hindu loving a Muslim or a Muslim loving a Sikh, but the lovers become united without trying or wanting to change anything about the other; they represent the impossible reconciliation of differences by uniting them without changing anything about them.

It was established earlier that narratives of superiority are the hardest NoDs to overcome because they are often pathological. Love (*Ishq*) is a force that is equally strong, as it compels the individual to act on it, despite him/herself and against his/her better judgement. This is illustrated in *Maps for Lost Lovers* with the metaphor of the moth that is irresistibly drawn towards the deathly flame. Sadly, Brain Aldiss' *HARM* does not comprise a love story, which is perhaps the reason why it did not read like a potential antidote to NoDs to me. However, this is not meant to be a reproach because the NoDs need to be fought beyond the realms of fiction or literary discourse.

In conclusion, the literary remedy to NoDs offers the principle idea that might help in overcoming NoDs in everyday life as well: uniting different entities despite their differences, rather than trying to enforce change, adjustments or assimilation. The point of this discussion was not to promote the idea that there are no differences between the values of Islam and those of the West, nor was the idea to pretend all people are the same. The idea is that all people are different, regardless of their affiliation to Islam or the West or any other religion or ideology.

NODS IN LITERATURE, HISTORY AND BEYOND

The NoDs-paradigm consisting of narratives of distinctive identity, narratives of inadequacy, narratives of mutual distrust and narratives of superiority were applied in the interpretations of novels depicting different versions of the conflict between Islamic and Western values. The paradigm helped identify some of the most commonly used narratives of disparity in history and fiction, and explains how they hinder the commingling of these two – often imaginary – entities.

NoDs define the entity they propagate, in this case either the West or Islam, almost arbitrarily as utopian images of the best possible way of life. The resulting ideals are presented in absolute terms with unrealistically high standards which cannot be met – at least not without hypocrisy or bigotry – because these standards only serve to evaluate the merit of one's views rather than one's practice. In other words, the conflict between Islam and the West is a war of ideas and the objective is not to invade each other's territory; this war is a race to reach the summit of moral superiority. In this conflict, both sides have turned their struggle for perfection and progress into a struggle to sustain the self-image of perfection and progress, which bestows the power of legitimacy.

Thus novels offer a useful field of study to take different perspectives and see how NoDs play out and unfold their divisive effect. But the idea was to demonstrate on only four different novels, what can hopefully be identified in other forms of literary fiction as well as historical narratives and several forms of public discourse. An awareness of the omnipresence of NoDs between Islam and the West can potentially help deconstruct the old narratives that maintain the conflict in history as well as present politics and might perhaps also facilitate a curb in the post-9/11 torrent of new narratives of disparity between Islam and the West.

While it is alright to try to define Islam and the West respectively, one must refrain from speaking in absolutes and from defining them only by their differences to each other. An awareness of the NoDs should also help restrain the urge to respond with equally biased and divisive counter-narratives. The discourse around Islam or the West must be subdued, so that inadequacies, weaknesses and/or maladies of people can be discussed and investigated without detours along the lines of judgement or defensiveness based on their real or assumed group-affiliations. A solution-oriented discussion of faults and problems should be given the same attention on both sides. And finally, there certainly must be a struggle for perfection in every civilization, instead of a struggle to sustain a perfect image deserving of moral and global hegemony.

A successful amalgamation of the values which both sides can believe in might enable a coexistence without diasporic experiences. So far, history has witnessed many centuries of a battle from which one side was supposed to emerge victorious as representing the utopia, eliminating all alternative ideals of civilizations as options. But instead of wanting to eliminate the competitor by either persuading or coercing all adherents to change sides, the intellectual efforts should now be concentrated on uniting the two entities without making demands for change or assimilation. Obviously, the aim of that is only the awareness itself and the progress towards an attitude that is free from the influence of powerful NoDs. The new ideal which might serve as inspiration might be Goethe's attempt to unite the two sides in the title of his *West-Eastern Divan,* without seeing the need to adjust either of them to enforce an assimilate or integration with the 'other'. Goethe did not deny that East and West were different in many ways. But rather than seeing their differences as a reason to divide them or to make them compete against each other, he celebrated the distinctions of each and even tried to imitate what he admired about 'the other' – e.g. typical features of Persian poetry – without fearing the loss of his European or German identity.

In summary, the complex intellectual exercise of accepting two or more different states at once is not new to humankind, but it has been something that, so far, only the truly great minds have achieved.

Conclusion

When Islam and the West are faced with each other within a discourse, the terms 'Islam' and 'the West' often denote two mutually exclusive markers of identity. This is due to the narratives of distinctive identity, which fabricate the two as distinct entities from a one-sided, subjective and partial vantage point into 'in-group' and 'out-group'. These narratives define 'Islam' and 'the West' not by the values and characteristics their adherents/affiliates display, but by the ideal conceptions of what the perceived 'in-group' or 'out-group' *should* represent. For instance, within this discourse, 'the West' might represent Christian, rationalist and modernist ideals and values *because* 'Islam' might represent Muslim, dogmatic, and traditionalist ones.

The 'Narratives of Disparity (NoDs)' paradigm was designed to explain how and why the nucleus of this discourse is relocated from *logos* to *pathos*. The NoDs – other than the abovementioned narratives of distinctive identity – are responsible for the prevalence of emotions and religious or ethnocentric sentimentalities in this discourse that force individuals to choose one side: narratives of mutual distrust trigger emotional responses like fear; and narratives of superiority and inadequacy appeal to the (collective) ego (see pp. 46-7).

Narratives of disparity usually build on recurring tropes from historical narratives. Most recurring historical tropes in NoDs about the West are related to its geopolitics, i.e. colonialism, imperialism, violent invasion of foreign countries, genocide, etc. The purpose of these powerful narratives – most successfully propagated by Islamists – is to blame the decline of the so-called Muslim world entirely on the West. At the same time, a western NoD contends that Islam's allegedly inherent incompatibility with secularism is the reason for its decline. On the one hand, this narrative disregards the vast variety of interpretations of Islamic teachings some of which do assert a strict separation between religion and politics. On the other hand, a diachronic view across the political development of many so-called 'Muslim countries' (see chapter 3) offers two reasons for the perseverance of this narrative. Firstly, the deeply religious masses in many Muslim empires and countries enabled leaders over many centuries to use the Machiavellian concept of a divine calling to validate their authoritarian rule. Secondly, Muslim countries and empires often sought 'Islam's' approval, so as not to hurt the public's religious sentimentalities, before implementing any changes in politics. For example, when reformists from the era of Islamic Modernism saw the need to travel to the West to learn more about it, they first discussed theologically whether it is permissible for Muslims to visit non-Muslim countries.

NoDs about Islam and Muslims often also include sexuality related tropes like hypersexual Arab men, sexually heteronomous women who are forced to veil, forced marriages, FGM, etc. Interestingly, the accusation of misogyny is a recurring trope in NoDs on both sides. The point is that the interdependent relationship between divisive narratives composed by each side about the 'self' and the 'other' ensures their further existence and perpetuation. The cycle can be broken by deconstructing a narrative instead of offering an equally divisive and partial counter-narrative.

In the preliminary chapter, we established that ethnocentric impulses and exclusivist attitudes facilitate the divisive effects of NoDs between Islam and the West and that these impulses and attitudes can be overcome and unlearned. This is a matter to be further studied by scholars of intercultural education as well as religious education. I believe that pedagogy is the very discipline to study ways to implement a pluralist society. Scholars of Islamic Religious Education and Didactics in Germany are already applying several models and concepts of intercultural and interreligious education, some of which have been derived from studies in Christian Theology. The existing methodology of overcoming ethnocentric impulses and exclusivist attitudes might be supplemented with a concept about raising awareness of NoDs from a young age.

The NoDs-paradigm can be used to analyse the discourse around Islam and the West and deconstruct divisive narratives in all kinds of writings – historical, political, fictional or otherwise. It can also be extended to discourses beyond the topics of Islam and the West; for instance, the NoDs-paradigm might be utilized in gender studies to explain how girls and boys are convinced from a young age that they cannot wear the same clothes, like the same colours, play with the same toys, and excel in the same kinds of sports. The concept of education derived from these findings should include a methodology that teaches a poststructuralist outlook to children and young adults.

BIBLIOGRAPHY

Abbas, S. (2011), "Leila Aboulela, Religion, and the Challenge of the Novel", *Contemporary Literature*, Vol. 52 Issue 3, pp. 430–461.

Aboulela, L. (2006), *Minaret*, Bloomsbury, London.

Aldiss, B.W. (2007), *HARM*, Duckworth, London.

Armstrong, K. (2002), *Islam: A Short History, Universal history*, Vol. 2, Phoenix, London.

Asad, M. and Moustafa, A. (2004), *The Message of the Qur'ān: The Full Account of the Revealed Arabic Text Accompanied by Parallel Transliteration*, Book Foundation, Bitton.

Aslam, N. (2004), *Maps for Lost Lovers*, Faber and Faber, London.

Baldick, C. (2008), *The Oxford Dictionary of Literary Terms*, available at: http://www.oxfordreference.com/ (accessed 27 May 2016)

Bickley, P. (2008), *Contemporary Fiction: The Novel Since 1990, Cambridge Contexts in Literature*, Cambridge Univ. Press, Cambridge.

Blackburn, S. (2008), *The Oxford Dictionary of Philosophy*, available at: http://www.oxfordreference.com/ (accessed 27 May 2016).

Brace, M. (2004), "Nadeem Aslam: A Question of Honour", available at: http://www.independent.co.uk/arts-entertainment/books/features/nadeem-aslam-a-question-of-honour-731732.html (accessed 27 February 2017).

Bukhari, *Sahih al-Bukhari* (Vol. 6, Book 60, Hadith 414): Book of Judgements, Chapter 49: The *Bai'a* (pledge of allegiance) Given by Women; https://sunnah.com (accessed 27 May 2016)

Bukhari, *Sahih al-Bukhari* (Vol. 1, Book 9, Hadith 490): Book of Prayers, Chapter 102: A Man Facing a Man While Offering *Salat* (Prayer); https://sunnah.com (accessed 27 May 2017)

Cobley, P. (2001), *Narrative, The New Critical Idiom*, Routledge, London, New York.

Currie, M. (1998), *Postmodern Narrative Theory, Transitions*, Macmillan Press, Basingstoke.

Davies, N. (1997), *Europe: A History,* Oxford Univ. Press, Oxford.

D'Costa, G. (2009), *Christianity and World Religions: Disputed Questions in the Theology of Religions*, Wiley-Blackwell, Oxford.

De Groot, J. (2009), *The Historical Novel, The New Critical Idiom*, Routledge, London, New York.

Fludernik, M. (2009), *An Introduction to Narratology*, Routledge, London, New York.

Furet, F. (1983), "Beyond the Annales", *The Journal of Modern History*, No. Vol. 55, No. 3, pp. 389–410.

Hamid, M. (2008), *The Reluctant Fundamentalist*, Penguin, London.

Hankins, R. (2009), "Fictional Islam. A Literary Review and Comparative Essay on Islam in Science Fiction and Fantasy", *Foundation*, No. 105, pp. 73–92.

Haug, S., Müssig, S. and Stichs, A. (2009), *Muslim life in Germany: A study conducted on behalf of the German Conference on Islam, Research report*, Vol. 6, Federal Office for Migration and Refugees, Nürnberg, Germany.

Hick, J. (2007), "Religious Pluralism", in Meister, C.V. and Copan, P. (Eds.), *The Routledge Companion to Philosophy of Religion, Routledge Philosophy Companions*, Routledge, London, New York, pp. 216–225.

Hunter, E. (2013), "The Muslim 'Who Has Faith' in Leila Aboulela's Novels *Minaret* (2005) and Lyrics Alley (2009)", *Current Writing*, Vol. 25 No. 1, pp. 88–99.

Huntington, S.P. (1996), *The Clash of Civilizations and The Remaking of World Order*, Simon & Schuster, New York.

Ilott, S. (2014), "Generic Frameworks and Active Readership in *The Reluctant Fundamentalist*", *Journal of Postcolonial Writing*, Vol. 50 No. 5, pp. 571–583.

Kaye, Jeffrey S. (2009), "Isolation, Sensory Deprivation, and Sensory Overload: History, Research, and Interrogation Policy from the 1950s to the Present Day", *Guild Practitioner,* Vol. 66 No. 1, pp. 2-18

King, N.L. (2008), "Religious Diversity and its Challenges to Religious Belief", *Philosophy Compass*, Vol. 8 No. 3, pp. 830–853.

Lewis, B. (2002), *What Went Wrong? Western Impact and Middle Eastern Response*, Oxford University Press, Oxford, New York.

MacPhee, G. (2011), *Postwar British Literature and Postcolonial Studies, Postcolonial literary studies*, Edinburgh University Press, Edinburgh.

McSmith, A. (2001), "Short Attacks Bush for 'Crusade' Quote", available at: http://www.telegraph.co.uk/news/worldnews/northamerica/usa/1341188 (accessed 11 November 2017).

Meister, C.V. (2014), *Philosophy of Religion, Palgrave Philosophy Today*, Palgrave Macmillan, Hampshire, New York.

Moore, L. (2014), "Voyages Out and In. Two (British) Arab Muslim Women's *Bildungsromane*", in Ahmed, R., Morey, P. and Yaqin, A. (Eds.), *Culture, Diaspora, and Modernity in Muslim Writing, Routledge Research in Postcolonial Literatures*, Routledge Taylor et Francis Group, New York, London, pp. 68–84.

Munos, D. (2012), "Possessed by Whiteness. Interracial Affiliations and Racial Melancholia in Mohsin Hamid's '*The Reluctant Fundamentalist*'", *Journal of Postcolonial Writing*, Vol. 48 No. 4, pp. 396–405.

Nawaz, M. and Bromley, T. (2013), *Radical,* WH Allen, UK.

Netland, H.A. (2007), "Inclusivism and Exclusivism", in Meister, C.V. and Copan, P. (Eds.), *The Routledge Companion to Philosophy of Religion*, *Routledge Philosophy Companions*, Routledge, London, New York.

Nicol, B. (2009), *The Cambridge Introduction to Postmodern Fiction, Cambridge Introductions to Literature*, Cambridge University Press, Cambridge, UK, New York.

Noack, R. (2016), "Leaked Document Says 2,000 Men Allegedly Assaulted 1,200 German Women on New Year's Eve", available at: https://www.washingtonpost.com/news/worldviews/wp/2016/07/10/ (accessed 11 November 2017)

Nochlin, L. (1989), "The Politics of Vision: Essays on Nineteenth-Century Art and Society".

Nünning, A. (1998), *Unreliable Narration: Studien zur Theorie und Praxis unglaubwürdigen Erzählens in der englischsprachigen Erzählliteratur*, WVT, Wiss. Verl. Trier, Trier.

Nünning, V. and Lusin, C. (Eds.) (2007), *Der Zeitgenössische Englische Roman, WVT-Handbücher zum Literaturwissenschaftlichen Studium*, Vol. 9, Wiss. Verlag Trier.

The Pew Forum on Religion and Public Life (2013), *The World's Muslims: Religion, Politics and Society*, Washington D.C., available at: http://www.pewforum.org/Muslim/the-worlds-muslims-religion-politics-society.aspx (accessed 11 November 2017)

Reynolds, V., Falger, V.S.E. and Vine, I. (Eds.) (1987), *The Sociobiology of Ethnocentrism: Evolutionary Dimensions of Xenophobia, Discrimination, Racism, and Nationalism*, Croom Helm, London.

Ritzer, G. (2005), *Encyclopaedia of Social Theory*, Sage Publications, Thousand Oaks, CA.

Rüsen, J. (2004), *History: Narration, Interpretation, Orientation, Making Sense of History*, Vol. 2, Berghahn Books, New York.

Sarikaya, Y. (2012), "Die Authentizität des al-Ǧāmiʿ aṣ-ṣaḥīḥ: Eine Skizze der Klassischen Ḥadīṯ-Kritik an dem Ṣaḥīḥ von al-Buḫārī. Teil I: Kritik hinsichtlich der Überlieferer", *Zeitschrift für Islamische Studien*, Vol. 2 No. 3, pp. 17–32.

Schneiders, T.G. (Ed.) (2012), *Islamfeindlichkeit: Wenn die Grenzen der Kritik Verschwimmen*, VS Verlag Sozialwissenschaften, Wiesbaden.

Taleb, N.N. (2007), *The Black Swan: The Impact of the Highly Improbable*, Random House, New York.

UNICEF (2013), *Pakistan Statistics UNICEF*, available at: https://www.unicef.org/infobycountry/pakistan_pakistan_statistics.html (accessed 10 November 2017).

van der Dennen, Johan M. G. (1987), "Ethnocentrism and In-Group/Out-Group Differentiation. A Review and Interpretation of the Literature", Introduction, in Reynolds, V., Falger, V.S.E. and Vine, I. (Eds.), *The Sociobiology of Ethnocentrism: Evolutionary Dimensions of Xenophobia, Discrimination, Racism, and Nationalism*, Croom Helm, London.

Warraq, I. (2003), *Why I Am Not a Muslim,* Amherst, N.Y.

Watt, W.M. (1999), *Islam: A Short History,* Oneworld, Oxford.

Williams, P. and Chrisman, L. (Eds.) (1995), *Colonial Discourse and Post-Colonial Theory,* 3rd ed., Harvester Wheatsheaf, New York.

Yaqin, A. (2013), "Cosmopolitan Ventures During Times of Crisis. A Postcolonial Reading of Faiz Ahmad Faiz' 'Dasht-e-Tanhaii' and Nadeem Aslam's *Maps for Lost Lovers*'", *Pakistaniaat: A Journal of Pakistan Studies*, Vol. 5, No. 1.

Yaqin, A. (2014), "Muslims as Multicultural Misfits in Nadeem Aslam's '*Maps for Lost Lovers*'", in Ahmed, R., Morey, P. and Yaqin, A. (Eds.), *Culture, Diaspora, and Modernity in Muslim writing, Routledge Research in Postcolonial Literatures*, Routledge Taylor et Francis Group, New York, London, pp. 101–116.